CW01360202

Airline Payments Handbook

A complete guide to payments in the air transport industry

Thomas Helldorff

Payments.aero

Published by Payments.aero
50 Bridgman Road
London, W4 5BD, United Kingdom

info@payments.aero
www.payments.aero

First edition published in 2012

© Copyright Thomas Helldorff 2012 – 2014

All rights reserved. No part of this book may be reproduced or transmitted in any form or by any means, electronic or mechanical, including photocopying, recording, or by any information storage and retrieval system without express written permission from the author / publisher.

A catalogue record for this book is available from the British Library

ISBN 978-0-9572730-0-9 (Paperback)

Typeset and cover design by Boston Graphics, Acton, London
Printed and bound in the UK by Blissett Bookbinders, Acton, London

NOTE: The material contained in this book is set out in good faith for general guidance and no liability can be accepted for loss or expense incurred as a result of relying in particular circumstances on statements made in the book. We assume no responsibility for errors, inaccuracies, omissions or any inconsistency herein. The rules, laws and regulations around payments are complex and liable to change, and readers should check the current position with the relevant organisations and authorities before making any arrangements.

Contents

PREFACE 15

ACKNOWLEDGEMENTS 19

INTRODUCTION 23

THE AIRLINE PAYMENTS HANDBOOK – UNDERSTANDING THE AIRLINE
PAYMENTS WORLD 25

PART I. THINGS YOU SHOULD KNOW BEFORE YOU START 29

1 HISTORY OF PAYMENT CARDS 29
- 1.1 INTRODUCTION 29
- 1.2 CHARGE CARDS AND THE ORIGINS OF PAYMENT CARDS 30
- 1.3 CREDIT CARDS 32
- 1.4 CHEQUE AND DEBIT CARDS 33

2 PAYMENT TECHNOLOGY – FROM SIGNATURE TO 3D SECURE 36
- 2.1 SECURE DESIGN ELEMENTS – SIGNATURE TO HOLOGRAM 37
- 2.2 IMPRINTERS 41
- 2.3 ELECTRONIC AUTHORISATIONS AND THE MAGNETIC STRIPE 41
- 2.4 THE CARD SECURITY CODE 42
- 2.5 CHIP AND PIN 43
- 2.6 3D SECURE PASSWORD – THE PIN FOR THE INTERNET 44
- 2.7 CONTACTLESS PAYMENTS – RFID AND NFC 46

3 SETTING THE STAGE - WHO DOES WHAT TO MAKE A PAYMENT HAPPEN? 48

    3.1   Cardholder 48
    3.2   Issuer 50
    3.3   Merchant (Airline) 51
    3.4   Acquirer 51
    3.5   Payment Scheme (Card Association) 52
    3.6   Processor (Transaction Processing Company) 53
    3.7   Payment Service Provider (PSP) 53
    3.8   Clearing Houses 54
    3.9   Players with Multiple Roles 54

4 MESSAGE AND FINANCIAL FLOW – PAYMENTS STEP BY STEP 55

    4.1   Overview 55
    4.2   Authorisation 56
    4.3   Payment Confirmation 60
    4.4   Airline Data 62
    4.5   Reversals, Cancellations, Refunds and Credits 64
    4.6   Transaction Submission (Capture) 65
    4.7   Clearing and Settlement 65
    4.8   Billing the Cardholder 67
    4.9   Settlement with the Merchant 67
    4.10 Transaction Dispute Process 68
    4.11 Additional Transaction Types 70

5 COSTS OF A PAYMENT TRANSACTION – WHO EARNS WHAT? 72

    5.1   Transaction Cost Model 73
    5.2   Surcharging 80
    5.3   Dynamic Currency Conversion 82

6 PAYMENT LIABILITY – WHO TAKES THE RISK? 88

    6.1   Participant's Risks and Responsibilities 88
    6.2   Shift of Liability – The Weakest Link 92
    6.3   Types of Fraud 94
    6.4   Costs of Fraud 96

7 LAWS, RULES, STANDARDS AND COMPLIANCE 97

    7.1 PAYMENT SCHEME RULES 98
    7.2 INDUSTRY STANDARDS AND RULES 98
    7.3 NATIONAL AND SUPRANATIONAL REGULATORY INFLUENCE 102
    7.4 AIRLINE INDUSTRY RULES 105

8 AIRLINE AFFILIATED PAYMENT INSTITUTIONS 106

    8.1 IATA 106
    8.2 AIRLINE CLEARING HOUSE (ACH) 112
    8.3 UATP 112
    8.4 AIRLINE REPORTING CORPORATION (ARC) 114

9 AIRLINE PAYMENT SYSTEM INTEGRATORS 115

    9.1 SITA 115
    9.2 AMADEUS TRAVEL PAYMENTS 120
    9.3 NAVITAIRE 122
    9.4 SABRE 122
    9.5 TRAVELPORT – ENETT 122

10 PAYMENT METHODS USED IN THE AIRLINE INDUSTRY 123

    10.1 IATA APPROVED FORM OF PAYMENT CODES 123
    10.2 CASH AND CHEQUE 125
    10.3 INTERNATIONAL CREDIT CARDS AND DOMESTIC PAYMENT INSTRUMENTS 125
    10.4 CO-BRANDED CARDS 128
    10.5 ALTERNATIVE PAYMENT METHODS 128
    10.6 DEBIT CARDS 128
    10.7 REAL-TIME BANK TRANSFERS 129
    10.8 DIRECT DEBIT AND BANK TRANSFERS 130
    10.9 CASH PAYMENTS OPTIONS 130
    10.10 ELECTRONIC WALLETS 131
    10.11 PREPAID CARDS 133
    10.12 MOBILE PAYMENTS 134
    10.13 FREQUENT FLYER MILES 135
    10.14 VOUCHERS AND GIFT CARDS 136

11 SUMMARY 138

PART II. PAYMENTS IN THE AIRLINE INDUSTRY – WHERE AND HOW ARE THEY PROCESSED? 141

1 INTRODUCTION 141
2 TRADITIONAL AIRLINE AUTHORISATION AND SETTLEMENT FLOW 142
2.1 Overview 142
2.2 Sales Transaction 144
2.3 Authorisation Request 145
2.4 Extraction and Submission of Credit Card Transactions 149
2.5 Settlement and Reporting 149
2.6 Implications of Separating the Message Flow 150

3 TRAVEL AGENCY 151
3.1 Bookings through a GDS 152
3.2 Airline Direct to Agent Sales 155

4 AIRLINE TICKET DESK 158
4.1 Cash and Cheque 158
4.2 POS Terminal 158
4.3 Payment Processing through the Reservation System 160

5 CHECK-IN DESK 161

6 CALL CENTRE 162
6.1 Cash Collection 162
6.2 Credit Cards 162
6.3 Payment Processing through the Reservation System 163
6.4 POS Terminal 163
6.5 Virtual POS Terminal 164
6.6 Interactive Voice Recognition Systems 164
6.7 Hybrid Solutions – Separation between Authorisation and Capture Message 165

7 E-COMMERCE 166
7.1 Payment Processing through the Reservation System 166
7.2 Payment Service Provider (PSP) 167
7.3 PSP Integration Options 168

8 PASSENGER MOBILE APPLICATIONS 172
8.1 Mobile Browser and Mobile Applications 173

9 SELF-SERVICE KIOSK 176
9.1 Kiosk as Distribution Channel 176
9.2 Magnetic Stripe Card Reader 178
9.3 POS Terminal 180

10 AGENT MOBILE APPLICATIONS 185

11 ON-BOARD RETAIL 187
11.1 Cash and Credit Card Imprinters 188
11.2 On-board POS Devices 190
11.3 Chip & PIN Devices with GSM Communication Capability 191
11.4 Real-time Authorisations through Satellite Communication 192

12 ON-BOARD TELEPHONE SYSTEMS 196

13 STAFF TRAVEL OFFICE 196

14 LOUNGE ACCESS 197

15 COMPENSATION PAYMENTS – SERVICE RECOVERY PAYMENTS 197
15.1 Cash, Cash Vouchers and MCOs 197
15.2 Card Based Solutions – Chip and Prepaid Cards 199

16 TAKING PAYMENTS FOR 3RD PARTY ANCILLARY SERVICES 202
16.1 Airline takes Payment for the Entire Shopping Basket 203
16.2 Airline Charges Deposit or Booking Fee 203
16.3 Payment Details are used for Two or More Transactions 204
16.4 3rd Party Provider takes Payment 204

17 SUMMARY 205

PART III. BACK-OFFICE SUPPORT PROCESSES 209
1 ORDER SCREENING 210
2 TRANSACTION RECONCILIATION 213
3 CARD OPERATIONS – TRANSACTION CORRECTION PROCESSES 214
4 COLLECTION – CHARGE-BACK PROCESSING 215
5 CREDIT CARD VALIDATION BEFORE CHECK-IN 217

PART IV. PLANNING YOUR PAYMENT PROJECT – A STEP BY STEP GUIDE 221
1 INTRODUCTION – HOW TO USE THIS GUIDE 221
2 STRATEGY DEVELOPMENT 223
    2.1 Evaluation of Current Set-up 223
    2.2 Goal Setting and Strategy Development 225
    2.3 Project Set-up and Kick-off 227
3 SUPPLIER AND PARTNER SELECTION 228
    3.1 Acquiring Bank 228
    3.2 Payment Service Provider 240
    3.3 Fraud Management Solution Provider 252
    3.4 Currency Exchange Service Provider 262
    3.5 Secure Card Number Storage - Token Solutions 268
    3.6 Passenger Service Systems Providers and Payment Integrators 269
4 SELECTING PAYMENT METHODS 270
    4.1 Penetration and Reach 271
    4.2 Potential Additional Sales 271
    4.3 Costs 272
    4.4 Strategic Value 272
    4.5 Liability for Bad Transactions and Fraud 272
    4.6 Costs for Risk Mitigation, Fraud Prevention and Monitoring 273
    4.7 Regulatory Requirements 273
    4.8 Transaction Processes and Integration Consideration 274
    4.9 Operational Impact 274

5	**IMPLEMENTATION**	**275**
	5.1 ADAPTATION OF DISTRIBUTION SOFTWARE	275
	5.2 INTERNAL PROCESS ADAPTATION	277
6	**END-TO-END TESTING**	**280**
	6.1 TRANSACTION FLOW	280
	6.2 SUPPORT PROCESSES	281
7	**GO-LIVE**	**281**
8	**MONITORING AND REVIEW**	**281**
9	**SUMMARY**	**283**

PART V. SUPPLIER DIRECTORY 285

INDEX		**329**
TABLE OF FIGURES AND TABLES		**337**
1	TABLES	337
2	FIGURES	338
REFERENCES		**341**

Preface

On the first day of my MBA course the Dean of the Business School stood up and said to the assembled class: "What you will learn on this MBA course is a blinding glimpse of the obvious" and perhaps you're feeling like me sitting in the class and hearing that, and thinking why I am studying for this degree if it is blindingly obvious? He paused at this point, and as the collective intake of breath in the room subsided, added "trouble is, most of us are blinded".

That insight came back to me as I started to read the "Airline Payments Handbook". After all, what is there new to know? Airlines have been collecting payment for tickets since commercial flying began and have been innovators in the online world. Surprisingly, not only is this the first comprehensive guide on the subject but there is a lot you probably don't know (but should) as well as practical insights into leading edge strategies that can mean the difference between payments being a cost or an enabler to even great sales (and profits.)

Whether you are new to the airline payments industry or a seasoned expert, this guide hits the just the right levels of detail and insight. Covering the complex world that gets the money from passengers worldwide into airline bank accounts is no easy task and this guide offers a comprehensive road map not only for seasoned payment professionals but their colleagues in distribution, e-commerce, ancillary revenue,

revenue accounting and marketing. Investing your time in reading the guide and keeping it handy as a reference will not only make for a better experience for your customers, but also make your CFO happy as you not only add revenue but save costs too.

With this excellent and comprehensive roadmap there are no reasons for any of us to be blinded by the obvious - this is a truly illuminating guide to Airline Payments.

Michael Smith

Chairman, Airline and Travel Payment Summit &
Managing Partner, Airline Information

payments.aero

Acknowledgements

I wish to thank numerous individuals for their assistance in the researching, writing and publication of this book: Anna Almqvist, Birgit Aflenzer, Brian Geary, Cameron Olsen, Celine Helderman, Celia Pereiro, Chiara Quaia, Chris Leadbeater, Christophe Kato, Christopher Saab, Dan Hayter, David Smith, Eamonn O'Shea, Eoin McGillycuddy, Helen Smith, Jan-Jaap Kramer, Jeremy Dyball, Johanna Waara, Jörg Möller, Kate Sloan, Lars Bergvind, Maarten Rooijers, Manuel Brunnader, Mike Smith, Milesh Shah, Nadja Sittler, Neill Butcher, Patrick van der Knoop, Paul van Alfen, Peter Harvy, Philip McGriskin, Robin Philip, Rupesh Fatani, Sander Maertens, Tuli Faas, Vivienne Grace and Wendy Ward.

Two individuals deserve my special thanks: Peter Parke, whose support encouraged me to write the book and Michael Smith who helped me promote it among my industry colleagues.

The people who helped in the editorial and production process: Urvashi Patankar from Boston Graphics, Dan Petter for the logo, my editor Kathryn Potter, and for cross reading and their feedback, Emma Swinnerton and John Davies.

I am also grateful to all the sponsors who have made this project possible: Adyen, Airline Information, Air Transport Publications, Alaric, Amadeus, Continuum Commerce, CyberSource, Elavon, FEXCO, FirstData Merchant Solutions, Headcount, IATA, Initium Onboard, Ogone, PayGate, ReD, SEB Euroline, SITA, UATP, WireCard and Worldpay.

The book, of course, does not necessarily reflect the views of any of the organisations or people who have generously provided me with all forms of assistance.

This work is the result of 14 years of experience in the airline and payment industry, many discussions with airlines, suppliers and colleagues, anecdotes, conferences and my own experiences as a passenger. It is a snapshot of the current environment and I have tried to capture it as accurately as possible.

I am looking forward to feedback, especially from you, the specialists in many of the areas that I have covered. The aim is to make this the basis of a "living document" for the airline payments community, reflecting our common understanding of the industry.

payments
.aero

Introduction

"Accepting payment is a core activity of EVERY business, even airlines." This is how Ralph Kaiser, the CEO of UATP recently opened a discussion on "Managing the Evolving World of Payments". If an airline does not receive payments, it won't fly for very long. It is not only a core activity; it is an absolutely vital activity.

Traditionally this part of the distribution activity has been performed by travel agents. They processed the payments on behalf of the airlines and the funds arrived at the airlines' accounts almost automatically through various systems like the IATA Billing and Settlement Plan (BSP).

To reduce the distribution costs associated with distribution through travel agents and Global Distribution Systems (GDS), airlines were keen to increase the proportion of direct distribution - through call centres, the internet and more recently through mobiles, social media etc. The percentage of direct distribution has grown significantly since the early 90s and for low cost carriers it has become the core of their business models.

Airlines were quick to celebrate the savings made in this way, but this victory brought its own challenges, which many airlines around the world are still trying to get their heads around:

Being responsible for taking payment direct from the customer.

Travel agencies and traditional airline ticket offices had great flexibility when it came to taking payments, as even customers who had no banking relationship and no access to any sort of card-based payment methods could still purchase tickets – with cash. However, cash does not really work with these new, remote direct distribution channels, or through a call centre, over the internet or via a mobile phone.

So, what forms of payment are available to your customers? How would you sell flights online in a country with limited credit card usage?

How can my customers pay?

All of a sudden this has become a major question. As airlines want to enter new markets and reach new, emerging customer segments, they need to be familiar with local payment behaviours and the payment methods relevant to that market.

But every payment method works slightly differently, is governed by various national rules and regulations; requires integration of additional partners and triggers adjustments to internal procedures. The risk and fraud potential have to be understood and financial flows adopted. All this has to be achieved within a very regulated and complex technical and organisational environment, as airlines typically are.

Taking payments is a complex and challenging task.

It involves multiple entities both inside and outside the organisation and as it is not really the core business of an airline, it is very often not fully understood.

The economic downturn that started in 2008 and the resulting need to further reduce every cost element within the airline business tabled another uncomfortable fact:

Taking payments is not only complex, it is also expensive.

Payment costs can be the biggest distribution cost element after GDS fees. Merchant fees of up to 3% are not uncommon, manual handling, and high fraud and fraud related costs can add anything up to 4% on top of that. Many of the payment related costs are still not fully understood by the airlines, as they occur in different parts of the organisation and are not always directly attributed to the distribution business case.

These are only some of the challenges that those involved in payment processing often face. And they very often wish they had some

HELP!

The Airline Payments Handbook – Understanding the Airline Payments World

This is what this book is all about: Help. It is an attempt to put together "all there is to know about airline payments" into a single reference guide, helping you to answer some of the most prominent payments questions.

- **How do payments work?**
- **How do payments work in the airline industry?**
- **How do I define a payment strategy for my airline?**
- **How can I reduce my payment costs?**
- **How can I improve fraud and risk management?**
- **How can I manage and reduce the complexity of payments?**
- **How do I select my suppliers?**
- **How do I structure a payment implementation project?**

For those new to airline payments, it is a perfect first step to a better understanding of this topic and a great reference book for ad hoc "What is that?" and "How does that work?" questions. For all those who work or "have to work" with payments, without it being their primary field of expertise, this book will be a welcome step-by-step guide through the challenges that the world of payments brings with it. For the advanced payment reader, it is a superb reference guide for "best in class" payment handling and a source of inspiration for improvements in their day-to-day business.

The guide is divided into four parts: Payment Basics, Payments in the airline industry (distribution channels and back-office processes), "Your Payment Project" and a Supplier Directory.

Payment Basics – How does it all work?
The first part of the book focuses on payment basics, giving the history of payments and the development of payment methods from coins and cash through to credit cards and alternative payment methods like contactless and mobile payments. It examines the individual elements of a payment transaction and the costs and players involved in making that transaction happen. It also discusses the relevant legal frameworks, industry standards and compliance rules such as the Payment Card Industry (PCI) Standards. It analyses the risk management aspects for dealing with payments, looks at the responsibilities and risks of each of the players, payment fraud, fraud scenarios and fraud prevention tools. This part concludes with an analysis of the major institutions and organisations relevant to this industry.

Payments in the Airline Industry –
A Channel by Channel Analysis and Back-office Processes
The second and third parts apply the information from the first chapters to the airline industry. They provide analysis of the various distribution channels, discuss the challenges of traditional channels such as travel agencies, call centres and ticket desks versus newer, direct distribution channels e.g. e-commerce and mobile. It also gives a window into on-board retail transactions, on-board telephone authorisations and emerging 'Chip & PIN' payments at kiosks. Each of these channels requires their own approach as the underlying infrastructure and the environment in which payment is taken varies greatly. They further investigate the airline back-office processes that are required to support the payments processing within the airline, such as order screening, transaction corrections, charge-back processing and transaction reconciliation and accounting.

My Payment Project – A Step-by-Step Guide
The fourth part provides a blue-print for an implementation of a payment project, offering step-by-step guidance through the set-up of such a project. It helps you to define a payment strategy for your organisation balancing (often opposing) requirements from various internal departments. It gives you tools to evaluate existing and potential new suppliers and understand their product offerings and pricing strategies. It draws up an outline implementation plan and explains its execution, touching on support process adaptations, testing and on-going monitoring processes.

The book concludes with a directory of contact details for a variety of industry players and suppliers including payment service providers, acquiring banks, fraud management solution providers, currency conversion experts, consultants, conferences and media.

The web-site to the book will provide further, up-to date information about this topic:

www.payments.aero
info@payments.aero

Part I. Things you should know before you start

Have you ever wondered how it is that you can fly halfway around the world to arrive in some foreign country, where you get in a taxi and ask the driver to take you to your final destination; and to pay for all this, all you have to do is pull out a colourful little piece of plastic and sign a piece of paper. The driver does not know you and no money changed hands... a miracle?

How was this system of paying for your purchases developed? Where did it come from? It may look easy from the user's perspective, but behind it lies a very complex system of relationships and technology. This section takes a look behind the scenes at payments and explores the systems, the players and the infrastructure that allows this to happen.

1 History of Payment Cards

1.1 Introduction

The exchange of goods and services has always been a central part of society. Coins and bills support this exchange and go back as far as 3000

B.C. in Mesopotamia. However, it is not always convenient to carry money around to pay for what you need, especially for larger value purchases or when travelling. If you can't pay immediately though, how do you get a potential merchant to trust you and hand over the items or services you want in return for a promise to be paid later? It was this need, the ability to have access to your funds at a distance, which drove the development of the payment systems we have today.

1.2   Charge Cards and the Origins of Payment Cards

Payment cards have been around for a just over 100 years. The first paper cards were introduced in the early 1900s by big department stores in the U.S. They were issued to preferred customers, who were allowed to defer payments for purchases they made. In 1914, Western Union were the first to hand out small metal cards (later known as "Metal Money") to their premium customers, again allowing them to get interest-free deferred payments. In the early 20s, large oil companies picked up on this idea and started to issue similar metal cards, specifically for petrol and automotive services. They took the concept one step further though and allowed the cards to be used not only within their own organisations, but across different companies. Different regions began to accept one another's cards, for the first time making them usable on a broader geographical scale. (Evans & Schmalensee, 2005)

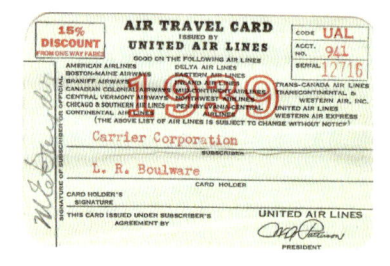

Fig 1: The "Air Travel Card", Predecessor of the UATP Card (Courtesy of UATP)

The "Universal Air Travel Plan" or UATP led the development in the business travel industry. Founded in 1936, the Air Travel Card, as it was known initially, was an early innovator and pioneer in the payment industry (see also page 112). It developed industry standards such as the magnetic stripe, lodged accounts and the credit card numbering system. (UATP were the first cards in the world and thus start with the number 1.)

Then World War II came along and with it- "Regulation W", restricting the use of all credit and charge cards. While prohibited for public use, the US Military kept using its own version of the "metal money" – the Charga-Plate – to record and process payment transactions. These were yet another predecessor of today's credit cards. The first bank-issued card was introduced in 1946 by a New York banker. The card was called "charge-it" and could be used to make purchases from local merchants. To get reimbursed the merchants then deposited the bills with the bank. The bank later charged the customer against their account.

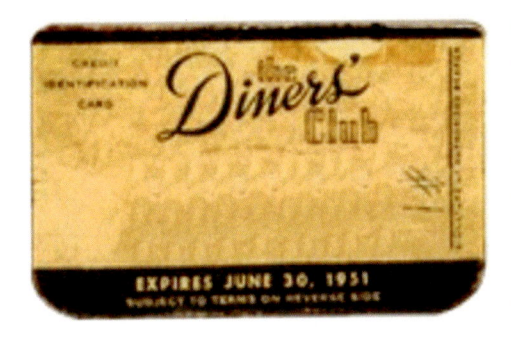

Fig 2: First Diners Club Card (Courtesy of Diners Club)

1950 was a turning point for the Credit Card business, when a man named Frank McNamara invented the Diners Club Card. Although originally intended to pay for dinners only (hence the name of the card), cardholders were soon able to make purchases at a wider range of travel and entertainment related merchants, making it the first "universal card". It was also the first card scheme that acted as a guarantor, ensuring the cardholder's credibility and guaranteeing for all its transactions. The merchant no longer needed to have a direct relationship with the cardholder. Within a year there were 20,000 Diners Club cardholders (Diners Club 2012).

Diners Club had no real competition until 1959, when American Express entered the market with a similar charge card. It was the first card to be made out of plastic, and benefitting from American Express' global footprint it was also the first to be issued in multiple countries in multiple local currencies – one of the first world-wide card schemes. All of these cards were charge cards, where the purchases were made on credit, but the full bill had to be paid at the end of the month.

1.3   Credit Cards

The BankAmericard, issued in 1959 by Bank of America was the first real credit card, introducing the concept of a revolving credit. Customers could either pay the bill in full or in monthly instalments, while the bank charged interest. As travel became more common and people began to equip their homes with more costly modern conveniences– like kitchen appliances and washing machines, there was a growing need for credit. Credit cards were a convenient way to finance these "big-ticket" items, which people could otherwise not afford. Other banks quickly followed and the credit card industry was born.

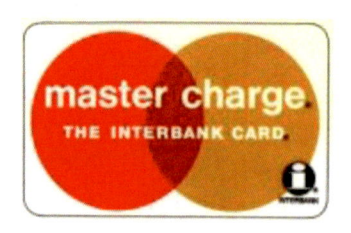

Fig 3: MasterCharge Logo

To increase their market share beyond their own network, Bank of America started to form licensing agreements with other banks to issue BankAmericards. This was the foundation of the card associations. In 1966 four Californian banks formed their own card associations and introduced the MasterCharge program to compete with the BankAmericard program. MasterCharge was later renamed MasterCard (MasterCard 2011).

These programs were so successful that soon the administrative infrastructure in place was no longer sufficient to cope with the volume of transactions being processed. The handling of paper slips became unmanageable and fraud and card misuse skyrocketed. It got to the point where Bank of America decided to spin off its card organisation to form an independent, member owned organisation – the predecessor to Visa. Both Visa and MasterCard started to introduce automated processing systems to handle the information and financial flows between its members. (The U.S. Interlink system was established at around this time.) Electronic dial-up terminals and magnetic stripes on the back of the cards automated the data capture and authorisation process at the merchant location. The card associations introduced common rules and agreed on procedures to settle disputes between them. Sharing the card program costs between multiple members made joining viable even for smaller banks. Soon these card schemes also started to expand their issuing and acceptance network beyond the U.S. (Evans & Schmalensee, 2005; Hock, 1990).

1.4 Cheque and Debit Cards

In Europe, the card business developed quite differently to that in the U.S. Cheques dominated the cash-less payments market. Over time though, they became increasingly subject to fraud. As printing machines became easily accessible, cheques became easier to counterfeit (think of the film *"Catch Me if You Can"*). Cheque verification services (e.g. calling somebody/an institution to check if a cheque was good and there was sufficient credit associated with it) became too tedious and time consuming in a merchant's day-to-day business. Credit cards only arrived much later.

To stay ahead of the fraudsters, banks came up with an additional piece of identification that was less easy to come by and counterfeit and which would increase the probability of genuine transactions. They started to issue cheque cards (cheque guarantee cards). The cheque card, first introduced in the UK in 1965, took over the function of identifying the cardholder to the merchant. The card number, which the merchant had to copy onto the cheque, provided them with a payment guarantee. The cheque itself remained the origination of the fund transfer and was handed to the merchant's bank for clearing and settlement.

The introduction of the Automated Teller Machine (ATM) in the 70s sparked an additional use for cheque guarantee cards. Equipped with a magnetic stripe and a Personal Identification Number (PIN) they became known as "Bank Cards" and were the access mechanism to cash and other bank transactions. 1985 saw the birth of the first Electronic Fund Transfers at Point of Sale (EFTPOS or POS terminals). They helped merchants and banks around to world to reduce the number of cheques being used at point of sale. Swiping the bank card through the reader initiated the transaction that was then authorised by the cardholder with either a signature or a PIN entry. The bank card then became the "Debit Card" that we know today.

Debit card schemes originally only worked in a single country and sometimes even only within a specific bank's network or within a group of banks. At the beginning every country had its own technical standards, networks and processing centres. Over time though, reciprocal acceptance agreements began to be put in place and common standards were adopted, allowing the cards to be used on each other's networks. Banks from 14 European countries launched the Eurocard program as early as 1984. In 1988 Eurocard International and MasterCard International entered into a strategic alliance, allowing the cards of each issuer to be accepted by each other's network. In an effort to further spread card usage and drive the interoperability of debit cards, they started a common joint venture called "Maestro" in 1991. Maestro has since replaced many of the domestic debit card brands around the world (e.g. Switch in the UK). In many countries it co-resides on the card together with the domestic acceptance brands. Eurocard and Eurocheque eventually merged into Europay in 1992. 10 years later Europay merged with MasterCard to form MasterCard International. (MasterCard, 2011; Eurocheque, 2011)

The adoption of credit cards in Europe was much slower than in the U.S. or Canada and the percentage market-penetration levels in countries like Germany and France are still below 30%. In those countries alternative payment methods therefore are playing an increasingly important role for online payments. **Fig 4** compares the preferred online payment methods in Germany, Europe and Brazil.

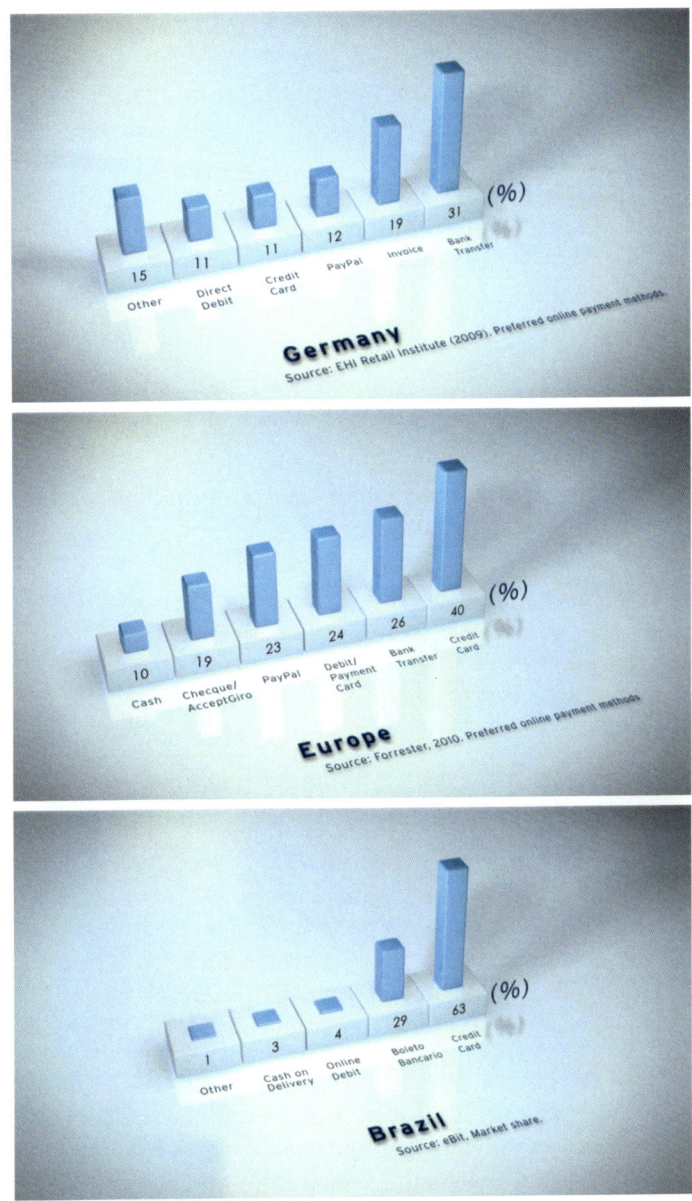

Fig 4: Preferred Online Payment Methods in Germany, Europe and Brazil (Courtesy of DataCash)

2 Payment Technology – From Signature to 3D Secure

Previously the success of a payment scheme was dependent on a constant improvement of the functions below, the main drivers in the development of payment technology:

- Identifying the user of the card as the owner of the card
- Verifying that the card is linked to a valid account that has enough funds available
- Increasing the speed of the sales process
- Improving the recording, processing and reconciliation of the sale.

Dee Hock, one of the founding fathers of Visa, identified three requirements that every payment system has to fulfil (Hock, 1999):

- **It has to identify the buyer to the seller and the seller to the buyer:** The buyer needs to know that the seller accepts certain payment methods in place of cash (e.g. by sticking a list of credit card logos to the entrance door of the shop). The seller needs to recognise the buyer as a member of a certain payment scheme. This is particularly important as the seller does not have any direct relationship with the buyer. The identification token (from a signet ring years ago to a plastic card with a card scheme logo today) identifies the customer as "one of us" and as such worthy of credit.

- **It has to be a guarantor to both the seller and the merchant:** Both parties have to be able to trust in the system to make it work. The buyer relies on his payment card to work and takes it along instead of cash (have you ever been on a holiday or a business trip, where they did not accept the only payment card that you had with you? Horror!). And even more importantly, the seller has to have the confidence that he will eventually get paid through the system.

- **It has to be the initiator of a payment transaction:** To allow the seller to be paid, the exchange of goods or services and the use of the payment method or token instead of cash have to trigger a payment transaction – a money-flow from the seller's account to the buyer's account. This was initially done via paper slips and today via electronic transaction messages.

This section of the book looks at some of the innovations that evolved out of the need to improve these areas. Some of them are focused on increasing the security of identification between the merchant (the seller) and the cardholder (the buyer), such as the secure design elements, Card Security Codes, chip technology and 3D Secure. Others substantially improved transaction processing, such as imprinters, the magnetic stripe and electronic processing. These chapters finish with an overview of contactless payments, another improvement in speed and convenience.

2.1   Secure Design Elements – Signature to Hologram

From the beginning credit cards have held the signature of their bearer. The signature plays a dual role in payment processing. By signing the payment receipt the cardholder indicates that he agrees to the payment transaction that is about to be initiated as well as to the price being charged for the goods or services received. Comparing that signature against the one on the signature strip on the back (earlier in the front) of the card identifies the customer as the legal bearer of the card that has been used for the purchase.

This concept has two main flaws: either the card is a fake, even if the signature on it is the fraudster's "real" signature; or the signature can be imitated by an unauthorised cardholder – allowing the card to be stolen and misused by another person.

Initially effort went into ensuring that the payment token, the credit card, was more difficult to counterfeit. Introducing plastic cards was the first step. Not only were these cards more durable, but they were also more difficult to produce without expensive equipment that was initially harder to obtain. As a next step MasterCard and Visa began featuring holographic emblems on their cards. Ultraviolet prints (e.g. all MasterCard cards must have an M and a C printed on the front with ultraviolet inks) and special embossing characters (e.g. Visa cards had a stylized V embossed on the line next to the valid date, MasterCard a stylized MC) were further initiatives to make them harder to forge.

1 Guillochen

Guilloches are printed security lines - the layout of the intersections and geometry is unique. Copying is inhibited by the layout arrangements of fine lines, rainbow print and the exact colour calibration.
Level 1, printed

2 Iris Print

The colours gradually change their shade from one colour to the next. Colour copiers cannot reproduce this effect and counterfeits can be detected very easily.
Level 1, printed

3 Microtext

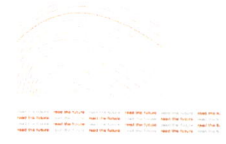

Fineline or microprinting refers to very thin and small printed characters or entire words. Without the use of a lens the structure appears as a continuous line. The characters contained in these lines cannot be reproduced with conventional copy methods.
Level 1-2, printed

5 Holographic Stripe

A holographic stripe may contain individual logos, characters or other information. The holographic stripe can be implemented horizontally or vertically under the top layer of the card.
Level 1-2, apllied

4 Printed Hidden Image

The Printed Hidden Image will be produced by means of a halftone displacement of the hidden image. The printed hidden image is only visible with a special decoding lens.
Level 2, printed

6 OVI

OVI – Optical Variable Ink is a high security feature showing different colors as the angle of view changes. Optical Variable Ink requires a support printing by a dark colour shade to get a luscious colour effect.
Level 1-2, printed

7 UV Print

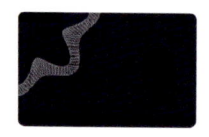

UV (Ultraviolet) ink is invisible under regular illumination. By viewing the card under UV light, all logos, design structures or texts become visible either in blue, red or green/yellow. The UV printing element cannot be copied.
Level 2, printed

8 M - Feature

The M-feature is defined as a special pigment ink, which is mixed with printing ink. If the element is viewed under IR light, the special pigment ink reflects brown and green colours.
Level 2, printed

10 IR Feature

By means of a special decoding lens applied to an IR enabled camera, the printed IR colour becomes invisible whereas all logos, design structures or texts remain visible on the monitor. Infrared colours are invisible under the light spectrum of 800 - 1300 nm.
Level 2, printed

9 Kinegram®

A Kinegram® consists of microscopically tiny areas with refractive characteristics. When viewing a Kinegram® from different angles, various designs or structures become visible. A Kinegram® can be implemented in clear transparent or in metallic silver.
Level 1-3, applied

11 See-through Register

A see-through register combines both sides of the card. Parts of any shape or character will be printed on either side of the card. When holding the card against a light source, both parts merge to form a combined picture.
Level 1, printed

12 CLI - Changeable Laser Image
MLI - Multiple Laser Image

In a highly specialised processing, the CLI or MLI is integrated into the transparent overlay as a live screen. Up to 2 partial pictures are engraved into the live screen in 2 different angles. The optical equivalent for this feature is a tilting image. **Level 1, special processing**

13 Positive - Negative Embossing

By means of a special laminating process, a perceptible relief is produced on the surface of the card. Positive and negative line patterns show a relief including guilloches and microtext. Due to the special characteristics of the embossing, it is actually possible to feel the structure with the fingertip.
Level 1-2, special processing

15 OVI Chip Cover

The chip has to be covered on the reverse side of the card. The OVI features is a common choice for this protection.
Level 1-2, printed

14 Hologram

Holograms are applied to the card surface in a 2-or 3-dimensional appearance. Holograms are well known from credit cards.

The range of classifications is a result of the great variety of hologram designs. There are holograms with machine readable features which can only be read with special equipment..
Level 1-3, applied

17 Laser Engraving

High secure laser engraving makes the identification document practically "impossible to forge". It is possible to laser engrave any kind of personalized information – i.e. text, photos and signatures.
Level 1, personalised

16 Magnetic Stripe

The magnetic stripe can be printed with customized logos and design elements as well as special color effects.
Level 1, applied/printed

18 Signature Panel

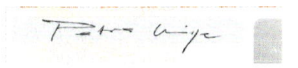

A customized signature panel applied on the surface of the card can hold numerous separate security features – i.e. microtext or guilloches.
Level 1, applied/printed

19 MRZ - Machine readable zone

```
ID<AUT<UNIQUE<<P
7007007<READ<<TH
AUSTRIA<CARD<<HI
```

The ICAO compliant machine readable zone is personalized using high secure laser engraving.
Level 1, personalised

20 Hidden Image IPI

By means of a special software tool, hidden images can be applied to existing pictures on the card – i.e. a photo, cardholders date of birth or any other personalised information. The hidden image only becomes visible under a special lens. The hidden image cannot be copied.
Level 2, personalised

Level 1
A level one security feature is visible to the naked eye and can be detected without any verification device.

Level 2
The second level feature can only be detected by means of appropriate verification tools - i.e. magnifying glass, ultraviolet lamp or infrared pointer.

Level 3
A feature categorised in the third level can only be veified and made visible in dedicated laboratories with special equipment and tools.

Level 4
Only the manufacturer of a security feature classfied in level four has the knowlege about the feature itself. Only the certified prouction company can detect the feature with special equipment in their very own laboratory.

To curtail the use of arbitrary account numbers, card schemes introduced a verification algorithm based on the Luhn formula (invented by Hans P.Luhn in 1960). In this method, the last digit of the card number is a "checksum" generated by performing a fixed set of calculations on the other digits. This system allowed anybody processing a card to test a number for compliance. Today the system is used to protect against accidental data entry errors rather than malicious attacks.

The benefit of these features however only ever lasted until the production techniques (and the calculation formula) became common knowledge; they were then more easily accessible to fraudsters and affordable even for small scale productions. Holographic signature panels later replaced the holograms at the front of the card and the special embossing characters disappeared after 2006. Both became too easy and cheap to reproduce.

Previous page:

Fig 5: Secure Design Elements (Courtesy of AustriaCard)

2.2 Imprinters

Imprinters have been around since the introduction of credit cards. They were designed to speed up the recording of card details onto the sales slip. The initial models were stamping machines that pressed the paper slips onto the card, leading to cards becoming unreadable after being used too many times. Later models use a rolling technique that better protected the embossed card numbers. These imprinters are still in use today, either as back-up devices or for off-line sales situations, were electronic POS terminals are not available or not practical to use (e.g. where there are no electricity or communication links available).

Fig 6: Manual Imprinter

2.3 Electronic Authorisations and the Magnetic Stripe

Authorisations were initially obtained over the phone by calling an authorisation service. This process often took five minutes or more and was therefore only used for larger transaction amounts. The first automated authorisation devices "felt" the imprinted card numbers and transmitted them to an authorisation system. A central computer system determined that the card was valid, not listed as lost or stolen and the amount charged within the limits of the card.

In 1979, both Visa and MasterCard started to equip their cards with magnetic stripes, greatly enhancing the electronic processing potential. Cards could be read by swiping them through a POS terminal or inserting them into an ATM. Modems connected these devices to the authorisation systems and enabled a response within one or two minutes. This significantly reduced card fraud – for a while anyway – until card readers and writers became off-the-shelf equipment.

The magnetic stripe gets embedded into the plastic card during a multi-layered production process. It is one stripe made up of three tracks. Track 1 is the only one that contains the name of the cardholder. It is used in the airline industry to identify the passenger in self-service environments. The banking industry uses the Track 2 to store card account data such as the credit card number, expiry date, the Card Security Code, and a service code indicating if the card is equipped with a chip, if a PIN entry is required and if it can be used off-line. Track 3 is only rarely used. It generally contains issuer or card scheme specific information, such as additional service or security codes as well as membership and reward program numbers.

2.4 The Card Security Code

In an attempt to prevent credit card or debit card data on the magnetic stripe from being generated or modified, card schemes introduced an additional security feature - the Card Security Code (CSC), or Card Verification Value 1 (CVV1). This number is generated by the issuing bank and added to the magnetic stripe data. It is derived from a calculation similar to the Luhn-check digit using a secret algorithm across all numbers and all other characters of the magnetic stripe. Being transmitted along with the authorisation request, the issuing bank can verify that the magnetic stripe date is genuine.

This technique however did not protect from skimming attacks where merchants simply copied the magnetic stripe details of a card and later used on counterfeit cards. To help prevent that kind of fraud, card schemes have introduced an additional security code: The Card Verification Value 2 (CVV2), as it is known by Visa and Diners Club. MasterCard refers to it as the Card Verification Code 2 (CVC2). The three digit code is usually printed onto or indented into the card; on or next to the signature panel at the back of the card. The American Express Card ID (CID) is four digits long and printed on the face of the card. Similar to the CVC1, the code is unique to each card and can be generated and verified only with the secret algorithm of the card issuer.

Merchants are advised to request this code for every purchase transaction over the phone, mail or internet. This practice has since become compulsory for card-not-present transactions in Europe (EPC 2010). Knowing the code is intended to verify that the cardholder is in possession of the card that he is using for the purchase. Not all issuers however consistently respond to an incorrectly supplied code. European card issuers have committed to decline authorization requests in case of a card security code mismatch (EPC 2010). Visa Asia Pacific issuers lose all fraud charge-back rights if they approve an authorization request with the wrong card security code. In other regions issuers are free to approve authorisation requests made with false card security codes, making it a solution that is not yet really reliable across the world. As merchants are not permitted to store the code after a transaction (see PCI-DSS on page 99), compromised cardholder details never contain them, hence making the numbers less valuable to fraudsters. Merchants requesting the code during a purchase are better protected from card fraud.

The airline industry does have difficulties in fully adopting this practice as some airline systems cannot process these security codes and in other sales scenarios they are not even an available option. An example of this are the large proportion of tickets purchased with lodged cards or purchasing cards. There, usually only the card number and expiry date is available to the travel agent making bookings on behalf of corporate customers. As the CSC must not be stored, it cannot, of course, be submitted during the authorisation process.

2.5   Chip and PIN

Smart cards have been around since the mid-70s. They are plastic cards with mini computer chips embedded into their surface (hence they are also called "Chip Cards"). The standard processing power equates to some of the first PCs (64KB). The chip contains multiple embedded digital security keys that are exchanged with the card reader during a payment transaction, allowing them to mutually authenticate each other. Some keys are transmitted to the issuing bank's host system for verification and some are used to encrypt the messages on the way.

The chip is also able to verify if the PIN entered into the PIN pad of the card reader is correct. Contrary to common belief the PIN itself however is never stored within the card. It is rather used as part of a complex mathematical calculation of which the result is compared against the result that is stored on the chip. If the results are the same, the PIN is correct. This local PIN validation enables payment transactions to be authorised off-line, without a link to the issuing bank.

Commercialisation of smart cards first started in the early 80s with the introduction of telephone cards. The banking industry quickly realised the potential of these chip cards to reduce fraud and started issuing smart card based domestic debit card programs (e.g. France in the early 90s, Austria in 1995). In 1993 Europay, MasterCard and Visa agreed to work together on specifications for a common debit and credit card smartcard programs (see chapter 7.1 for more information on Europay, MasterCard and Visa (EMV) Standards).

Chip & PIN will ultimately be the "death" of the magnetic strip. In December 2010 the European Payment Council (EPC) approved a resolution to remove the magnetic stripe requirement for debit cards across the Single European Payment Area (SEPA) (European Payments Council, 2011). This is likely to become standard across all payment cards over the next decade.

2.6   3D Secure Password – the PIN for the Internet

The introduction of chip and PIN has significantly reduced fraud in card-present environments. Fraud itself however has not gone away, but rather moved on to a more vulnerable sales scenario: card-not-present transactions. For payments over the internet the chip on the card has no real value. For security reasons card schemes would also not want the regular card PINs to be revealed on the internet. So, card schemes were eager to find an equivalent technology that would work for e-commerce transactions.

Visa was the first to offer 3D secure, an XML-based protocol that was designed to add an additional layer of security to internet payments. It became known as "Verified by Visa". MasterCard has since adopted a similar service called MasterCard SecureCode, JCB adopted J/Secure and the American Express equivalent is called SafeKey.

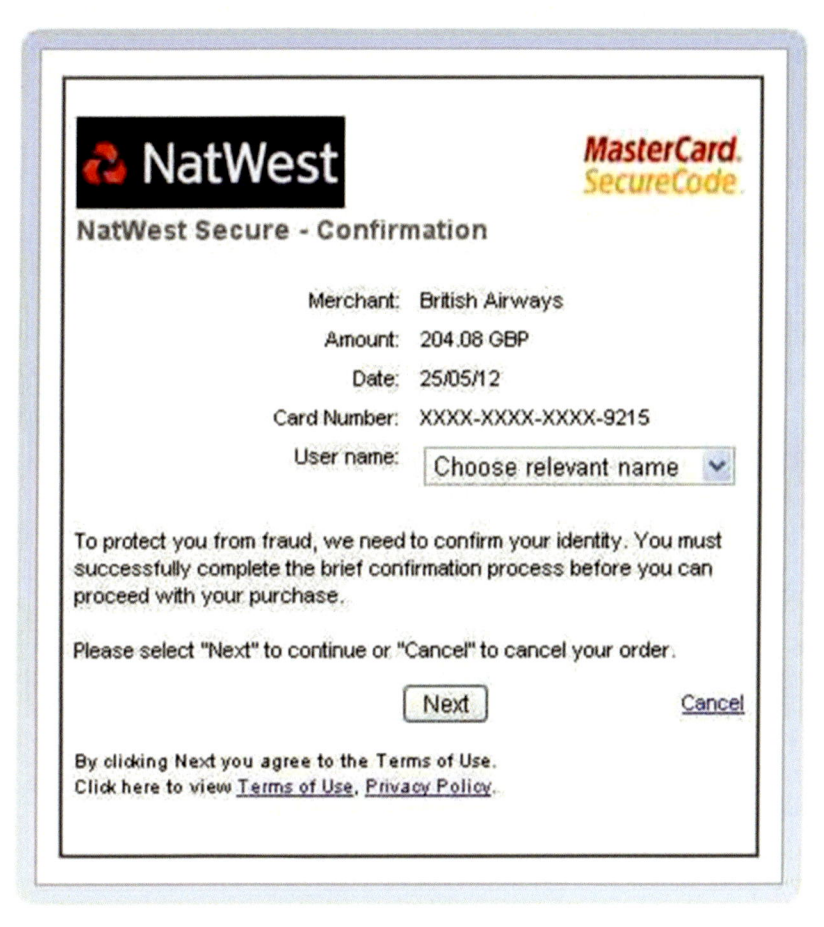

Fig 7: Example of MasterCard SecureCode Screen

For all of these programs the issuing bank provides the cardholder with an additional internet-only code (e.g. a user name and/or a password). During the payment process the cardholder is re-directed to an authorisation dialog with his issuing bank (usually a pop-up window branded by the bank). The cardholder then enters the 3D Secure Code. The bank uses this code to verify the identity of the payer and returns the dialog to the merchant. The merchant receives a confirmation code that he then sends along with the authorisation request.

Visa and MasterCard have also developed standards for using EMV cards in combination with portable mini-card readers to authenticate card-not-present transactions over the telephone and Internet. These devices require the card to be inserted and the PIN to be entered. They then generate a one-time password that needs to be submitted during the transaction process. MasterCard call it the Chip Authentication Program (CAP) EMV-CAP. Visa named it the Dynamic Password Authentication (DPA) scheme.

2.7 Contactless Payments – RFID and NFC

Radio-frequency Identification (RFID) is a technology used to read information from an electronic tag (a label or card) without physical interaction – making it contactless.

The most common usage of RFID tags is to affix them to an object and use them to track inventory, people or assets. The International Air Travel Association (IATA) for example has introduced standards for RFID based bag tags as alternative to the paper based ones. Public transport operators were the first to adopt contactless payments to increase convenience and speed, critical in their business. Credit card schemes quickly followed with MasterCard introducing PayPass, Visa introducing PayWave and American Express following suit with Expresspay.

To prevent credit card data from being retrieved or read without the consent or even the awareness of the cardholder, card schemes have introduced various security measures. The approach though differs in the U.S. and in countries where EMV chip card technology is used. Contactless payments there leverage the EMV cryptogram security to encrypt the card account number before it is transmitted. Transactions can therefore also be authenticated by the Point of Sales terminal – also in an off-line mode, similar to a regular chip transaction. U.S. based implementations rely on Dynamic Data Authentication (DDA). With this technology the RFID chip creates an additional Card Security Code (CVV3), individual to each payment transaction. For an authorisation request the card transmits the magnetic stripe data to the POS terminal, replacing the Card Security Code stored on the magnetic stripe (CVV1) with the contactless specific one. The information is forwarded to the issuing bank's host for authentication and authorisation. All transactions therefore have to be on-line (Smart Card Alliance, 2011).

Fig 8: Antenna in RFID enabled Cards (Courtesy of AustriaCard)

Near Field Communication (NFC) takes this concept one step further. Enabling a wireless data exchange between two devices (e.g. a chip card and a card reader) it allows a more elaborate two-way communication between both devices. However, this technology requires both the sending and the reading device to be (battery) powered, whereas RFID tags use the radio energy transmitted by the reader as its energy source.

The use of NFC-enabled mobile phones for mobile contactless payments and other mobile applications, such as access, loyalty and coupons is expected to grow dramatically over the next few years. The NFC transmitter module is either embedded within the mobile phone device or within the Subscriber Identity Module (SIM card) provided by the mobile phone operator. The credit card data is held either within an application on the phone or within the SIM card itself. NFC-enabled mobile phones will be able to carry multiple payment applications and accounts from different issuers. (NFC Forum.)

3 Setting the Stage - Who does what to make a Payment happen?

A payment network is a system of trust between many entities, each fulfilling a specific role. Here is an overview of the participants and their roles, in the context of the airline business.

This chapter provides a brief overview of the eight major participants involved in the payment process: cardholders, making a purchase with a payment card, issued by an issuing bank; merchants accepting card payment for goods and services that the cardholder wishes to purchase; the acquiring banks, payment processors, payment service providers and the card associations themselves, as well as their respective clearing houses. Later chapters further analyse each of their roles and responsibilities (see section 6.1), the transaction flow that links them together as well as the financial benefit for each of the participants.

3.1 Cardholder

Let's start with the cardholder—who can be you and I as private individuals wanting to purchase goods or services. Instead of using cash, you use a payment card that is provided by the bank, building society or a financial institution that you have a relationship with (issuer).

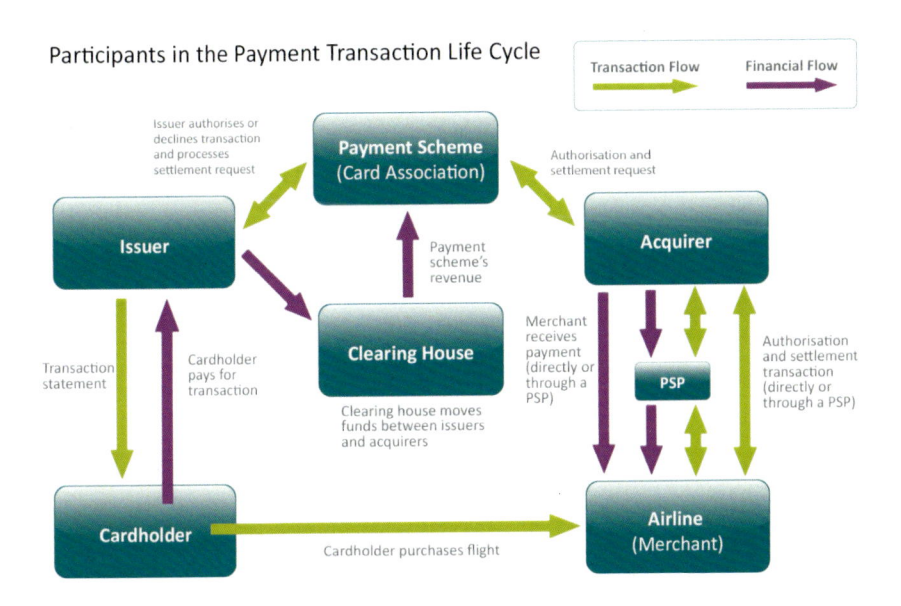

Fig 9: Participants in the Payment Transaction Life Cycle – Overview

By completing a purchase transaction using a card, you are instructing the card issuer to make a payment to the seller (merchant) on your behalf. You are equally promising your bank that you will ultimately pay back the amount of the purchase.

As discussed in later chapters, the "payment card" does not necessarily have to be a physical card. It can be an account number, a voucher, an electronic wallet, a user name, a mobile phone number or an NFC sticker that you affix to the back of your mobile phone. It is a means of identification that the cardholder has been given or assigned by the issuer allowing them to uniquely identify themselves to the seller (the merchant, e.g. the airline).

3.2 Issuer

The issuer (also called issuing bank or card issuer) is the entity issuing/providing the payment card, the cardholder uses for his cashless payments.

The issuer has a legal relationship with the cardholder and manages the funds associated with each payment card. As such, it authorises or declines transactions (purchases) the cardholder wants to perform with the card(s) and bills the cardholder for all purchases made using the card(s).

Depending on the payment method, these payments can be taken out of the cardholder's current account, immediately at the time of transaction ("pay now", e.g. debit card and on-line banking transactions) or paid back at a future date ("pay later"), as in the case of credit cards or charge cards, where the amount is deducted from a line of credit. Prepaid cards and electronic wallets have to be pre-funded before they can be used ("pay before"). The issuer pays for purchases out of those funds. By authorising a payment the issuing bank indicates that there is credit available to cover the transaction at the time.

In many cases the issuing bank is also the bank that manages the cardholder's current account (usually the case for debit cards).Many of the alternative payment methods are managed by non-financial institutions (e.g. prepaid cards, air miles, electronic wallets, mobile wallets, voucher systems). Such organisations either work with a bank or obtain a banking licence themselves to become an issuer. In Europe they can apply for a less regulated "Payment Institution" licence, rather than a full banking licence.

Issuing a Visa or MasterCard requires the issuing bank to have a license agreement with the respective card scheme. Some card schemes (Diners Club and American Express to a large extent) issue cards directly to the cardholder without the need for a separate issuing entity (three party model).

3.3 Merchant (Airline)

The merchant (or Merchant of Record) is the contractual entity selling the goods or service. In the airline world, the merchant could be either the airline directly, the travel agent or a third party content provider (e.g. car rental company, hotel or ground transport provider), selling anything from flights, excess baggage, lounge access or hotel accommodation to souvenir toys. The merchant is the entity entitled to receive the funds from the cardholder.

In some situations the Merchant of Record does not keep the entire transaction amount, but passes part of it on to downstream partners. If an airline sells a flight segment that is operated by a code-share partner, it acts as the Merchant of Record for the entire transaction but will eventually forward part of the revenue on to the partner airline. Travel agencies selling a holiday package and accepting a credit card as payment method usually act as the Merchant of Record for the entire transaction. They then pass the relevant portion of the revenue on to the respective airlines and other service providers.

Being the entity who accepted the payment, it is also ultimately the merchant's responsibility to carry the associated risks should things go wrong. If the customer is not happy with the goods or service that they receive, they have the right to claim their money back – from the merchant that is. If the transaction turns out to be fraudulent it is ultimately the merchant's risk (although there are some levels of protection for the merchant).

3.4 Acquirer

The acquirer (also known as acquiring bank or merchant acquirer) is the bank working with the merchant. It collects all the payment transactions the merchant has performed during a day and submits them to the respective card schemes for settlement. Once they are processed, it accepts the deposits from the card schemes (i.e. its respective clearing houses) and forwards them to the merchant's accounts.

For face-to-face transactions the acquirer traditionally also provides the merchant with the necessary payment infrastructure (card imprinters, POS devices). For card-not-present transactions (e.g. call centre or e-commerce), acquiring banks usually cooperate with Payment Service Provider (PSP) to supply the required payment infrastructure.

The acquiring bank is responsible for charging the merchant a fee a share of the transaction value that is then divided between all the participants involved in processing the payment.

Acquiring payments requires a license from the respective card scheme. As a license holder the bank guarantees to take on the responsibilities and risks associated with acquiring a merchant (see more in chapter6.1). Some card schemes have direct acquiring relationships with their merchants (e.g. American Express, UATP).

3.5 Payment Scheme (Card Association)

The Payment Scheme ties all the participants together. It is made up of a strong brand name, wide ranging contractual networks with many issuing banks and acquiring banks, a communication network infrastructure that links them together and a corporate framework – the card association. The brand name itself, such as "Visa", "MasterCard" etc. is probably its most valuable asset.

A scheme's main responsibility is to develop and enforce the rules and regulations governing how transactions, services and disputes are to be handled and to manage the routing of transactions between their participants. As their value grows with the number of acceptance points, cards in use and the transaction volume, they actively promote and support their brands. They work with governments and trade organisation and interface with national and international banking legislations.

Not every card scheme is structured the same way. Some are operated centrally (e.g. JCB, UATP, and American Express), some are set-up as autonomous regional entities (e.g. Visa). Some of the organisations are member-owned, giving their owners an influence on their governance (e.g. UATP).

3.6 Processor (Transaction Processing Company)

Processing payment transactions has become a commodity and many issuing acquiring banks as well as card schemes have outsourced this task to a payment processor. Large processing groups such as First Data, process 56 billion transactions per year for over 4,000 financial institutions worldwide (First Data).They provide the processing software and the data centres as well as the communication infrastructure.

3.7 Payment Service Provider (PSP)

Nothing stops an airline from connecting directly to their acquiring bank, but there are a number of reasons why they may not want, or be able to. Integrating direct distribution channels (such as e-commerce) with a bank is a very complex time-consuming and costly procedure that most merchants do not want to have to worry about. Instead they choose to use a third party to connect them with their specific acquiring bank(s). These third parties are called Payment Service Providers (PSP) or payment gateway provider.

PSPs established themselves at the time of the arrival of e-commerce. Acquiring banks were very familiar with acquiring ATM and POS transactions. They were struggling however with the need for more flexible web-based payment integrations. PSPs resolved this issue by providing and managing a simplified interface between the airline's distribution application and multiple acquiring banks, card and other payment networks.

The range of services typically provided by a PSP has evolved over the years from simple connectivity to end-to-end transaction management solutions (full service provider). Most of them today offer ancillary services such as consolidated reporting, risk management tools and currency conversion services. Some PSPs go even further and engage in managing the merchant's funds. They collect the payment streams from multiple acquiring banks and payment schemes the airline is contracted with and consolidate them into one or multiple accounts in one or more currencies. At agreed intervals they forward the funds to the airline.

Regardless of whether the merchant uses a PSP or not, they will still have to set up an agreement with an acquiring bank. There can however be a very close relationship between the PSP and the bank. Banks often have a strategic PSP partner or their own in-house PSP. Some PSPs have gone the opposite way and either work closely with one or more acquiring banks, or set themselves up as a bank or payment institution. Having a banking licence enables them to provide acquiring business directly, without needing a partner bank.

3.8 Clearing Houses

Clearing houses are responsible for collating and settling large amounts of transactions between multiple counterparties. Within a payment card scheme they are responsible for clearing and settling (moving) the funds between the issuing banks and the acquiring banks. By adding up and netting out the multiple credit and debit transactions each member submits they reduce the number of financial movements for each member to a single daily settlement – either a credit or a debit transfer from or to the account that the member has with the clearing house.

3.9 Players with Multiple Roles

It is important to understand that many of the providers in the payment market cover more than just one of the roles described above. Each of the players have continually been adding more and more services to their portfolios, covering additional roles in the payment value chain.

Some card schemes acquire their transactions and issue the cards themselves (e.g. American Express). As mentioned above PSPs can obtain acquiring licences and are starting to compete with acquiring banks. Banks in turn build in-house PSPs and compete with external providers. Card schemes have recently bought PSPs (e.g. MasterCard has acquired DataCash and Visa has bought CyberSource) and are now providing services similar to those of their member banks and other PSPs. Merchants are getting smarter about processing payments and integrate directly with acquiring banks, by-passing the PSPs. Transaction processing companies are offering acquiring services, competing with their own bank clients.

4 Message and Financial Flow – Payments Step by Step

4.1 Overview

Completing a payment requires that multiple sub-transactions go back and forth between the various payment entities described above. These include the authorisation request, the confirmation or capture message and the transaction submission, the clearing and settlement process and the fund transfer to the merchant. These transactions are supported by reversal, cancellation and credit transactions as well as by a dispute process.

A payment transaction usually consists of two parts: a request for authorisation to perform a certain financial transaction; followed by the payment confirmation message that indicates the requested transaction has been completed. As proof of authorisation the merchant receives an authorisation code from the issuer. This code has to be submitted along with the confirmation message[1]. That message is the merchant's request for the money for the goods or services they have given to the cardholder. Airlines can enrich the transaction message with passenger itinerary data to qualify for lower transaction fees.

Most card schemes offer corrective transactions, such as reversals, cancellations or refunds to cater for situations where either the merchant or the cardholder has changed their mind about the transaction or the amount involved.

All transactions are submitted to the acquiring banks and then transmitted on to the card schemes. The clearing and settlement process moves the funds from the issuing banks to the acquiring banks that ultimately pay the merchants the promised funds.

The dispute process gives all the participants an opportunity to dispute and correct a payment transaction.

---

[1] Confirmation messages without the authorisation code are more likely to be challenged by the cardholder and attract a higher merchant fee.

4.2 Authorisation

There are two types of authorisation: A pre-authorisation and the actual authorisation.

4.2.1 Pre-authorisation

Pre-authorisations are performed to validate a payment token (e.g. credit card) that will be used during a transaction in the near future.

If you open a bar tab with your credit card, for example, the bartender may want to perform a pre-authorisation to ensure that the credit card is "good" (i.e. is active and has not been reported lost or stolen). This can be done by sending a "Pre-authorisation Request". Where issuers don't support this transaction type an authorisation request with a minimal value of 0.01 would have the same result. A positive response indicates that the card is OK and any subsequent transactions are likely to be authorised. If the transaction is declined, any subsequent payment transaction is very likely to fail as well, suggesting the merchant should ask for another card.

A pre-authorisation validates a card but does not give a payment guarantee for a future transaction. To ensure enough funds are available for a particular transaction, the merchant will need to initiate an authorisation request.

4.2.2 Authorisation Request

An authorisation transaction or request is a request to the cardholder's issuing bank to authorise a payment transaction the customer would like to perform in return for the goods or services that they are purchasing from a merchant. Authorising the transaction indicates that the Issuer accepts the transaction and promises to pay the merchant the requested amount.

Authorisation Request and Response Transaction Flow

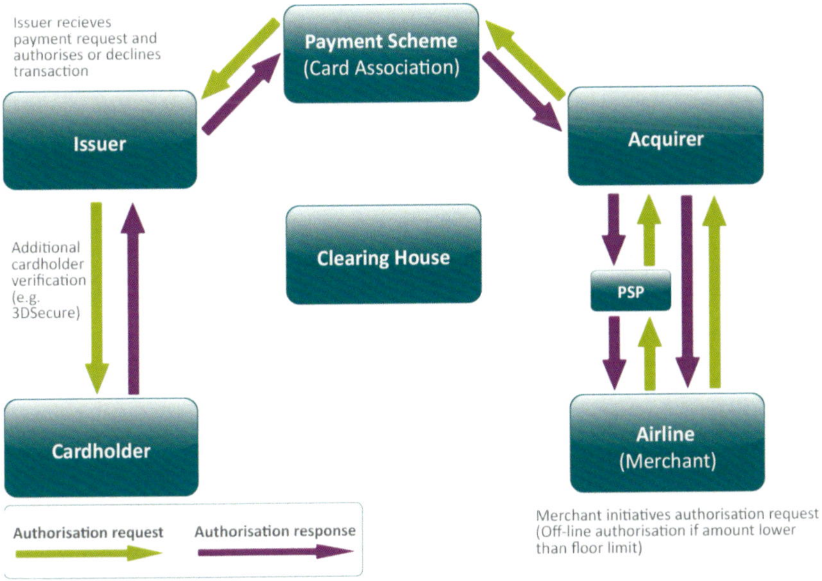

Fig 10: Authorisation Request and Response Transaction Flow

Issuing banks don't take this promise lightly. Upon receiving an authorisation request, the issuing bank would follow a number of checks to ensure the transaction is genuine (that the cardholder is the real cardholder) and that the cardholder has sufficient funds to cover the transaction.

Validating the transaction against available funds is easy enough. The bank checks if the requested amount is within the available balance (this can be a credit line, available funds on a current account or pre-loaded funds in a wallet/prepaid account). To avoid promising the same funds to multiple merchants, the bank reduces the available amount by the authorised amount. The money is then "put aside" for that merchant to claim later on[2]. That "promise" however is not open ended. If not used within a certain time frame (depending on the card scheme rules this can be between a few days and a few weeks) those funds are released and available for other transactions.

The second check, to ensure the cardholder is genuine, is ever increasing in complexity and a never-ending battle between fraudsters and those who fight them. Beside various techniques to increase the security of the payment token and the payment process (see chapter 2 on payment technology) banks use rules, algorithms and behavioural patterning to spot possible fraudulent transactions within the vast amount of good transactions. It is for example very unlikely that a cardholder will make three consecutive transactions in three different countries within a short period of time. Such transactions would automatically be declined – unlucky for those of us who have a transaction declined after arriving from a flight with a stop-over, where we have made a transaction in each of the previous airports...

Later in the book we will discuss various fraud management systems that are used not only within banks, but also increasingly by merchants and their providers (see page 252 for Fraud Management Systems).

Info box: Floor limits

Prior to electronic POS terminals and on-line shops, authorisations were obtained by calling the merchant's acquiring bank who forwarded the request to the card holder's bank. This was a complicated and expensive operation, especially when banks from abroad were involved. In many cases the costs of obtaining an authorisation outweighed the risk and associated costs of that transaction being fraudulent or not covered by available funds.

---

[2] This is the reason why the bank account balance is sometimes different from the amount that you have available to spend.

This is why card schemes introduced floor limits (or off-line limits), guaranteeing transactions up to a certain amount. Merchants were no longer required to obtain an authorisation request for amounts below this limit. The floor limits were dependent on the type of merchant, meaning that jewellery shops had higher limits than restaurants. The highest limits were those for airline transactions at $500 and included on-board retail transactions.

While the amounts of these floor limits have been reduced over time, they still exist today. Despite communication costs having dropped dramatically, the reasons remains the same – for transactions under a certain value, it is not worthwhile establishing a communication link for an authorisation. Some sales scenarios, like unattended parking terminals, are completely off-line – they don't even have the communication infrastructure to go on-line. For attended sales situations, dialling the acquiring bank for an authorisation can be an alternative to using a floor limit (e.g. taxi drivers).

4.2.3   Authorisation Response

The result of an authorisation request is either: "OK", "Declined", or "Refer to Issuer". The OK, or transaction acknowledgement, is sent together with an authorisation code. Declines and referrals are accompanied by a reason (code or message) to guide the merchant on any further action that can be taken.

A "Referral" requires the merchant to contact the acquiring bank for further transaction verification before the transaction is authorised. In some cases it is enough for the merchant to confirm verbally that the transaction is valid and intended. In other cases they may be requested to ask for further customer identification (e.g. passport details). The authorisation code is then manually issued to the merchant. This obviously works only in face-to-face situations where the cardholder is present and where the merchant can initiate such a call. In all other situations a referral would translate into the transaction being declined.

"Pick up card" indicates that the card is fraudulent and the merchant is requested to retain the card. Depending on the circumstances, the merchant may be more or less likely to actually do so (single shop keeper vs. supermarket with lots of security staff on hand). Merchants are rewarded by card schemes for retaining fraudulent cards.

The transaction authorisation itself does not constitute a payment. The authorisation code is the merchant's proof that they have obtained authorisation for a particular transaction. It provides a payment guarantee (which is actually more a payment promise) for a transaction that they may now perform. This actual payment has to be submitted as a subsequent transaction: the "payment confirmation" or "capture" message.

4.3 Payment Confirmation

This part of the payment transaction constitutes the actual payment request. Depending on the circumstances, it can be sent from any time immediately after the authorisation request[3] up until several days later. A key condition for the initiation of this message is that the goods or services have been provided to the cardholder. That point in time where this happens is called "delivery of goods".

When paying at the check-out counter of a shopping mall, the customer usually has all the things he has bought with him and the confirmation transaction is automatically created immediately after the issuing bank has authorised the transaction. When buying books on-line the payment authorisation happens during check-out at the payment page. The confirmation message however should not be created, until all the books have actually been delivered/ shipped.

Here are a few more examples: When you check-in at a hotel, the front desk agent asks for your credit card and usually performs an authorisation of the amount that you are likely to spend over the days

---

[3] Some card schemes provide a "combined message", but it is not widely used.

that you have booked for[4]. On check-out they create the payment transaction with the amount that you have actually spent, using the authorisation code obtained during check-in. A similar transaction happens with car rentals. When you collect the car, the agent obtains an authorisation for the rental amount plus the deposit. When you return the car the final rental amount is submitted.

The amount in the confirmation transaction has to be equal to, or lower than the authorised amount. For any amount larger than requested in the authorisation message, the merchant loses the payment guarantee. He may be lucky to get the funds, but he has no right to them. If there are insufficient funds available to cover the transaction, the issuing bank can decline the request for the money.

There is a small tolerance factor however for things like tips at restaurants (e.g. the waiter authorises the original amount on the bill and adds any tips to the confirmation message) and to accommodate currency exchange fluctuations between the time of authorisation and the transaction submission.

Info Box: Delivery of Goods in the Air Travel Industry.

Prior to electronic tickets, handing over the paper ticket to the passenger was considered the "delivery of goods". Although the passenger had not actually used the service (flown), the airline industry was successful in arguing that the paper ticket represented enough value in itself to justify that the passenger had to pay at that point. And it did: The paper ticket was the accountable document that could be used in exchange for a seat on a particular flight. But it could equally be used as a form of payment in exchange for another ticket, or it could be refunded against money (depending on the rules).

---

[4] Alternatively they only perform a pre-authorisation, verifying the card.

With the introduction of the electronic tickets, this topic came up for debate again. What does the passenger get, when he gets an electronic ticket number? Not much really – a number in an email or SMS usually. But again, the airline industry was allowed to carry on with the practice of charging the passenger as soon as this number was issued to them.

In normal circumstances this does not really matter. It does however become an issue, should the airline go out of business and the passenger does not get to use the promise to fly. According to most card scheme rules the cardholder has the right to challenge (and refuse to pay for) a transaction, where they did not receive the promised the goods or service. As the acquiring bank would have long ago forwarded the cardholder's money to the airline it would now no longer be available to be refunded to the cardholder. Chapter 6 further discusses cardholder rights and investigates who picks up the bill in those circumstances.

4.4 Airline Data

A regular payment transaction includes very little information about the goods or services purchased. Card schemes however are keen to get this additional transaction information as they can sell this data on to their corporate customers for all their business and purchasing cards. This supports them in matching the card transactions with the travel and entertainment expenses or order references in their Enterprise Resource Planning (ERP) systems. Additionally, knowing more about who they purchase from allows them to negotiate better rates with frequently used suppliers.

To encourage merchants to provide this extra information the card schemes reward them with lower merchant fees. To qualify for these preferential airline rates (which can be 0.2-0.3% lower than regular fees!), airlines need to make sure that their own systems as well as those of their PSPs and integrators can record and forward the relevant purchase details (commonly called Level II and Level III data). These need to be submitted as part of the capture transaction message.

Visa and MasterCard require passenger name, ticket number, issuing carrier, travel date, carrier code, service class code and the airport codes of the origin and the destination cities. Other card schemes, like American Express and UATP cards allow even further details (Descriptive Billing Information, or DBI) to be captured and transmitted including agent numeric code, the staff ID of the traveller, cost centre, project code or department code.

Some card schemes are preparing to be able to receive this information along with the authorisation request to further improve fraud prevention (e.g. American Express).

Level II Airline Data	
Issuing Carrier	Detailed data for up to four legs of travel:
Original ticket number	- Carrier code
Passenger name	- Services class
Departure date	- Stop-over code
Travel agency code/name	- Destination city/airport code
Origination city/airport code	

Level III Airline Data	
Restricted ticket indicator	Electronic ticket indicator
Total fare/tax/fee amount	Internet indicator
Currency code	Conjunction ticket number
Exchange ticket number and amount	Ticket issue date
Control ID detailed information for up to 198 legs of travel	Fare basis code

Table 1: Examples of Level II and Level III Airline Data

4.5 Reversals, Cancellations, Refunds and Credits

There are endless situations that require a payment to be modified or cancelled. People changing their minds during the booking process, customers who no longer want to use a flight and want the ticket refunded... Equally the airline may want to cancel/end a payment transaction (e.g. when the itinerary quoted to the passenger is no longer available). For these situations most payment methods provide corrective transactions, such as reversals, refunds and credits.

Reversing a transaction can be compared to tearing up the paper credit card slip before it is sent to the acquiring bank. Electronic transactions can equally be reversed or cancelled before they are submitted (see below). In both cases, the cardholder will not see the transaction on his transaction statement. The transaction is simply deleted (although still available for audit purposes) before it is submitted.

After a transaction has been submitted to the acquiring bank (or the paper slip has been sent off), it needs a refund transaction to balance out the original transaction. In that case the value of the transaction is credited back to the card. To avoid fraud it is vital to credit the amount back to the card that was used for the original transaction (see chapter 6.3 for more on "Types of fraud"). Refund amounts need to be lower or equal to the original payment amount. Some payment methods can only be manually refunded (e.g. as cash payment options). There the refunds have to be made using alternative payment methods such as cash, cheques or bank transfers.

Credits can be given independent of any previous payment transactions. They occur for example in situations where passengers need to be compensated (see page 197 for compensation payments). Not all payment methods allow this type of transaction. The access rights to this functionality needs to be carefully managed —as it allows a merchant's agent to put funds onto an individual's card from the merchant's account.

4.6 Transaction Submission (Capture)

At the end of a day (or a shift) the airline submits all the capture, refund and credit transactions to the acquiring bank. In the days of paper, this would have been when the paper slips were sent off to the bank. Today, most transactions are transmitted electronically. On a POS terminal all transactions that have occurred during the day would be submitted with an "End of Day" procedure (the transmission is either initiated manually at the terminal or centrally by a service that "polls" the terminal for the transactions. i.e. it dial up the POS terminal). Reservation systems extract the credit card transactions from the sales reports and submit them in batch files to the acquiring banks. For e-commerce transactions it is usually the PSP who submits the transactions to the various acquiring banks at the end of the day (the next section discusses submission by various channels in more detail). Depending on the card scheme, a merchant may have up to several months to submit transactions before they lose the payment guarantee.

4.7 Clearing and Settlement

This process initiates and controls the movement of funds from issuing banks to the acquiring banks and on to the merchants.

At the end of every day (sometimes several times a day), acquiring banks around the world collect the transactions their merchants have performed during the day, sort them and forward them to the respective clearing and settlement systems for each of the card schemes.

The card schemes receive the transactions and once a day (the bigger schemes may do this several times per day at different times per region and time zone) and forward them to the various card issuing banks – the banks of the cardholders who initiated the payment. The issuing banks need to pay the total of all transactions performed by their cardholders the previous day. This amount is debited from the account that the issuing bank has set up with the clearing house of the card scheme. At the same time acquiring banks receive the total amount of all transactions performed by their merchants, transferred onto their accounts with the clearing bank. Where banks operate in multiple settlement currencies, they would receive them separately.

In many cases the banks are both acquiring and issuing institutions. Instead of sending to and receiving amounts from the card schemes, clearing houses settle the difference between the two amounts, either a credit or a debit transaction, depending which part of the business is bigger.

Clearing and Settlement Process

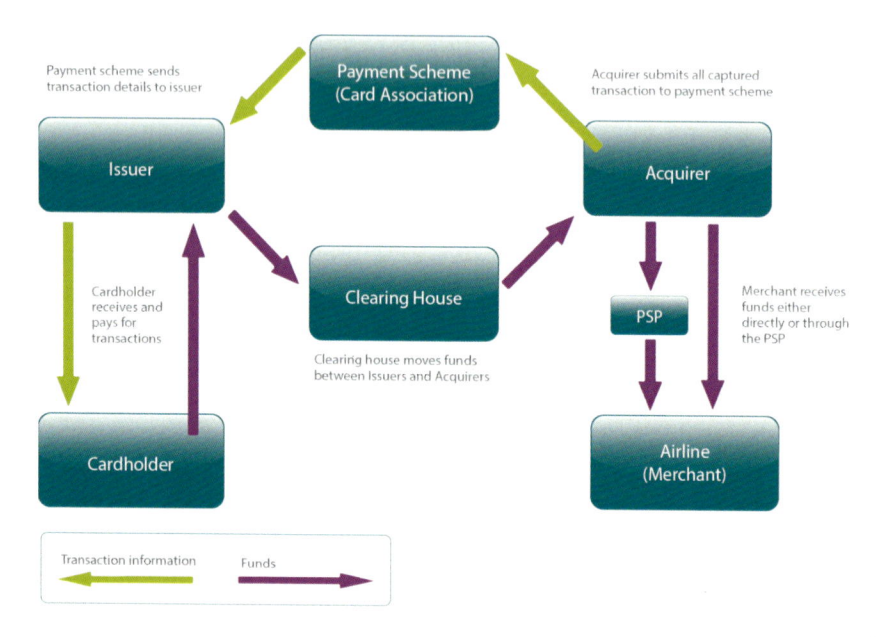

Fig 11: Clearing and Settlement Flow

Banks who acquire transactions that were generated with cards belonging to their own cardholders ("on us" transactions) usually do not forward them to the card schemes for clearing and settlement, but process them internally. This saves them some of the fees associated with the clearing and settlement process. Airlines with a large amount of domestic transactions may be able to negotiate to share some of those savings with their acquiring banks. Refund and credit transactions trigger funds to flow in the opposite direction. So do charge-backs.

4.8 Billing the Cardholder

As described above, the issuing bank pretty much immediately has to provide the funds for all its cardholders' transactions. This does not necessarily have to correlate with the time that the cardholder has to pay for it. The payment method determines when the issuing bank will present the cardholder with the "bill" and when the cardholder actually has to pay for a particular transaction.

With credit cards, as the name suggests, the cardholder has a credit line he can use to make purchases. At the end of a billing cycle he may have to pay the total of his purchases immediately (these types of credit cards are "charge cards"). With "real" credit cards the cardholder has the option to even further defer the payment of the transactions (revolving credit). Usually only a minimum percentage of the total outstanding amount has to be paid at the time. The remaining amount can be accumulated up to the credit limit of the card. Debit card transactions, as well as direct debits and bank transfers are immediately (the day after they have been submitted by the merchant) deducted from the cardholder's current account.

Prepaid cards, as well as any wallets or on-line prepaid accounts require the cardholder to fill the account with funds first, before any transactions can be made. The issuer immediately deducts any transactions from those available funds.

4.9 Settlement with the Merchant

Settlement can be equally unsynchronised: whilst the acquiring banks receive funds from the card scheme immediately (daily) after the transaction submission, they do not necessarily immediately re-distribute them to the merchants. The settlement cycle is usually negotiated between the merchant and the bank and depends on various factors:
The longer the merchant agrees to wait for their money, the lower they will be able to negotiate the merchant fee. Many acquiring banks now hold onto a "balance" which is used to cover bad transactions (charge-back claims from cardholders) or a potential merchant bankruptcy. The higher the perceived risk, the longer they delay pay out (see page 234 for more information about the risk evaluation process).

4.10 Transaction Dispute Process

Most of the card scheme rules protect their cardholders against illegitimate transactions on their accounts. This includes scenarios where they have not made the transaction (authorisation not obtained - somebody else has misused their card for a fraudulent transaction), the charged amount differs from the amount that they had agreed to pay, they did not receive the goods or services they had ordered (goods not delivered) or situations where they have not received quite what they had ordered and/or expected to receive. In all those situations the cardholder has the right to dispute a transaction. Unfortunately merchants also have to face cases where the cardholder is purposely seeking to dispute a legitimate purchase they made ("friendly fraud"). The merchants of course have the opportunity to defend their position, providing evidence to support their claim. There are several stages to such a dispute process, clearly defined by the rules of every card scheme:

4.10.1 Retrieval Request or Request for Copy

If a cardholder is unsure about a transaction that has occurred on their statement they can request additional transaction information from the merchant to sustain the claim for the amount that they have been charged. This is called a "request for information", or a "request for copy" – a copy of the sales ticket that the customer has signed. The merchant needs to respond to this request within a certain time frame, supplying additional information about the purchase. Providing the full name of the merchant (not just the short, often cryptic description on the statement) usually helps the cardholder to either identify the transaction as valid, or be sure that the transaction was certainly not theirs.

4.10.2 Charge-back

If the cardholder does not accept the transaction charge, they can initiate a process to get a partial or a full refund: a charge-back. To dispute a transaction the cardholder needs to contact their card issuer. The issuer pre-evaluates the claim and temporarily credits the cardholder with the transaction amount, if they think there is sufficient evidence to support the dispute.

The bank then submits the charge-back to the card scheme to claim the money back. The charge-back windows that are available to the cardholder vary from scheme to scheme and from region to region. The cardholder does not have to go through the request for information process first.

The merchant's acquiring bank receives the charge-back, debits the merchant account with the transaction amount and notifies them via the transaction management console and the daily transaction report. The airline now has two options: either accept the charge-back or collect enough evidence to support a re-presentment.

4.10.3 Second Presentment or Re-Presentment

The merchant has about seven days to respond to a charge-back. The information submitted together with a re-presentment is often more extensive than that submitted during the request-of-information process. A copy of the order, signed payment receipts (where available), booking summary, delivery confirmations (copies of the email confirmation), copy of the Passenger Name Record (PNR) and evidence that the passenger has flown (such as flight number, seat number) will be included. If the merchant agrees to some of the customer's concerns they can reduce the amount of the second presentment accordingly.

As there are transaction fees associated with a re-presentment it may not be worthwhile processing them for small transaction amounts (on-board meals for example). Some airlines on the other hand have a policy to defend every single charge-back, regardless of the costs, to deter fraudsters from systematically abusing the system.

The issuing bank will evaluate the information presented. If it is deemed sufficient to support the claim, then the cardholder is debited again with the transaction amount and the airline receives the funds (minus the processing fees). The bank may get in touch directly with the airline to request further information before accepting or declining a claim.

4.10.4 Second Charge-back and Arbitration Process

The cardholder may still refuse to accept the transaction and can initiate a second charge-back to fight the charge to their account. If the merchant continues to disagree with the cardholder and the issuing bank, then all parties involved have an opportunity to escalate and present their case to the card scheme in an arbitration process. An arbitration analyst will evaluate the evidence against the scheme rules and decide on the case. Split decisions are possible when one party offers a reasonable compromise solution to the dispute. The losing party has to pay the filing and review fees (which can be several hundred dollars).

In addition to cardholder initiated charge-backs, there may be reasons for an issuing bank itself to initiate a charge-back. The most common are:
- Duplicate transaction
- Card/account not valid or expired
- Late presentment
- Incorrect transaction details (currency code etc.)

Defending charge-backs can cost a merchant a lot of effort, but it is a vital process in protecting revenue.

4.11 Additional Transaction Types

This section covers two additional transaction types. They refer more to the way a payment is taken as opposed to the steps within a payment transaction: Split payments, where multiple payment methods are used for a single purchase or one authorisation code is used for multiple transactions; and dual merchant payments, where the same cardholder details are used for multiple purchase transactions.

4.11.1 Split Payments

The term "split payment" can either refer to a process where multiple payment methods are used to pay for a single purchase or to the situation where a single authorisation is used to buy multiple items that are shipped and charged for at different times.

The first scenario refers to a practice quite common in the airline environment, where tickets are paid for using multiple payment cards or multiple payment methods. This can be two passengers in one booking, each paying their share of the ticket price with their own credit card.

Single Payment	**Split Payments**

Payment method

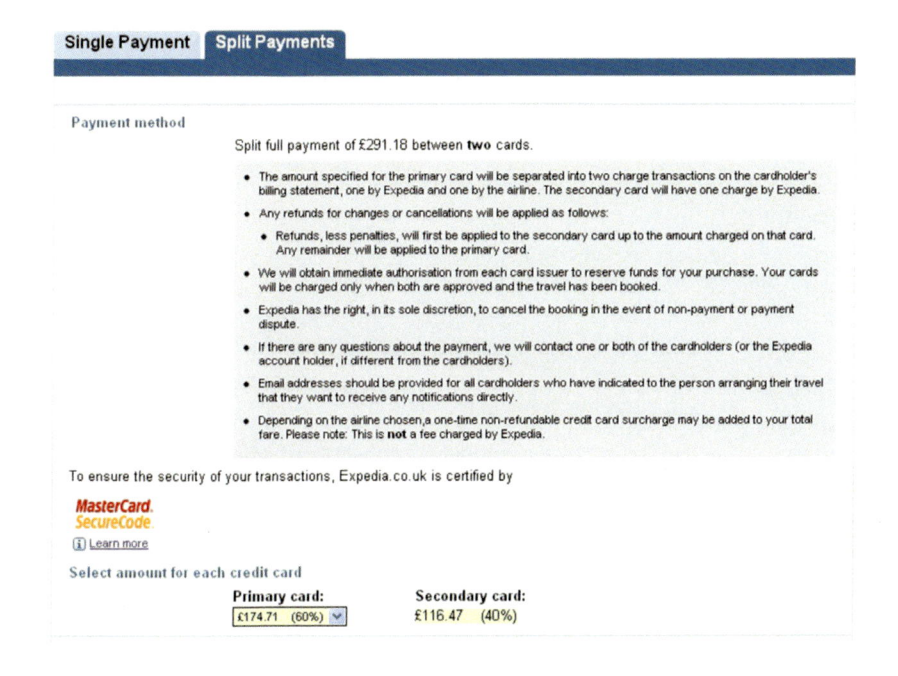

Split full payment of £291.18 between **two** cards.

- The amount specified for the primary card will be separated into two charge transactions on the cardholder's billing statement, one by Expedia and one by the airline. The secondary card will have one charge by Expedia.
- Any refunds for changes or cancellations will be applied as follows:
  - Refunds, less penalties, will first be applied to the secondary card up to the amount charged on that card. Any remainder will be applied to the primary card.
- We will obtain immediate authorisation from each card issuer to reserve funds for your purchase. Your cards will be charged only when both are approved and the travel has been booked.
- Expedia has the right, in its sole discretion, to cancel the booking in the event of non-payment or payment dispute.
- If there are any questions about the payment, we will contact one or both of the cardholders (or the Expedia account holder, if different from the cardholders).
- Email addresses should be provided for all cardholders who have indicated to the person arranging their travel that they want to receive any notifications directly.
- Depending on the airline chosen, a one-time non-refundable credit card surcharge may be added to your total fare. Please note: This is **not** a fee charged by Expedia.

To ensure the security of your transactions, Expedia.co.uk is certified by

MasterCard. SecureCode.
(i) Learn more

Select amount for each credit card

Primary card:	Secondary card:
£174.71 (60%)	£116.47 (40%)

Fig 12: Example of Split Payment Processing

But it can equally be one ticket being paid with a combination of cash and credit card, cheque and credit card, a miles redemption and partial cash payment, Miscellaneous Cash Orders (MCOs), prepaid tickets etc. or any other combination of these. The ticketing systems are usually able to record multiple payments with multiple payment methods. Carriers can set rules to determine the combinations permitted.

The second scenario where the term split payment (or "multiple transaction sequencing") is used is when a merchant obtains an authorisation code for a purchase comprising multiple items (tickets or any other goods such as books). The same authorisation code is then used for multiple capture transactions, each one with a partial value of the entire order. This may be operationally required when the tickets are issued or the books shipped at different times. Not all card schemes and acquiring banks support this transaction type. It can cause reconciliation issues and merchants may lose their payment guarantee.

4.11.2 Dual-Merchant Payments

For a dual-merchant payment the cardholder details, which have been recorded during the purchase process are used for two or more individual payment transactions with two or more merchants. A typical example is a situation where an airline sells a flight and a car rental booking together through their e-commerce portal. The payment details are captured once during the check-out process and then sent for authorisation to the airline's acquiring bank for the value of the ticket and then to the car rental company's acquiring bank for the value of the car rental. They form two separate transactions with two separate merchants of record, using the same cardholder information.

It is recommended that this process is kept visible to the cardholder, as it enables payer authentication (3D secure, if required) for each transaction. It equally avoids misunderstandings and possible charge-backs from cardholder who was not aware of the second transaction with the other merchant (e.g. the car rental company) and may be under the impression they are being charged twice.

5   Costs of a Payment Transaction – Who Earns What?

For each of the transaction types discussed in the chapters above, all the players discussed earlier on in the book have a role to fill. It is complex, involves a lot of technology and implies commercial risk on all sides. So, why are they doing it?

At the end of the day they perform these roles to make money. In this section we will discuss each of the players in terms of what their share is in the fees that the merchant (and ultimately the customer or passenger) has to pay for processing each transaction. Understanding this will help you to optimise your business costs.

The end of this chapter looks at two options that allow the merchant to recover some of these transaction processing costs: Surcharging and Dynamic Currency Conversion (DCC).

5.1 Transaction Cost Model

The transaction model below (**Fig 13**) describes a typical Visa and MasterCard fee structure. Depending on the number of parties involved, other payment methods may follow a similar or slightly simpler version of this model (e.g. simpler interchange structure, less entities).

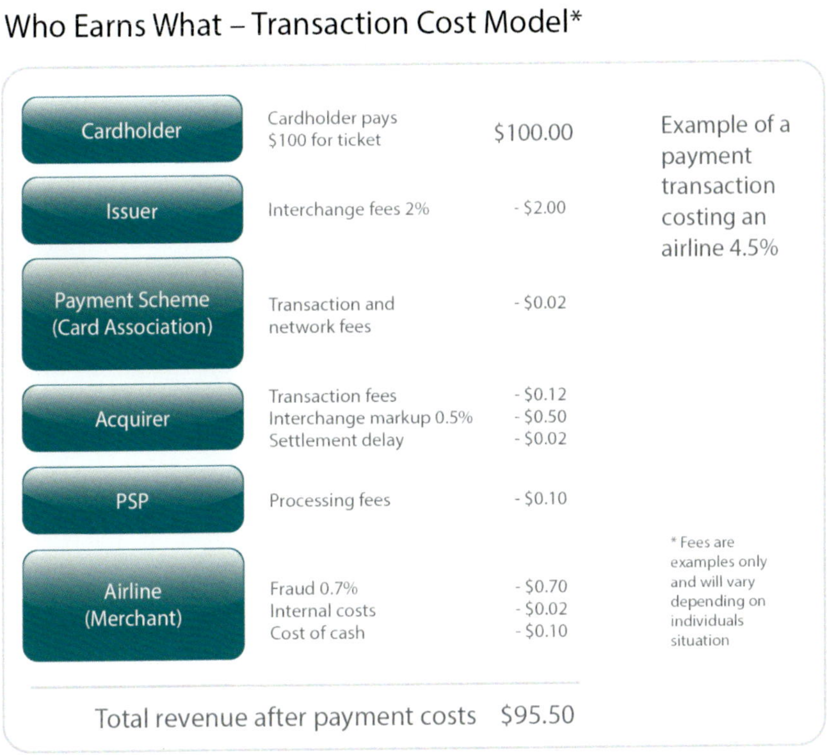

Who Earns What – Transaction Cost Model*

Cardholder	Cardholder pays $100 for ticket	$100.00	Example of a payment transaction costing an airline 4.5%
Issuer	Interchange fees 2%	- $2.00	
Payment Scheme (Card Association)	Transaction and network fees	- $0.02	
Acquirer	Transaction fees Interchange markup 0.5% Settlement delay	- $0.12 - $0.50 - $0.02	
PSP	Processing fees	- $0.10	
Airline (Merchant)	Fraud 0.7% Internal costs Cost of cash	- $0.70 - $0.02 - $0.10	*Fees are examples only and will vary depending on individuals situation
	Total revenue after payment costs	$95.50	

Fig 13: Who Earns What? Transaction Cost Model

The model starts with the entity furthest away from the merchant – the issuing bank – and adds its costs to the costs of the card scheme, the acquiring bank and the Service Providers. The sum of these elements adds up to the fees that the merchant ultimately needs to pay for processing a transaction.

5.1.1   Issuing Bank – Cardholder and Interchange Fees

The issuing bank has two revenue streams from a payment transaction: cardholder fees and interchange fees. These fees allow them to cover the expenses associated with processing the payments: administration and system costs; the costs of defaults (in cases when the cardholder cannot pay) and for credit cards the costs of pre-financing the transaction amount between the time the issuing bank pays the card scheme (next working day) and the time they charge the cardholder (at the end of the billing cycle, when the cardholder gets their statement). Some of that fee will obviously contribute to the issuer's profit.

Cardholder fees – These are levied in particular for transactions in foreign currencies. For those, the issuing bank usually charges a transaction fee and a mark-up on top of the currency exchange rate that is applied to convert foreign currencies into the card's currency. Transactions in local currency are normally free of charge to the cardholder. The exceptions are pre-paid cards, where banks sometimes charge a transaction fee for purchases.

Interchange fees – The interchange fees are by far the largest part of the transaction revenue for the issuing bank. They are set by the card schemes and paid out as part of the daily settlement[5] from the card scheme. The fees contain variable elements, set as a percentage of the transaction and fixed transaction fee element. They are not actually a set fee, but rather a complicated matrix of different fees, based on the circumstances under which the payment was taken. There are different matrices for almost every country. To calculate the actual fee, several parameters are taken into consideration.

---

[5] Or rather subtracted from the amount that is settled with the clearing house.

The most important fee parameters are:

- **Country** – in what country was the transaction acquired and where is that in relation to the location of the issuing bank? Interchange fees for domestic transactions (where the issuer and acquirer are in the same country) are a lot lower than "intra-regional" (or cross-border) transactions – where they are in the same region. "Inter-regional" transactions, where they are outside the region (e.g. a passenger shopping in Asia with their American card) attract the highest interchange fees.
- **Payment product** – debit card transactions are priced lower than credit card transactions.
- **Card-present indicator** – was the card present during the transaction? "Card-not-present" transactions attract a higher fee than transactions that were processed in a "card-present" mode.
- **Data Entry Mode** – what technology was used to enter the cardholder information? The fee is the highest for transactions where the cardholder information has been keyed in, followed by swiped transactions and then those where the chip was the source of the data.
- **Number of days between authorisation and transaction submission** – transactions captured more than 2-3 days after they were authorised attract higher interchange fees.
- **Card and terminal technology** – what technology was used for the interaction between the terminal and the payment card? Fees vary for full EMV transactions, where both the card and the terminal were EMV compliant and the transaction was done using the EMV protocol (digital interaction between the chip card and the card reader), partial EMV transactions, where either the card or the POS terminal were EMV compliant, magnetic swipe transactions and transactions where 3D secure was used to authenticate the cardholder.
- **Card type** – what type of payment card was used? Corporate, purchasing, premium cards (e.g. "Platinum" cards) and reward cards (e.g. those where the cardholder gets miles for every purchase) all attract a higher interchange fee than regular consumer cards.

- **Preferential rates** for airline, hotel and car rental transactions – transactions acquired for a merchant with an airline Merchant Category Code (MCC) that contain all the additional airline itinerary data (Level II data), as well as hotel and car rental transactions with the equivalent set of data attract a special, lower interchange fee.
- **Volume** – Merchants processing a certain volume (well above 500 million USD) can agree special interchange rates directly with the card schemes.

The difference in interchange fees helps card schemes to incentivise scheme participants to follow certain behaviours and use certain products and technologies over others. To reward merchants for using more advanced chip technology, for example, the interchange fees for EMV transactions are lower than those for swiped transactions. If transactions are submitted late, the merchant is penalised with a higher interchange fee. Higher fees also help issuers finance reward programs.

Understanding the different interchange rates can help airlines to better negotiate their fees with the acquiring banks. By optimising the payment strategy and the payment systems, they can qualify their transactions for lower interchange rates, incurring lower costs to their acquiring bank. Depending on the negotiation skills and the agreements, some of these savings can then be passed on to the airline (see below, merchant fees).

5.1.2 Card Scheme - Network Fees

Card schemes only add a very small fee to the overall cost of a transaction, typically based on the transaction type and the card product that has been used for the payment. The revenue is used to cover the costs of processing the payment, managing the card scheme and to create brand awareness. It also contributes to the card scheme's profit.

5.1.3 Acquiring Bank – Merchant Fee

The acquiring bank charges the merchant a Merchant Service Fee (also known as Merchant Discount Fee and Merchant Discount Rate). As it is the entity that has the commercial relationship with the merchant these fees needs to cover not only acquiring bank's own costs, but also the costs of the other participants in the scheme – the interchange fees for the issuing bank and the card scheme fees.

The acquiring bank itself charges an additional transaction mark-up to cover its own costs as well as the commercial risk that is associated with acquiring a merchant's transactions. The level of mark-up is predominantly influenced by the merchant's transaction volumes, the type of business they are in and the merchant's risk profile (see Acquiring Bank – Risk evaluation process, page 234).

There are three common ways an acquiring bank can structure its own fees on top of the interchange and scheme fee: a blended rate, an "Interchange+" model, and a tiered pricing model.

Blended rate

The blended rate is a single rate per payment method, independent of the transaction profile and its associated interchange rates. For this rate the acquiring bank evaluates the transaction profile of the merchant's business, estimates the average applicable interchange rate and adds its internal mark-up. For the merchant this simplifies the rate structure, protects them from variable fee elements and allows them to better predict their transaction costs.

Illustration of a Blend Fee Pricing

Blend fee pricing

- Merchant agrees fixed blended rate with bank.
- Cost price of transactions varies depending on country, card type and sales channel.

Example (right):

- UK registered business
- Blend fee of 1.55%
- 5 transactions from DE, UK, NL and US
- Cost to merchant average 1.55%

Fixed transaction costs 1.55%

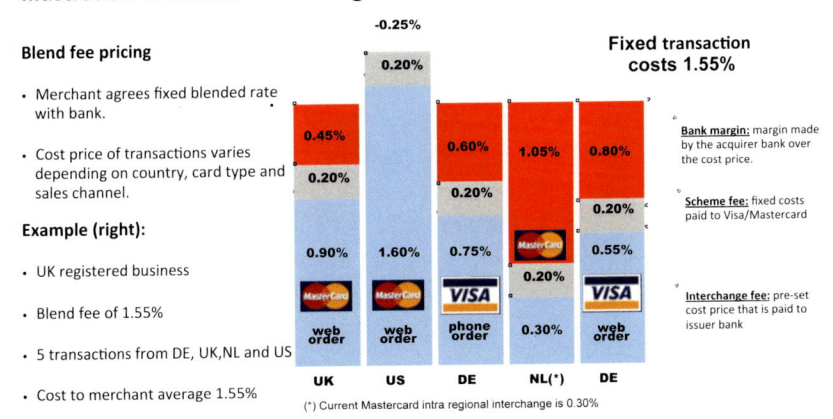

Bank margin: margin made by the acquirer bank over the cost price.

Scheme fee: fixed costs paid to Visa/Mastercard

Interchange fee: pre-set cost price that is paid to issuer bank

(*) Current Mastercard intra regional interchange is 0.30%

Fig 14: Illustration of Blend Fee Pricing (Courtesy of Adyen)

"Interchange+"

This model works quite the opposite way. The merchant agrees to pay the actual applicable interchange and card scheme fees for each transaction plus a fixed mark-up. This gives the merchant full transparency of the actual interchange costs that apply per transaction. But as the fees vary per transaction, it makes them more difficult to understand, plan and administer.

Illustration of an interchange+ Pricing

Interchange+ pricing

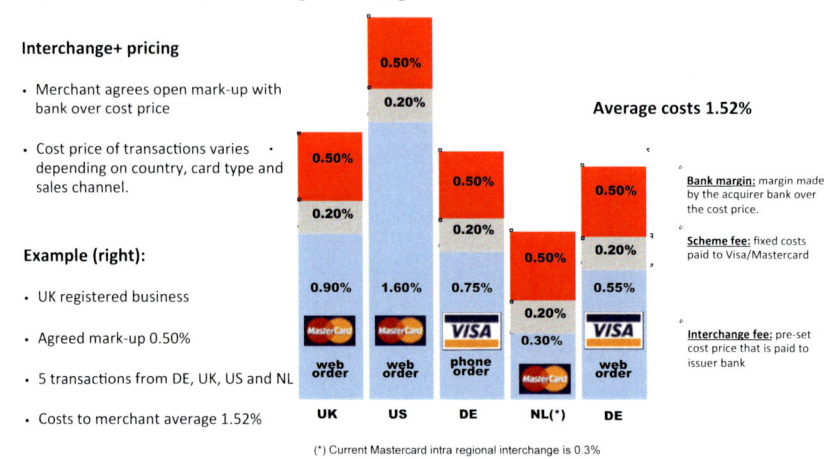

- Merchant agrees open mark-up with bank over cost price
- Cost price of transactions varies depending on country, card type and sales channel.

Example (right):

- UK registered business
- Agreed mark-up 0.50%
- 5 transactions from DE, UK, US and NL
- Costs to merchant average 1.52%

Average costs 1.52%

Bank margin: margin made by the acquirer bank over the cost price.

Scheme fee: fixed costs paid to Visa/Mastercard

Interchange fee: pre-set cost price that is paid to issuer bank

(*) Current Mastercard intra regional interchange is 0.3%

Fig 15: Illustration of Interchange+ Pricing (Courtesy of Adyen)

Tiered Pricing

Tiered pricing is a combination of both of the above models. The acquiring bank re-categorises the interchange matrix and the various associated costs into three to six tiers. The merchant and the acquiring bank agree on a transaction price per tier. This method better exposes the merchant to the true costs, gives an incentive to improve the transaction quality (e.g. submitting them on time), but protects them from the complexity of the entire interchange matrix.

Depending on the transaction volume, the nature of the business and the actual rates that the merchant is able to negotiate, one or the other model may be more beneficial. The more advanced the merchant's payment strategy and the more control they have over their operations, the more likely they are to be able to benefit from an Interchange+ model. For smaller merchants and for merchants with less control over their payment infrastructure a simple, blended rate may be better.

5.1.4 Payment Processor and Ancillary Service Provider Fees

The merchant fees are only a part of the fees that the merchant will have to pay to have their transactions processed. They only cover the costs of the card scheme and its participants and do not yet include the costs of the various other providers that are involved in accepting, processing and forwarding payment transactions on behalf of a merchant: payment processors, Network Service Providers (NSP), PSPs and ancillary service providers.

These fees are usually charged directly by the various providers. Some of them can bundle all of the fee elements (including the merchant fees) into a single price for the merchant (see Supplier and Partner Selection for detailed pricing structure – Page 228ff).

This section covered the external costs of a payment transaction. Later parts of the book will discuss the internal costs of taking payments: the administration and processing costs as well as the costs of fraud.

The following section looks at two methods that are available to merchants to recoup some of the expenses associated with taking payments: Surcharging and Dynamic Currency Conversion.

80　Things you should know before you start

5.2　Surcharging

Surcharging is the "art" of charging additional fees for accepting payments with certain payment methods.

In the airline industry this practice was first picked up by low cost carriers for their internet based distribution channels. It has since been widely adopted across the industry. Low cost carriers as well as traditional full service carriers are applying it to e-commerce transactions and all other direct and indirect distribution channels.

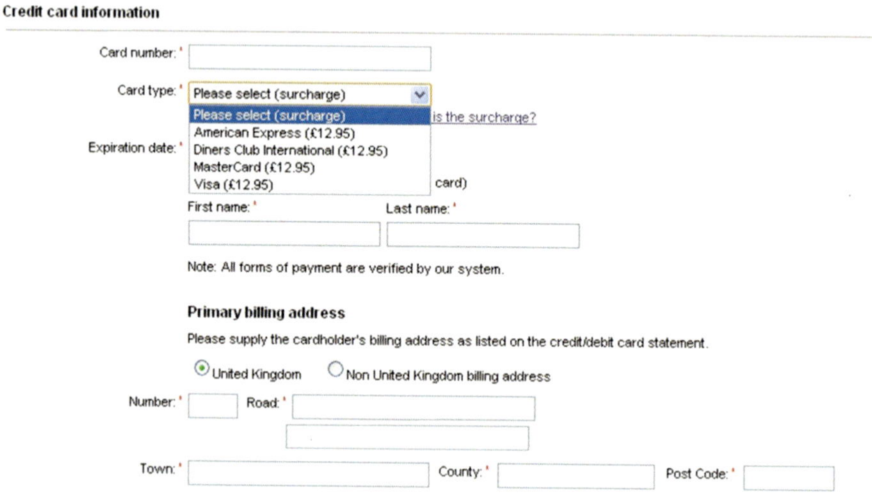

Fig 16: Surcharge Amount depending on the Payment Method

The fee structure follows one of three main models: A fee per person or per sector (sometimes subject to a minimum for one-way fares); a percentage of the ticket price; or a flat fee, independent of the value, amount of passengers or number of flight segments. The actual amount is also often dependent on the selected payment method. That usually correlates to the actual costs of the payment transaction – the higher the merchant fees, the higher the fees for the passenger. Debit card or UATP transactions for example are often charged less than credit cards. The airline's own co-branded cards are sometimes excluded from being surcharged – they are identified by the first six to nine digits of the card number.

Airline	Surcharging	Amount for credit card bookings*
American Airlines	YES	£4.50 per booking
British Airways	YES	£4.50 per person per booking
Bmibaby	YES	£4.50 per person per sector, minimum charge £6
BMI	YES	£4.50 per person per booking
Delta	NO	Zero
EasyJet	YES	2.5% of booking cost, minimum £4.95
Flybe	YES	£4.50 per person per sector, plus £1 per sector, min £5.50
Lufthansa	YES	£4
Monarch	YES	£10 per booking
Ryanair	YES	£6 per person per sector
United	NO	Zero
Virgin Atlantic	YES	1.5%

* Source information company websites at 1st August 2011

Table 2: Chart of Airlines Charging Credit Card Surcharges in the UK Market (Courtesy of Airline Information)

To avoid having to declare credit card fees upfront, together with the ticket price, airlines offer a niche payment method, such as Visa Electron, free of charge. In this way the payment fees remain an "optional" fee item and can be presented later on in the booking process – usually only as part of the final step – during the payment process. Some countries require credit card fees to be included upfront in the published ticket price (e.g. Australia, U.S.).

For many carriers these fees are a way of recovering their payment costs, for others surcharging is an obvious revenue generator. No wonder that, ever since its introduction, this practice has received criticism from customer protection groups. Their main concerns is that charges are disproportionate to the real cost of the payment and are not immediately apparent to customers. Governments are trying to regulate this practice to ensure fairness and price transparency. "Consumer laws agreed by the European parliament make it clear that unfair surcharges for all means of payment must be made illegal in the UK before 2014."(King, 2011).A consumer protection directive issued by the European Commission limits the airline's ability to add credit card fees to the actual costs of the transaction. This directive has to be transposed into national law by the end of 2013 (Cohen, 2011).

Although consumer protection groups may force airlines to revise the processes around surcharging, it will remain a part of the ticket buying process and a major ancillary revenue factor for the foreseeable future.

5.3   Dynamic Currency Conversion

Have you ever encountered the following dilemma: you are somewhere abroad and want to make a purchase? You put your credit or debit card into the terminal and the following question pops up:

'Do you want to pay in XYZ currency, or in your home currency?

"Hmm... Yes? No? Yes? What did everybody say I should do? Will I be overcharged? But wouldn't it be better to know how much it will cost me in my home currency immediately?"

This service is called Dynamic Currency Conversion (DCC). It offers Visa and MasterCard holders the choice to pay for goods and services in their home currency either when abroad or when the merchant's pricing currency differs to that of the customer's card currency. For any merchants, including airlines the DCC service can generate a profit or revenue stream from international card transactions.

5.3.1   Overview – How does the DCC Service work?

Once the credit card details are entered for payment, whether online or at the point of sale, the DCC provider immediately identifies the currency of the card (using the Bank Identification Number found in the first six digits of the card number). If the currency differs from that of the merchant, then the customer is given the option to make the payment in their home currency. When the conversion is made a margin, typically in the region of 3%, is added to the exchange rate thereby generating the additional revenue stream for the merchant.

The cardholder is presented with the option to either pay in the merchant's original pricing currency or in their home currency. The card schemes stipulate that the cardholder should be given the option of which currency to pay in and that the exchange rate used for the transaction as well as the source of the exchange rate are clearly displayed. If the cardholder agrees to DCC, it is this amount that is sent for authorisation and settlement.

It is important to note that without DCC it is the issuing bank together with the card schemes, i.e. either Visa or MasterCard who do the conversion – they apply a margin to the exchange rate and they enjoy the revenue stream. By offering DCC the cardholder is not charged any more for the transaction – the revenue is simply redirected away from the card schemes and issuing banks back to the merchant and the DCC provider. It is advisable to apply a margin in the region of 3% to the exchange rates to ensure the offer made to the cardholder is a competitive one. Airlines applying too high a margin to rates can expect that their customers will refuse to use the service or file complaints at a later stage.

5.3.2 Benefit to the Cardholder

The main benefit for the cardholder, when choosing DCC, is price transparency. The cardholder will know exactly what the merchant will charge them in their home currency, the exchange rate applied to the transaction and the margin to the exchange rate – the idea is that the cardholder has sufficient information to make a well informed choice. It is particularly popular with business travellers as it simplifies making expense claims (the amounts are already converted into the correct currency) and reduces the time involved in this otherwise tedious process.

⦿ **Pay in your home currency**
(USD) $501.05

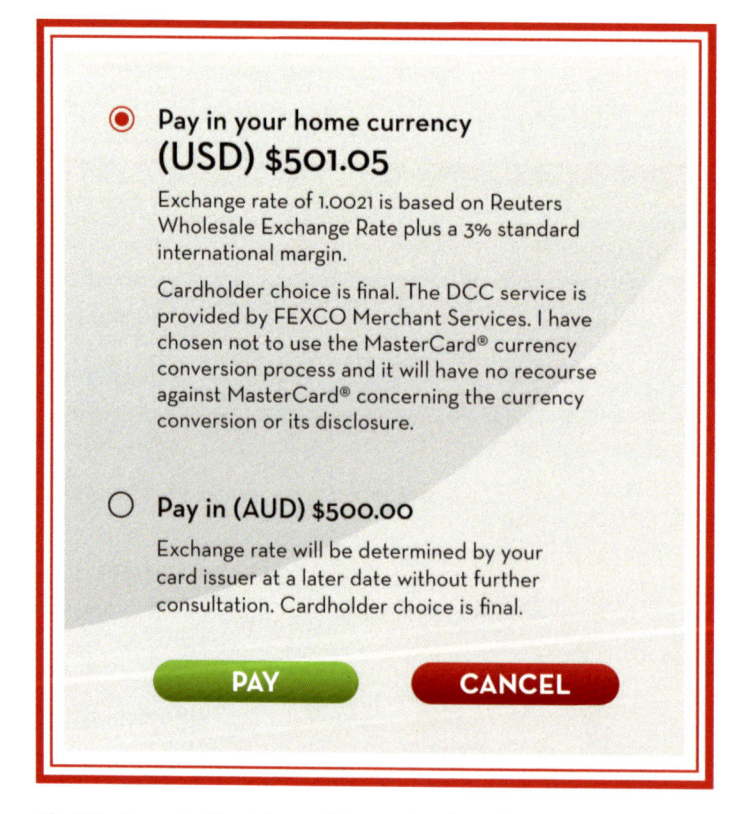

Exchange rate of 1.0021 is based on Reuters Wholesale Exchange Rate plus a 3% standard international margin.

Cardholder choice is final. The DCC service is provided by FEXCO Merchant Services. I have chosen not to use the MasterCard® currency conversion process and it will have no recourse against MasterCard® concerning the currency conversion or its disclosure.

○ **Pay in (AUD) $500.00**

Exchange rate will be determined by your card issuer at a later date without further consultation. Cardholder choice is final.

[**PAY**]   [**CANCEL**]

Fig 17: Sample Text for a MasterCard on-line DCC Transaction (Courtesy of FEXCO)

Benefits of DCC for an Airline

Talking to FEXCO who brought the service to market in 1996 there are a number of advantages of DCC for an airline. The chief benefit being revenue generation and the possibility of increasing the customer service offered to passengers. All DCC providers offer the technology to identify foreign credit cards and the relevant exchange rates for transactions and some DCC providers will also offer treasury and cash management i.e. a complete DCC solution, and manage all of the Foreign Exchange risk on your behalf. This means you can now sell in multiple currencies servicing your customers but still continue to receive settlement in your chosen base currencies. All of the Foreign Exchange risk attached to currency fluctuations is absorbed and managed by the DCC provider ensuring you enjoy a guaranteed share of the profits from the DCC service. Furthermore DCC will not interfere with your settlement and reconciliation as your settlement amount will always match the original price amount.

What is the Revenue Potential?

The good news for you as an airline is that DCC providers can run an analysis on historical transactions and can tell you how much DCC was worth to you on any given day. This exercise enables you to obtain a very good estimate as to the value of DCC for you. Airlines are often surprised by the volume of foreign transactions on their routes and this applies to both scheduled and low costs carriers on regional, long hauls, one-ways etc. Airlines are now also realising and enjoying substantial DCC revenue from non-ticket sales, such as charges for excess luggage, extra leg room seats and other miscellaneous sales.

Additional Benefits for Airlines

Airlines are continuously expanding the payment options available to their customers, but recognise that credit cards are still an important payment mechanism for many customers worldwide. For that reason merchants and indeed many airlines welcome DCC as the revenue it generates helps counteract the cost of accepting credit cards as a form of payment.

In summary DCC is rapidly becoming a popular service all over the world and not just with airlines with the result that cardholders are now expecting to be offered DCC when travelling or making a purchase in a foreign country.

5.3.3 Compliance

MasterCard and Visa have introduced regulations around the usage of DCC, ensuring the customer is provided with clear and comprehensive information to make an informed decision. DCC providers proactively advise on and provide sample compliant text to airlines, which can be used for the different sales channels (see **Fig 17** and **Fig 18** for sample texts that can be used in e-commerce and for POS transactions).

As well as giving customer the choice to pay in their home currency or in the merchant's currency, it is a compliance requirement that an airline provides a detailed receipt.

A compliant DCC receipt includes information on

- Margin applied
- Exchange rate and source
- DCC amount
- Amount in merchant's base currency
- DCC provider

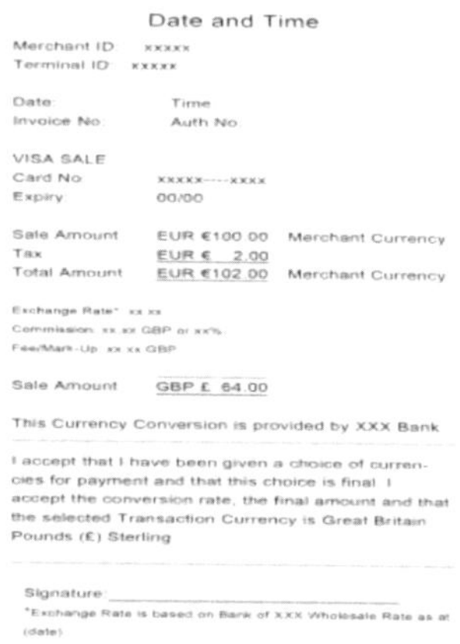
Date and Time

Merchant ID: xxxxx
Terminal ID: xxxxx

Date: Time
Invoice No: Auth No

VISA SALE
Card No: xxxxx----xxxx
Expiry: 00/00

Sale Amount EUR €100.00 Merchant Currency
Tax EUR € 2.00
Total Amount EUR €102.00 Merchant Currency

Exchange Rate*: xx.xx
Commission: xx.xx GBP or xx%
Fee/Mark-Up: xx.xx GBP

Sale Amount GBP £ 64.00

This Currency Conversion is provided by XXX Bank

I accept that I have been given a choice of currencies for payment and that this choice is final. I accept the conversion rate, the final amount and that the selected Transaction Currency is Great Britain Pounds (£) Sterling

Signature: ____________________
*Exchange Rate is based on Bank of XXX Wholesale Rate as at (date)

Fig 18: Sample Receipt (Courtesy of FEXCO)

DCC is applicable to all sales (not just tickets but also ancillary sales) and depending on the chosen DCC provider, may also be available across all channels including online, call centre, ticket desk and kiosk ensuring a consistent customer experience and maximising the revenue the airline can generate from international card transactions.

In summary DCC can be a 'win-win' for both the airline and its customers. The airline can enjoy substantial revenue from the DCC service with no FX risk while the airline's customers enjoy full price transparency. The mark-up strategy in combination with the customer perception about this service determines its ultimate success.

WHEREVER YOU FLY, WHATEVER YOU SELL...

FEXCO DCC (Dynamic Currency Conversion) generates revenue from international VISA & MasterCard transactions

- **EUROPE** 15%
- **N AMERICA** 7%
- **ASIA** 30%
- **M EAST** 50%
- **AFRICA** 12%
- **S AMERICA** 30%

FEXCO Merchant Services is a diverse, experienced and globally trusted organisation providing DCC solutions to approximately 45,000 merchants together with 30 acquiring banks across its operations in Europe, the Middle East, the Americas, Asia and Australia.

AVERAGE % OF DCC'ABLE TRANSACTIONS FOR AIRLINES GLOBALLY

- Full service solution provider
- DCC available across all sales channels
- Over 90 currencies supported
- Guaranteed commission earned on all FX transactions
- Risk free solution for airlines

WWW.FEXCOMS.COM

FEXCO Merchant Services
Part of the FEXCO Group

6   Payment Liability – Who Takes the Risk?

Accepting a promise to be paid at some time in the future in return for goods or services that a merchant hands over to a customer is always going to be a bit more risky than getting the cash in your hands immediately (not that cash handling doesn't bring along its own risks). The discussion of "Whose risk is it?" probably makes up two thirds of the big and heavy rule books of the payment schemes.

This chapter describes the various risk aspects as well as the responsibilities each of the players in the payment chain have in order to minimise them. And yes, it also gives answers to THAT question: Who takes the risk?

The risk comes from two sides, from the outside, where third parties try to misuse the system and from within the system, as each one of the players themselves can be a source of a certain amount of risk. Each participant takes a risk. The responsibility for fraud shifts between the parties and sticks with the one who has allowed it to happen or did the least to avoid it - the one exposing the biggest vulnerability to the system - the weakest link.

6.1   Participant's Risks and Responsibilities

6.1.1   Merchant

The merchant is the entry point of a transaction. As such they take on the role of "gate keeper" and must ensure that only "good" transactions get into the system. Good transactions are those that are carried out by genuine cardholders with genuine payment tokens (e.g. credit card). The merchant's responsibility is (among others) to check the security features of the credit card, the signature of the cardholder against the one on the card and if in doubt, the ID of the cardholder. If challenged by the cardholder (e.g. a charge-back) they need to be able to provide enough evidence that the cardholder has actually authorised the transaction. The introduction of "Chip & PIN" enabled POS terminals replaced the manual verification process to a large extent for regular shopping scenarios.

Verifying payments is relatively easy in a face-to-face scenario, where both the cardholder and the payment card are present. It does not work quite so well in situations, where the order is placed remotely (card-not-present scenarios). An example of distance selling would be a call centre, where the airline agent collects the credit card information for a ticket that they are about to issue over the phone. Other examples are mail order companies, where the card number is simply written on the order form (Mail Order; Telephone Order – MOTO transactions). My pizza delivery service around the corner operates the same way – they accept a card number for payment that I give them over the phone without checking if that card actually exists and I am the cardholder I claim to be. The same applies for transactions over the internet.

By accepting these kinds of transactions the merchant knowingly introduces a risk to the system. He consciously skips one of his responsibilities (i.e. verifying the card against the cardholder and his signature) and therefore takes the full risk of such a transaction being fraudulent, even after having received an authorisation code from his acquiring bank. This risk is a heavy burden to carry. For a long time however, credit cards were the only means for accepting payments over distance. And taking some risk was still better than not getting the business at all.

Later chapters in this section describe how the introduction of EMV technology (see Shift of Liability, page 92), as well as risk management solutions have helped them to reduce their share of the risk.

6.1.2   Acquiring bank

The acquiring bank is responsible for signing merchants up and accepting transactions initiated by them. A part of their role is to check and monitor the soundness of the businesses that they sign up. This is to ensure that the merchant does not all of a sudden disappear without actually shipping the goods or delivering the services that the cardholder has already paid for. It should also prevent money laundering and other criminal activities. The bank needs to check certificates of incorporation, the business premises (does the merchant actually exist), licenses to trade, bank statements etc.

A common fraud scenario is travel agencies that set themselves up and start selling non-existent travel packages and flights. Then the agency disappears overnight with the money it has collected but without actually providing any of the holidays. A similar risk scenario is an airline that goes out of business and can no longer provide the flights they have sold.

In all such cases it is the acquiring bank that will be held accountable for covering the damages. They are responsible for all transactions that they have accepted from that merchant. The card scheme and in particular the cardholder have to be kept indemnified.

6.1.3 Issuing bank

In the same way as the acquiring bank signs up merchants and covers their risk; the issuing bank signs up cardholders and is responsible for any potential cardholder defaults. If a cardholder is unable to pay for the transactions made with their card, it is the issuing bank that will ultimately have to step up and cover any outstanding amounts.

As this risk is quite substantial for credit cards, banks go through extensive credit checks before signing up a new cardholder. For debit and prepaid card accounts, where the issuing banks authorises a transaction against funds that they have immediate control over, the default risk of a cardholder is a lot lower.

6.1.4 Payment Scheme

The payment scheme itself does not take on a lot of responsibility. It guarantees the financial exchange between the issuing bank and the acquiring bank for all the transactions processed with cards carrying its brand. It does not however get involved in the relationship between the acquiring bank and a merchant or the issuing bank and the cardholder. Should a bank default and fail to pay a merchant, e.g. the deposit held, the merchant would have no right to go back to the card scheme with their claims. Equally, a cardholder cannot approach the card scheme with a claim against a defaulting bank that was for example, managing his prepaid account[6].

6.1.5 Cardholder

The cardholder is responsible for paying for the transactions that they have authorised – and only for those! Being the only private entity in this chain of responsibilities the cardholder is considered the most vulnerable participant and hence the one generally most protected by the rules of the payment schemes.

When using a credit card the cardholders are first and foremost protected against transactions made against their accounts, but not carried out by them – in other words, credit card fraud, in whatever way.

If your personal credit card number was copied in a restaurant, where you left the credit card with the waiter to pay and the card number is subsequently used by the waiter for on-line gambling, then you are protected and can request a charge-back.

Secondly cardholders are protected against merchants who do not or only partially deliver the promised services or goods. These are transactions for something (paying for something) that the cardholder has not or has only partially received ("Goods not Delivered" – see above for the responsibilities of a merchant), as well as situations where he has received something else than he has ordered.

This protection however only applies to cardholders who have fulfilled all their obligations: that is to do everything possible not to share their payment details with a potential fraudster. It is the cardholder's responsibility to keep their payment token (the card, account number etc.) safe. Even more importantly, they need to keep the PIN and/or password that they have been given secret. If a cardholder loses his debit card with his PIN written on the back of it (you won't believe how often this happens!!!) he will have very little grounds for claiming any money back in the case of his account being emptied within minutes.

---

[6] This does not apply for payment schemes that also act as issuers and hence do have a direct relationship with the cardholder.

Not all fraud cases though are easily attributed to a single perpetrator. What about manipulated ATMs with mini cameras and altered card readers stealing card numbers and PIN data? Should the cardholder be held liable for this kind of fraud? – For disclosing his PIN? Or should the ATM provider take the risk for such an attack? Such cases are the driver for continuous improvement of technology and refinement of the terms and conditions of the payment schemes and consumer protection laws.

6.1.6 All Participants

All participants in a card scheme have to ensure their systems are protected against system compromises and theft of cardholder details. This relates to external threats by hackers as well as internal security breaches, where employees misuse their access to card data. Security standards such as those issued by Payment Card Industry Security Standards Council should help reduce that risk. All participants of the major card schemes have to adhere to them (see PCI DSS, page99).

6.2 Shift of Liability – The Weakest Link

As discussed above, the biggest part of the risk is carried by the merchant. As the entry point of a transaction they have to ensure that the transaction is genuine. The introduction of safer technologies such as Chip & PIN for POS devices as well as 3D Secure for the internet brought a new dynamic into the risk distribution.

To incentivise merchants and issuers to migrate to these more secure technologies (i.e. upgrade cards and terminals to comply with EMV, enable 3D Secure on e-commerce sites), the card schemes have introduced the concept of "Shift of Liability". The basic idea is to move the responsibility for fraudulent transactions to the entity that operates the least secure payment technology. Merchants with upgraded infrastructure are promised an absolute payment guarantee. And they no longer have to go through the routine of manually checking cards and signatures as the POS terminal electronically checks the authenticity of the card (and vice versa).

Even in the event that the card does not have a chip or the cardholder does not have a PIN (the transaction is initiated through a card swipe and authorised by signature) the merchant remains protected. The liability "shifts" to the participant providing the least secure infrastructure. In cases of cards without chip, it is the issuing bank. As more and more merchants migrate, the issuers have started to pick up the huge fraud bill that was previously footed by the merchant.

For issuing banks, introducing Chip & PIN technology then started to make commercial sense as well and more and more countries in Europe, Asia, Middle East and South America started to introduce chips on their payment cards. This significantly reduced fraud in face-to-face transactions in regions with full EMV penetration. But fraud hasn't gone away – it's moved on to countries that still don't have EMV infrastructure (such as the US.A.), and even more pertinently – to card-not-present scenarios.

3D Secure was introduced to address fraud in e-commerce. It came with the same promise for all transactions made over the internet. Once a merchant upgrades their web site to accept 3D secure, they enjoyed a payment guarantee – again a shift of liability from the merchant to the issuing bank.

The adoption of 3D Secure however did not pick up as quickly as the card schemes had hoped. Merchants were concerned about the conversion rates, as the re-direct authorisation process extended and sometimes disrupted the sales process. The extra hurdles drove down "look to book" ratios. Cardholders, if they had one at the first place, tended to forget their on-line password, as they were not using it frequently enough (it is hard enough to remember your normal PIN...). This led to additional aborted purchases. As the merchants dragged their feet, issuing banks were less incentivised to act and equip their cardholders with on-line PINs.

Merchants with a high risk profile (such as on-line gambling) however were very quick to adopt this new technology. The promise of payment guarantee was worth the potentially lower conversion rate. The unintended side effect was that it also removed any incentive for them to have additional fraud control systems in place. The shift of liability automatically pushed all the fraud losses to the issuing banks. The losses with the issuing banks were huge and the card schemes had to react. To ensure that the merchant continues to reduce the chance of fraud at the entry point the rules were eventually amended: The Shift of Liability would only apply as the long as the merchant's overall fraud level remained less than 1-2% of the total transaction amount (depending on the card scheme and region).

The U.S., so far having managed to exempt themselves from the Shift of Liability rules, have now also agreed to introduce EMV and a shift of Liability by August 2015 (Smart Card Alliance, 2011).

6.3 Types of Fraud

Fraudsters understand the weaknesses and risks in the payment environment and systematically exploit them, at the cost of one or more participants. Making purchases with stolen credit card numbers is the most common fraud scenario, followed by customers who claim to have not, or have only partially received what they have paid for. The sections below describe those types of fraud in more detail. Later parts of book focus on systems that help merchants fight them.

6.3.1 Using Stolen Card Numbers

Most fraud happens with stolen credit card numbers. Traditionally, these numbers were collected through skimming attacks where the card data was copied in places like restaurants, bars, hotels or on rigged ATMs. More recently they are being stolen in large quantities by breaking into the databases of on-line merchants (hence the growing importance of PCI Data Security compliance). Fraudsters then use these card numbers themselves or sell them on through the internet.

To reduce the chances of triggering fraud detection systems individual merchants usually only get hit with one transaction per card. The card itself will get used multiple times in various situations, until either the cardholder realises the fraud (often only weeks later, when they receive their card statement) or the issuing bank detects abnormal activity, checks with the cardholder and blocks that card. More sophisticated fraud management solutions have access to transaction information across multiple merchants and are more likely to detect such fraud attacks.

6.3.2 "Friendly Fraud"

"Friendly Fraud" is a scheme in which a consumer denies a purchase they have previously made. They then call their issuing bank and use their right to dispute a transaction claiming that

- They never made that purchase (bought that flight) – somebody was misusing their card, or
- They never received the service (e.g. never got the booking confirmation).

These claims result in a charge-back, where the cardholder is refunded the payment amount. Airlines can fight and defend their transactions if you have the right processes in place to provide enough evidence and prove the legitimacy of the purchase. This is easy enough, if the cardholder himself has flown and the airline can provide the boarding confirmation. It does get more complicated though for third party bookings, where the cardholder differs from the passenger who actually flew.

6.3.3 Consumer Dissatisfaction Fraud

Consumer dissatisfaction fraud works in a similar way: A passenger can make use of their charge-back right, if they did not get the goods or service they contracted for. In an airline scenario the given reasons are most often something along the lines of "I did not get the seat I was promised", "… the food that I had ordered", or "… the service that I expected". Using these (sometimes even legitimate) complaints, the passenger contacts their issuing bank and requests a charge-back for the full or partial transaction amount.

6.3.4 Credit & Return Fraud

Credit & Return fraud is a scheme where a fraudster purchases a flight with a stolen card number and subsequently requests a refund either in cash or onto another payment card. Most merchants are already protecting themselves against this kind of fraud with strict instructions to refund only against the card used for the original purchase.

6.4 Costs of Fraud

Fighting fraud continues to be a significant and growing cost for merchants of all sizes, and in particular for airlines. "In 2010, airlines lost an estimated $1.4 billion dollars in revenue due to online fraud perpetrated on their websites, which represented 0.9% of total worldwide online airline ticket sales." (CyberSource, 2011)

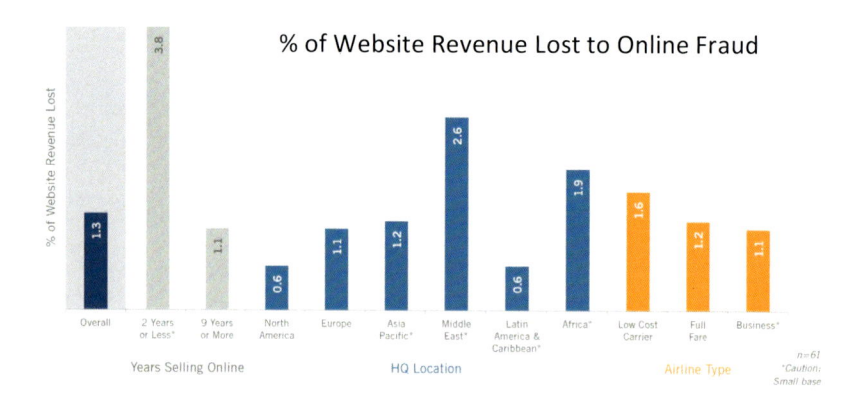

Fig 19: Airline Fraud (Source: Airline Online Fraud Report 2011- Courtesy of CyberSource)

The total cost of fraud is significantly higher than just the value of all tickets that have been paid for with fraudulent cards. They need to include the loss of valid orders that were incorrectly rejected by the fraud screening tools as well as the costs of fighting fraud and the associated administration costs:

- **Actual fraud losses** – measured by the accumulated charge-back amounts; including associated charge-back fees.

- **Rejected valid orders** – screening transactions for fraudulent behaviour can result in a decline of legitimate transactions (false positives). A passenger may retry a booking but will ultimately abort the purchase, if his payment is declined several times by the fraud management systems. In 2010, airlines reported that on average, for every fraudulent transaction, they rejected an additional 5.1 bookings due to suspicion of fraud. (CyberSource, 2011)

- **Costs associated with fighting fraud** – these include the cost of fraud management tools, the internal or external fraud specialists who configure and maintain them as well as the administrative costs to review orders and fight charge-backs.

Implementing a good fraud management system in combination with the appropriate back-office systems can help to significantly reduce these costs (see back-office processes, page 210).

7   Laws, Rules, Standards and Compliance

Processing payments is governed by several layers of laws, rules standards and compliancy regulations. The next chapter will analyse the most relevant ones, those that are applicable to the payment industry in general as well as those that are particular to the airline industry.

They can be grouped in three categories: First, at the lowest level, you have those laid out by the card schemes themselves. They govern the interaction between all participants of the scheme - their own rules as well as those that apply across multiple card schemes – industry rules and standards. Then, governments have their say on payment processing – to protect the financial markets, as well as its participants. Then there is a third set, the airline industry's own rules and standards around handling payments consistently between all entities.

7.1 Payment Scheme Rules

These rules touch every aspect of the payment scheme and the transaction life cycle. They describe everything from the colour codes of the logos, the technical aspects of the payment, the messages and transaction processing, the fees, as well as the rights and obligations of its participants.

These rules are all embedded in the Terms & Conditions and the operational manuals that the merchant has to agree and adhere to when taking payments through a particular card scheme.

7.2 Industry Standards and Rules

For some parts of their operations the larger payment schemes have agreed to a synchronised approach to these rules and introduced common standards across multiple schemes. EMV and PCI standards are examples of such rules. Both of them are self-imposed by the card schemes and as such can only be enforced by the card schemes themselves. They are not incorporated into any national laws.

7.2.1 EMV Standards

In an effort to increase the security of payment cards against fraud three major card schemes joined forces to create EMV (Europay, MasterCard and Visa – hence the name) –a global standard for credit and debit payment cards based on chip card technology. The standards define the interaction at the physical level (where the chip is positioned and what it looks like), electrical level (to make sure you don't read it using 220V), data level (what data is passed back and forth and its structure), and application levels (what applications are available) between chip cards and the card reader in the POS devices and ATMs. It is those standards that make your credit cards work all around the world.

Its founding members published the first version of the EMV standard in 1995. JCB joined the organisation in December 2004 and American Express joined in February 2009. Now the standard is defined and managed by the public corporation EMVCo, each of the four members (Europay having merged with MasterCard) owning a quarter and being equally represented in the working groups.

As at the end of 2010, there were more than 1.24 billion EMV compliant chip-based payment cards in use worldwide. The U.S. is one of the last major countries to agree to adopt the standard. (EMVCo, 2011)

7.2.2 Payment Card Industry Data Security Standard (PCI DSS)

PCI is another industry initiative, the aim being to reduce the fraud risk posed by unintended exposure of cardholder information to fraudsters.

It started off as five individual programs run by five card organisations (American Express, MasterCard, Visa, Discover and JCB) with roughly similar intentions: to create an additional level of protection for card issuers by ensuring that merchants meet minimum levels of security when they store, process and transmit cardholder data. Eventually they formed the Payment Card Industry Security Standard Council (PCI SSC) and aligned their individual policies. In December 2004 this council released the first version of the Payment Card Industry Data Security Standard.

The current version of the standard (released in October 2010) is version 2.0 (PCI Security Standards Council, 2011). If your organisation is processing, transmitting or storing credit card data of one of the major debit, credit, prepaid or e-purse programs, you should have adopted this standard in January 2011. Changes to the standard follow a defined 2-year life cycle, so expect a new release by the end of 2012.

Validation of your compliance is done annually, either by Self-Assessment (if you handle small transaction volumes), or by an external Qualified Security Assessor (QSA) if the volume that you handle exceeds a certain threshold.

Achieving compliance and remaining compliant can cost organisations a great deal of effort and financial resources. There are after all about 220 sub-requirements that have to be met. The application of those requirements can depend on the interpretation of the QSA that is performing the assessment. An important thing to bear in mind is that being compliant only reduces, but by no means eliminates the security risk. A security breach and subsequent compromise of payment card data can have far-reaching consequences for affected organisations, including:

- Regulatory notification requirements,
- Loss of reputation
- Loss of customers (as a result of loss of reputation)
- Potential financial liabilities (for example, regulatory and other fees and fines)
- Litigation.

Some famous companies have suffered great losses due to cardholder related security breaches (e.g. Heartland Payment Systems: 130m records, Sony: 77m records (DATALOSS db, 2011)). Most organisations therefore choose to seek certification, if nothing else than to remain a vendor of choice for its customers.

For a merchant to be compliant, all its sub-service providers need to be compliant as well. They need to be able to provide relevant, up to date certificates – not only at the time of contract signature, but on an on-going basis.

The Council has extended its remit by two additional standards. To help software vendors to develop secure payment applications, the Council maintains the Payment Application Data Security Standard (PA-DSS). For vendors and manufacturers of POS devices, PIN pads and unattended payment terminals (such as kiosks), the council provides the PIN Transaction Security (PTS) requirements. For airlines requiring any hardware or software of these types the Security Standards Council provides a list of approved companies and providers.

Control Objectives	The 12 PCI DSS Requirements for Compliance
Build and Maintain a Secure Network	1. Install and maintain a firewall configuration to protect cardholder data
	2. Do not use vendor-supplied defaults for system passwords and other security parameters
Protect Cardholder Data	3. Protect stored cardholder data
	4. Encrypt transmission of cardholder data across open, public networks
Maintain a Vulnerability Management Program	5. Use and regularly update anti-virus software on all systems commonly affected by malware
	6. Develop and maintain secure systems and applications
Implement Strong Access Control Measures	7. Restrict access to cardholder data by business need-to-know
	8. Assign a unique ID to each person with computer access
	9. Restrict physical access to cardholder data
Regularly Monitor and Test Networks	10. Track and monitor all access to network resources and cardholder data
	11. Regularly test security systems and processes
Maintain an Information Security Policy	12. Maintain a policy that addresses information security

Table 3: The 12 PCI-DSS Requirements (Source: PCI Security Standards Council, 2011)

7.2.3 IATA and PCI-DSS

In a recent attempt to move the Air Transport Industry into the age of PCI-DSS compliance IATA has established the PCI-DSS Work Group (PDWS). Its aim is to investigate the following areas:

- instances where a card number is transmitted for purposes other than payment (Form of Payment, or FOP) in industry messages
- instances where self-service devices use a card number as a form of identification (FOID)
- airline kiosks and other shared equipment, addressing both card number as FOID or FOP as well as the requirement to support Chip & PIN.

IATA has set up sub-groups for each of those topics to develop proposals, recommendations and implementation plans that are compliant with the PCI standards[7].

7.3 National and Supranational Regulatory Influence

Governments have a huge influence on the way payments are processed in a country. They have three main sets of interests to protect: control of the financial systems, regulating the market place and the rights of consumers.

As cash is being replaced more and more by electronic transactions, payment schemes have an increasingly important role to play in a national market place: they process and manage an ever larger proportion of a domestic payment volume. Any irregularities could therefore have a major impact on the financial stability of that country – just imagine no ATMs working for more than a week or that the POS network breaks down the last two days before Christmas. So, governments introduce regulation that ensure the financial as well as the technical stability of a payment scheme and its participants. They impose financial controls and require deposits with the central banks to secure

---

[7] Further information: http://www.iata.org/workgroups/Pages/pci-dss.aspx

the funds that they hold on behalf of their merchants and cardholders. This protects you, as a merchant as well as the individuals using a particular scheme.

As soon as transactions cross country borders, financial authorities begin to be interested in the flow of funds in and out of the country. Some countries are less open to this than others and impose strict rules on what is allowed and what not. Countries like India and South Africa heavily regulate the export of funds out of the country. Revenue earned by an international airline within those countries cannot easily be transferred to the airline's home market.

Some governments see card payments as a nice way to make some extra money and have imposed taxes on for example the issuance of payment cards or on the contract value of the merchant-acquirer agreement.

Consumer protection is the other major concern of governments, in particular when it comes to banks and payments. They regulate the issuance of credit cards to customers and the institutes who issue them as well the merchants who accept them.

Free market and fair competition is another area of interest for governments (in some geographies anyway). They introduce legislation to minimise trade barriers and ensure that the market is free of monopolies. Here are some examples:

In an attempt to spur economic growth with lower merchant fees, the U.S. introduced the Durbin Amendment in 2010, ruling that debit interchange fees would be capped at a relatively low level (Board of Governors of the Federal Reserve System, 2011).

The Payment Service Directive (PSD) and the Single European Payment Area (SEPA) are two examples in Europe where governments try to harmonise the payment infrastructure.

7.3.1 Single European Payment Area (SEPA)

Payment schemes in Europe were very diverse and not particularly interoperable. Almost every country had (and some still have) their own bank card schemes (e.g. Laser in Ireland, Carte Bleue in France, Switch and Solo in the UK, EC in Germany). Customers could not use the cards that they were using domestically when they went on holiday abroad. Organisations that operated in multiple countries, such as airlines, needed an acquiring agreement and separate technical integration in each country. Moving funds between countries was costly and slow.

The Single Euro Payments Area is an initiative of the European banking industry (represented by the European Payment Council - EPC) to make all electronic payments across the Euro area – e.g. by credit card, debit card, bank transfer or direct debit – as easy as domestic payments within one country. The aim is to harmonise the technology and the legal standards between all member states. This was achieved predominantly by replacing all domestic debit card schemes with one of the international schemes (Visa debit and Maestro). Many countries though are still running both systems in parallel, the international brands for international transactions, as well as their domestic schemes for domestic transactions. Chip card technology allows the two applications to co-reside on the same card. Depending on the terminal and country, the relevant application/scheme is activated for a particular transaction. Only some countries have replaced their domestic schemes completely. (European Central Bank, 2011)

7.3.2 Payment Service Directive (PSD)

The Payment Services Directive provides the necessary legal framework for SEPA. The PSD aims to establish a modern and comprehensive set of rules applicable to all payment services in the European Union. The PSD also seeks to improve competition by opening up payment markets to new entrants, fostering greater efficiency and cost-reduction. It reinforces the rights and protection of all the users of payment services (consumers, retailers, large and small companies and public authorities). The PSD was issued in 2007. Member States had until November 2009 to transpose the directive into national law. (European Commission, 2011)

7.4 Airline Industry Rules

7.4.1 IATA Passenger Service Conference Resolution Manual

Being the industry's regulatory body it is of no surprise, that IATA's rule books also cover the payment space. The rules describe the instances and formats in which credit card data has to be captured and passed on between internal systems and downstream partners that rely on this information. Here are some examples (IATA 2009):

Resolution 728 of the Passenger Service Conference Resolution Manual (Code Designators for Passenger Ticket and Baggage Check) defines the payment data elements that have to be captured along with a ticket. Chapter 7 describes the valid Form of Payment Codes, the names of the accepted card schemes and their respective identifiers. These rules are the major stumbling block for alternative payment methods. As they are not listed here, they are not compatible with legacy airline systems.

The rules further define the process of obtaining a credit card authorisation through the airline system (see Traditional Airline Authorisation and Settlement Flow, page 142)

Recommended Practice 1791 describes the Standard Specifications for Airline Issued Credit Cards – the rules for the usage of UATP cards.

IATA further sets a standard for transmitting financial data including credit card authorisation and billing transactions (Recommended Practice 1791b), a format compliant with the global standards for financial transactions (ANSI X4.21-1981 and the ISO 7580).

These rules are only applicable to transactions between participants. Payments information that is processed within an organisation can, but does not have to adhere to those standards. IATA is constantly updating them to ensure that they meet the market's needs as well as card scheme and legal requirements such as PCI-DSS.

These are just some of the examples of IATA's regulatory influence on the payment processes within the airline industry. The next chapter will look at airline affiliated payment institutions, IATA being the most prominent again.

8 Airline Affiliated Payment Institutions

Airlines pioneered the international payment domain in many ways. The creation of UATP, the airlines' own credit card scheme is just one example of this. From very early on airlines had to cooperate and organise themselves to allow financial settlements between them, supporting their interdependent businesses and operations. IATA's financial services grew out of the need to meet those requirements. Below is a detailed description of the main services components that continue to be a vital back-bone of the air transport industry:

8.1 IATA

Apart from its effort to improve rules and regulations concerning the handling of credit card data, IATA also provides services to support the processing of payments in the airline and travel industry: a Billing and Settlement plan (BSP) in combination with a clearing house (ICH) to support the settlement of payments between its members, systems to extract and process credit card transactions originating from BSP files, as well as a card fraud prevention tool, allowing its members to share card fraud information.

8.1.1 IATA Billing and Settlement Plan (BSP)

The IATA BSP system is(similar to a payment scheme) a network of trust that allows funds to flow between the participants without the need to have a direct relationship with one another. This network enables travel agents to sell tickets on behalf of an airline without a direct agreement between the two. The travel agent sells a flight on one or more airlines to a passenger and receives payment for them (in cash, by invoice or a card transaction where the travel agent is the Merchant of Record). The BSP system ensures that those funds (minus the commission for the travel agent) eventually make their way to the respective airline.

To make that work the agents submit all sales that have happened during a reporting period (daily or weekly) to a central point – the BSP in the country or region of the agent. This is usually done electronically, either directly between the agent and the BSP or, in most cases, via one of the GDSs used for bookings.

All ticket sales and refund transactions collected by the local BSP are forwarded to one of six Data Processing Centres (DPC), where they are captured and processed. Similar to the card schemes the DPC consolidates all incoming transactions and produces a set of summary reports for its participants. This set of reports, called the "Agent Billing Analysis", is produced for each travel agent and provides a statement of sales made by each agent to each participating BSP Airline. The airlines receive the Hand-Off Tape file (HOT file) containing the details of all sales transactions as well as a sales summary report.

The travel agent now has to make one net remittance covering all transactions for that period for all BSP airlines, usually via a direct debit initiated by the BSP that they have signed up with. The BSP makes one consolidated payment to each airline covering all sales made by all agents in the country/region. All BSP payments are processed through the ICH clearing house (see next section).

The accounting department of each airline audits incoming reports and funds. Should they detect differences between their own records and the transactions that have been submitted by the travel agents, they can submit Accounting Debit/Credit Memoranda (ADM/ACM) to the BSP system to correct outstanding or overpaid amounts.[8]

Next Page:
Fig 20: BSP Card Sales Process (Courtesy of IATA)

---

[8] See http://www.iata.org/ps/financial_services/bsp

Journey of an Airline card transaction

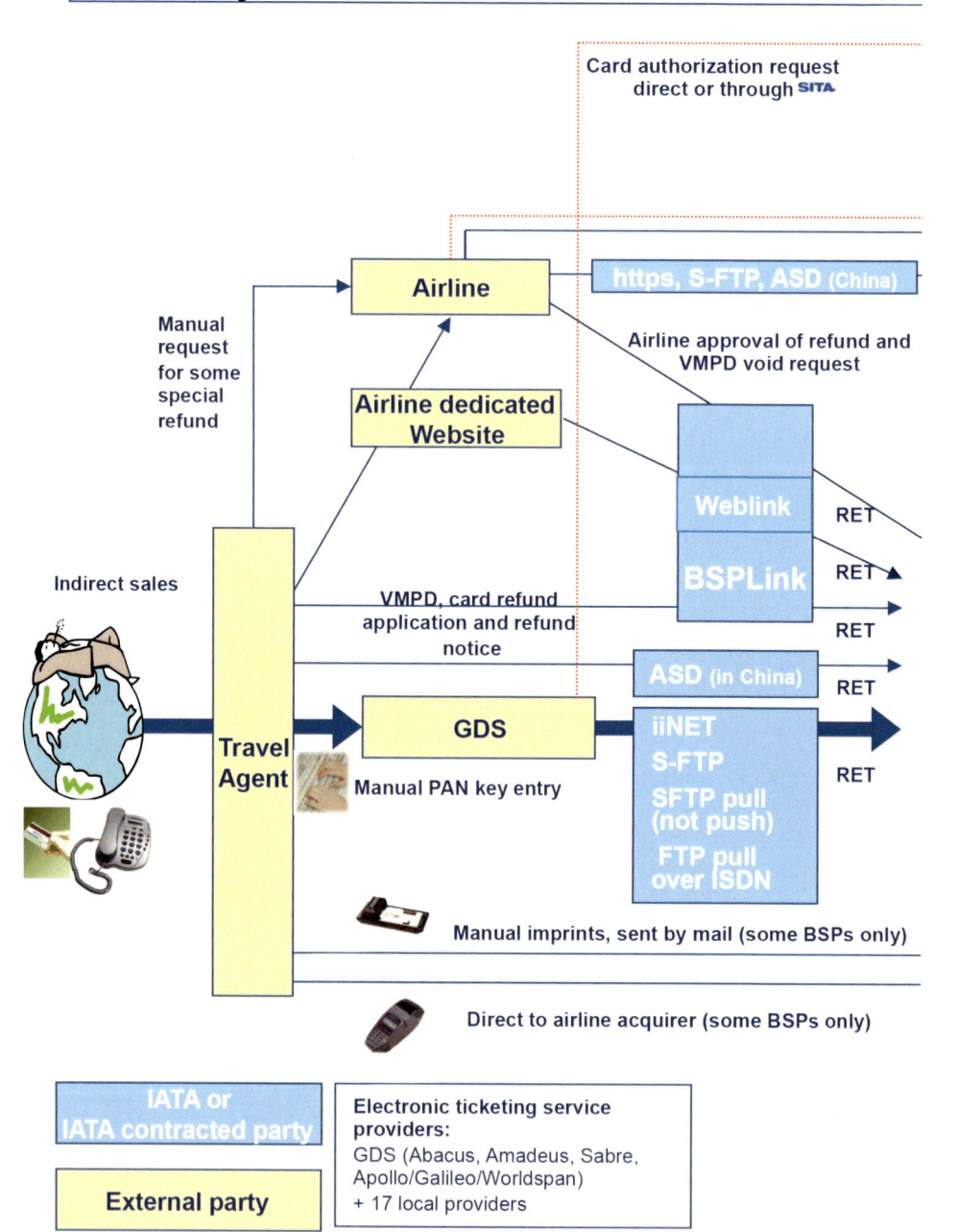

- BSP card sale process

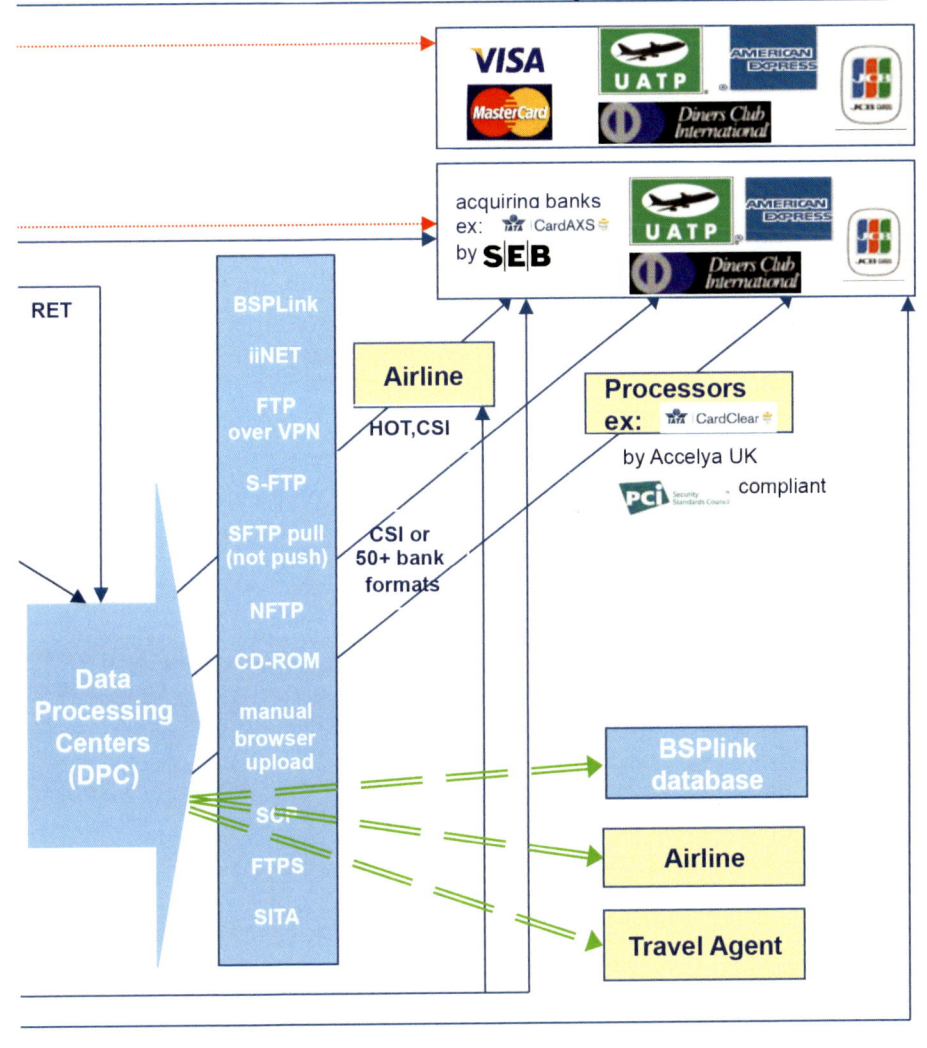

Multi-countries DPC:
ACCA (ISIS), Accelya (Maestro)
Mono-country DPC:
Deutsche Bank, India (ISIS)
KEB, South Korea (own software)
MHIR, Japan (own software)
Multicarta, Russia (ISIS)
T-Systems, Germany (own software)

Authorization request ....▶
Clearing transaction ─────▶
Reports ═══════▶

Data Processing Centers (DPC)

BSPLink, iiNET, FTP over VPN, S-FTP, SFTP pull (not push), NFTP, CD-ROM, manual browser upload, SCP, FTPS, SITA

RET

acquiring banks ex: CardAXS by SEB

Airline — HOT, CSI
CSI or 50+ bank formats

Processors ex: CardClear
by Accelya UK
PCI compliant

BSPlink database
Airline
Travel Agent

8.1.2 IATA Clearing House (ICH)

The IATA Clearing House (ICH) and the U.S.-based Airline Clearing House (ACH) enable the world's airlines and airline associated companies to settle their reciprocal billings.

By offsetting their mutual transactions through one of the clearing houses, they can reduce hundreds of bi-lateral transactions for passenger, cargo, baggage, catering, ground-handling and other services to one single payable or receivable amount in a currency of their choice.

The BSP payments between the airlines and the BSPs are also processed by this system. Instead of receiving multiple payments from multiple BSPs, airlines receive their funds as part of one net settlement credit or debit advice, covering also all other transactions that have been processed through the clearing house in a particular billing period.

Clearing houses are a corner stone of the air travel industry. It is this system that enables passengers and freight-shippers to purchase multi-sector journeys involving transportation on any number of airlines, as it allows airlines to settle their interline agreements. It enables its participants to share the revenue for passengers, baggage and freight transferred from one company to another.[9]

BSPs are set up on a country by country basis, sometimes there is a BSP covering a whole region. Travel agents have to be IATA accredited to be eligible to participate in a BSP. General Sales Agents (GSAs) and Airport Handling Agents (AHA) are equally entitled to join.

8.1.3 IATA CardClear

BSPs also manage credit card transactions that the travel agent initiated on behalf of the airline, with the airline as the Merchant of Record. These are payment transactions, where the travel agent collects the cardholder information, initiates the authorisation and then passes the transaction

---

[9] See http://www.iata.org/whatwedo/finance/clearing/Pages/ich.aspx

information on to the airline to submit them for settlement. The airline, as Merchant of Record, receives the funds directly from the acquiring bank. The travel agent does not directly get involved in the financial settlement (See Traditional Authorisation and Settlement Flow, page 142). The commissions for the travel agent are processed separately (also through the BSP).

As these transactions are not settled via the ICH or ACH, the airlines have to collect them from each BSP in the various countries individually and submit them to their acquiring bank of choice. Alternatively they can use the CardClear[10] service provided by IATA.

IATA CardClear collects card transactions from numerous BSPs, consolidates them and passes them on to one or more acquiring bank(s) selected by the airline for settlement. CardClear has direct links to acquiring banks, as well as to Diners Club International, American Express and UATP who act as acquirers for their transactions. For those, CardClear can submit the transactions on behalf of the airline. Another acquiring bank with a direct link is IATA's own acquiring service for Visa and MasterCard transactions, CardAXS.

8.1.4 CardAXS

CardAXS[11] is a partnership between IATA and Euroline/SEB a Swedish acquiring bank. Equipped with a global acquiring licence, it can process Visa and MasterCard transactions from most of the world (India, Central and South America are some of the exceptions). This partnership is the preferred choice for many airlines in countries where they have low transaction volumes. By consolidating all transactions to one bank they can get the advantage of lower merchant fees and reduce administrative effort. For countries with a high transaction volume it may be more advantageous to process them locally.

---

[10] See http://www.iata.org/ps/financial_services/Pages/cardclear.aspx
[11] See http://www.iata.org/ps/financial_services/Pages/cardaxs.aspx

8.1.5 Perseuss

Perseuss[12] was founded by a small group of airlines who were informally sharing information about fraud cases. In 2008 the group got too big to allow communication between each other purely based on phone calls, fax and email. Together with IATA they launched "Perseuss", a secure community platform, where airlines can legally share knowledge and information about fraud cases that they have encountered. Each member has access to the common database containing details of passengers who were involved in either suspicious transactions or in confirmed fraud cases. It also allows each airline to either manually, or automatically via an API, verify their own sales data to identify any suspicious transactions. The system can be accessed in real-time during the authorisation process, or some time after the booking, to re-verify previous sales. More than sixty airlines already use this system.

8.2 Airline Clearing House (ACH)

The Airline Clearing House (ACH) is the US based equivalent of the ICH. Both systems are linked, allowing airlines and airline associated companies to settle their reciprocal billings, regardless of their membership with either clearing house.

8.3 UATP

In 1936, just over 75 years ago at time of writing, a group of airlines set up their own credit card scheme: the Universal Air Travel Plan (UATP)– formerly known as the Air Travel Card. It is the pioneer of the charge card industry, developing such industry standards as the magnetic stripe (the card numbers starts with the number "1") and lodged accounts. Its main purpose is, even now, is to streamline the billing between airlines and their corporate clients, offering the lowest administrative costs of any travel payment product (UATP, 2011).

To avoid standard merchant fees, corporate clients are asked to purchase their tickets using a UATP card that the airline has issued to that

---

[12] See http://Perseuss.com

merchant, instead of using any other international card brand. At the end of a billing cycle, the airline invoices the corporate client for all its transactions[13]. By using their own cards airlines do not have to pay a merchant fee.

The corporate client can use the card for transactions with the issuing airline, as well as with any other airline accepting UATP cards as a form of payment. Over 260 airlines and thousands of travel agencies accept UATP today. For all transactions other than those with their own cards, airlines (and travel agencies) DO however have to pay a merchant fee (although it is usually a lot lower than standard credit card fees). The biggest part of that becomes revenue for the issuing airline, covering its costs for guaranteeing and collecting the funds from corporate clients[14].

The corporate clients benefit by receiving a large amount of travel data (Level II & Level III data) provided by UATP along with their invoices as well as through DATAMINE, an on-line reporting tool. This information is imported into their accounting systems to reconcile and analyse the flight elements of their staff travel expenses. Some airlines make the usage of UATP cards a pre-condition for special fare deals.

To allow corporate clients to use one card for all Travel & Entertainment (T&E) expenses, UATP supports co-branded cards. All air and rail tickets are charged against the UATP card number, all other non-air expenses are charged using a Visa or MasterCard number. Both transaction types are consolidated into a single invoice to the corporate client. UATP issuers need to cooperate with an issuing bank that can manage and process the transactions of both brands to enable such programs.

Additionally, UATP enables airlines to process alternative forms of payment on their e-commerce sites. To avoid costly software changes to integrate new payment methods in their back office systems, airlines

---

[13] This can be done using e.g. DATASTREAM, UATP's proprietary billing system.
[14] DATAVIEW is UATP's dashboard providing issuers summary level data for instant program review.

convert a PayPal transaction (for example) into a UATP card transaction and process it that way through legacy reservation and ticketing systems. Once it reaches UATP's processing centre the transaction is converted back into a PayPal transaction and forwarded to PayPal for authorisation. The confirmation message, as well as the settlement request follow the same logic – convert and re-convert. To the legacy airline systems the transaction looks like a known UATP transactions, to the passenger and to PayPal like a PayPal transaction.

UATP is integrated with ACH and ICH who perform the majority of the settlements between the IATA-certified UATP participants – from the airlines who have issued the cards to their corporate customers to the airlines who have accepted UATP cards for payment. For transactions made with their own cards for their own airline, no funds have to be moved.

For all other non- IATA, non-BSP members (e.g. low cost carriers) UATP has set up a proprietary in-house settlement system (UATP Settlement System - USS). It allows settlements between IATA-accredited and non-IATA-accredited participants.

Currently the usage of UATP cards is restricted to air and rail. UATP's strategic goals include the expansion of the merchant base to hotels and car rental companies.

8.4 Airline Reporting Corporation (ARC)

The Airline Reporting Corporation (ARC) provides the U.S.-based travel network with travel agency accreditation services and financial management tools. It's settlement services, used by nearly 16,000 travel agencies and 190 airlines, is the equivalent to IATA's BSP service. It was processing transactions worth more than $82 billion in 2011. (ARC, 2012)

9 Airline Payment System Integrators

Many airlines have outsourced the provision of their distribution software (reservation and departure control systems, call centre and ticket desk application, e-commerce and mobile platforms) to third party Passenger Service Systems providers. They are the ones who ultimately need to integrate all payment components into the distribution software to allow a payment to happen. To facilitate the integration process, most of these providers have built flexible payment modules within their infrastructure. Sometimes they use subsidiaries and external partners to manage their payment infrastructure. Below is a description of the major Passenger Service Systems provider, their payment integration components as well as a sample of external suppliers.

9.1 SITA

SITA is one of the world's leading specialists in air transport communications and IT solutions and delivers and manages business solutions for airline, airport, GDS, government and other customers. It is a "sister company" to IATA, equally structured as a member-owned organisation. As part of its portfolio it provides payment services to the air transport industry.

9.1.1 Credit Card Authorisation Service

SITA was one of the first IATA approved Authorisation Service Providers, processing authorisation requests for over 180 airlines and GDS. It has direct links to all the major credit card schemes (Visa, MasterCard, American Express, Diners Club, Discover, JCB and UATP) as well as to the database with lost and stolen paper ticket numbers.

Over time however most GDSs started to develop direct connections with the global credit card schemes to obtain credit card authorisations. Some of them use internal systems, some of them have outsources the payment handling to subsidiaries or external partners.

9.1.2 On-board Telephone Credit Card Authorisation

SITA processes most of the credit card authorisations initiated by the legacy on-board telephone phone systems that were popular prior to the introduction of GSM/WiFi services on-board planes.

9.1.3 Horizon Payment Services

For all its hosted carriers using its direct distribution applications (e-commerce, mobile, call centre etc.) SITA provides connectivity to multiple Payment Service Providers and acquiring banks and payment schemes around the world. Its recently introduced Horizon Payment Services will allow airlines to manage their own business rules, deciding what payment methods and what providers they wish to use in the various payment scenarios. Payment methods are displayed depending on the route, the currency, the value of the transaction, time to fly etc.

Fig 21: SITA Horizon Payment Services (Courtesy of SITA)

Airlines can use these parameters to dynamically decide about the suppliers (PSP, acquiring bank, fraud solution provider) they want to use for a particular transaction, allowing them to optimise costs and fund management. Several value added services, such as fraud management or currency conversion tools are pre-integrated into the solution and can be orchestrated into the transaction flow. In 2013 SITA will make this service available to the wider airline industry.

9.1.4 UATP's Next Generation Authorisation and Settlement System

As part of its community services role SITA is providing UATP with a next-generation authorisation and settlement infrastructure for its payment system, as well as hosting and customer support services.

DESCENDING AIRLINE PROFITS CALLS FOR TIGHTER COST CONTROL AT THE GATEWAY

THE CHALLENGE
The cost of payments has become a problem for airlines. Historically there was sufficient margin in the price of an airline ticket, typically sold over the counter by a travel agent, that the incremental cost of paying merchant service fees was acceptable.

Now with the introduction of low-cost airlines, rising fuel prices and intense competition, airlines are operating under severe cost pressures. In addition, the almost universal use of internet sales channels means fees from payment service providers represent a substantial cost. In this turbulent time, reducing the cost of payment processing is essential to improve the bottom line for airlines.

In an industry riddled with old, inflexible payment processing technology that dates back many years, the challenge is to bring payment processing into the 21st Century. Obliged to continue to support outdated payment standards, airlines nevertheless need to embrace new marketing and payment channels speedily and at a reasonable cost. They need a modern payments platform on which old and rigid payment standards can happily co-exist with fast-paced payment developments.

THE SOLUTION
Alaric offers Authentic, a flexible, low cost software solution that addresses the existing problems of airline payments. Its modern, open system architecture runs on the latest commodity hardware and software platforms, without the need for expensive specialist programming.

THE SUCCESSES
SITA, the world's leading specialist in air transport communications and IT solutions, has launched the SITA Payments Service for airlines using Authentic payments software from Alaric. As the gateway between the Global Distribution Systems and Payment Service Providers (PSPs), the Payments Service offers customers the flexibility to choose the way payments can be made.

SITA's key requirement was for flexibility to add new payment methods and service providers quickly, and react rapidly to

SITA has established numerous connections with a portfolio of PSPs that will be expanded over time to offer an unrivalled choice of payment methods for its international client base.

The success of the partnership with SITA has led to UATP, the low cost payment network privately owned by the world's airlines, upgrading its authorisation and settlements systems to Authentic. The new technology base will enable UATP to accept a wider range of transaction formats from existing scheme members. It will also be able to extend acceptance of the scheme to other travel-related merchants such as hotels and car rental firms. This will allow businesses to reduce their travel costs while offering airlines incremental opportunities to increase margins.

For airlines, Alaric offers not only an easy upgrade path to a modern payments platform but also the possibility to incorporate Fractals, an advanced fraud risk management service which already helps many on-line merchants control their exposure to CNP fraud.

CONCLUSION
Alaric opens a new generation of payment possibilities to the world's airlines. With Authentic enabling many airlines to seize full control over the manner in which they deliver new payment options, giving businesses the flexibility to make changes quickly, the travel industry is finally flying high in the payments space.

9.2 Amadeus Travel Payments

The Amadeus Travel Payments portfolio and technology brings together travel and payment expertise, offering the travel industry a unique set of attributes and capabilities.

The Amadeus Travel Payments portfolio is split into four categories: (Amadeus Travel Payments, 2014)

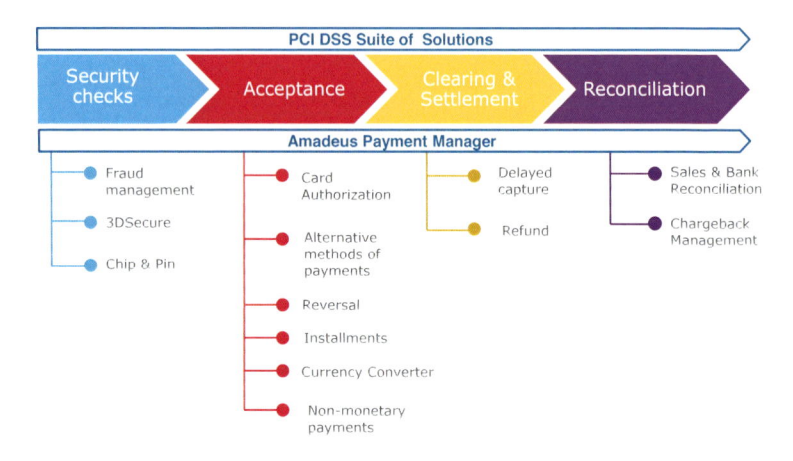

Fig 22: Amadeus Travel Payments Portfolio (Courtesy of Amadeus)

9.2.1 Security Checks

Amadeus Fraud Management offers a flexible and configurable omni-channel solution, fully adapted to the airline industry's specifics and with automatic action options.

Amadeus 3D Secure authenticates the cardholder in an online environment using a secret password validation.

Amadeus Chip and Pin is an innovative multi-merchant EMV device that allows airlines to authenticate face-to-face payments.

9.2.2 Acceptance

Amadeus Card Authorization offers real-time card authorisation integrated into the booking and issue flow for international and local credit or debit cards.

Amadeus Alternative Methods of Payments (AMOP) provides a single-interface framework including a wide range of AMOPs, from real-time bank transfers and eWallets to mobile payments.

Amadeus Instalments allows travel merchants to offer payments by instalments.

Dynamic Currency Converter (DCC) solution offers the merchant the possibility to allow travellers to pay in their card currency when the booking pricing currency is different.

9.2.3 Clearing and Settlement

Amadeus Delayed Capture is a two-step solution customised for the travel industry: first authorisation, then capture. This enables transactions to be reversed prior to being captured, avoiding refund processes.

Amadeus Refund enables automatic customer crediting when needed, based on the form of payment used.

9.2.4 Reconciliation

Amadeus Sales and Bank Reconciliation allows the airline to reconcile sales made against funds received, ensuring all payments have been collected and avoiding revenue leakage.

Travel and payment
expertise through our
unique Amadeus
Payment Platform.

Amadeus Travel Payments

End to end travel customized portfolio

Our solutions

- **Security Checks**
- **Acceptance**
- **Clearing and settlement**
- **Sales and bank reconciliation**

aMaDEUS

9.3 Navitaire

Navitaire's New Skies system provides real-time payment processing to all major credit cards, private credit cards and T&E card schemes. New acquiring banks and new payment methods can be integrated and configured centrally at a single point. It provides enhanced payment services, such as DCC and fraud management solutions. (Navitaire, 2011)

9.4 Sabre

Sabre Sonic Credit Suite is an option provided by SabreSonic® Ticket, providing integrated credit card authorisation and settlement services for all major credit cards (Sabre, 2011). It supports the direct submission of settlement files as well as airlines wishing to submit their own. Sabre is integrated with DataCash to provide 3D Secure services.

9.5 Travelport – eNett

Travelport has formed a joint venture with PSP International to provide an integrated payment and settlement system for its customers: eNett (Travelport, 2011). Its solutions focus on the transaction processing, settlement, reconciliation and reporting requirements of their travel agency, travel suppliers and corporate customer community.

In addition to its core business it provides credit card authorisation services with links to the major credit, charge and debit card schemes, across all channels.

10 Payment Methods used in the Airline Industry

For a very long time, cash, cheques and credit cards were the predominant payment methods used in the airline industry. The last decade though has seen a massive growth in alternative payment methods. Airlines are slowly adopting them into their payment operations to increase sales conversions in countries where credit cards are not commonly available and to reduce their merchant fees. This chapter gives you an overview of the methods that are available to airlines, from the IATA listed credit cards, debit cards, real time bank transfers, prepaid cards, electronic wallets, direct debits, cash payment options to mobile payments and payments with frequent flyer miles and gift cards.

10.1 IATA Approved Form of Payment Codes

Payment methods in the airline industry are standardised by IATA rules. Every ticket, Miscellaneous Cash Order (MCO) and every Electronic Miscellaneous Document (EMD) issued under these rules needs to contain one or more payment references to indicate how it has been paid for. The payment reference contains one of the IATA approved Form of Payment Codes (Form of Payment Identifier, or FOP ID) and the appropriate account details which are then used to initiate the payment (e.g. credit card number, government warrant number). There are codes available for cash, cheques, credit cards, prepaid tickets, government and United Nation transportation requests, credit sales and "pay later" plans.

There are currently no codes designated to alternative payment methods (the codes were defined long before these forms of payment became available). Carriers can either sub-submit them under one of the existing codes (e.g. "CA" for cash or "MS" for miscellaneous payment methods) or create new codes. New codes however can only be used for internal reporting. They would not be recognised in interlining or code-share scenarios where the payment information is passed on to external downstream partners. They would not know about them and would not be able to report on them.

Form of Payment Code	Description
CASH	Paid cash or by travellers cheque
CHECK or CHEQUE	Paid by cheque (other than travellers cheques)
PT	Prepaid Ticket Advice
GR	Government Transportation Request or Government Warrant
SGR	U.S. Government Transportation Request
UN	United Nations Transportation Request
NONREF	Refund is restricted
AGT	To be entered in the ticket when issued on behalf or in exchange for a document previously issued by a Sales Agent.
MS	Miscellaneous – any form of payment other than described above – sometimes used for alternative payment methods
DP	Direct form of payments (ARC)
CREDIT CARD CODES	Two-letter codes – see Table 5

Table 4: IATA Approved Form of Payment Codes

Low cost carrier and regional carriers who are not using e-tickets are a bit more flexible. As they do not necessarily have to follow IATA standards they can create their own ways of taking and recording payments.

10.2 Cash and Cheque

Cash is still very important in countries with limited banking infrastructure and low payment card penetration. There are no merchant fees associated with cash, but there is the risk of loss and theft and a cost to reconcile and deposit the money with the airline's bank. Cheques have commonly been replaced by debit card schemes and are hence only rarely accepted by airlines today. The payment guarantee is limited as banks have often reduced the cheque guarantees below the average ticket value and it takes a long time for the funds to clear.

10.3 International Credit Cards and Domestic Payment Instruments

Since their introduction by UATP, international credit cards are a corner stone of payments in the air transport industry. They account for a very large proportion of the airline payment transactions. Credit cards are fully embedded in all airline systems and processes, giving them an advantage over all other alternative payment options. Below is a list of all IATA approved international payment cards and domestic payment instruments with their respective two letter codes (IATA, 2012):

Card Scheme	Credit Card Code (Alpha)
American Express	AX
Discover Card	DS
Diners Club	DC
Japan Credit Bureau	JC
MasterCard	CA
VISA International	VI
Universal Air Travel Plan (UATP)	TP

Table 5: IATA Approved International Payment Cards

Domestic Payment Scheme	Credit Card Code (Alpha)	BSP
CreditoDirecto payment	AM	BSP Korea specific
Cards issued by BC	BC	BSP Korea specific
Cabal	CL	BSP Argentina, domestic
Cards issued by Kookmin	CN	BSP Korea specific
Cards issued by KEB	EB	BSP Korea specific
Card issued by Hyundai	HD	BSP Korea specific
Reserved for future use	KA	BSP Korea specific
Reserved for future use	KB	BSP Korea specific
Cards issued by Lotte	LC	BSP Korea specific
Card issued by Nonghyub	NH	BSP Korea specific
Cards issued by Naranja	NV	BSP Korea specific
OCA	OC	BSPUruguay, domestic card
Domestic payment voucher	OV	BSP Spain domestic voucher

Domestic Payment Scheme	Credit Card Code (Alpha)	BSP
Domestic payment voucher	OY	BSP Spain domestic voucher
Domestic payment voucher	PC	BSP Spain domestic voucher
Reserved for future use	PR	BSP Chile specific
PagaTodo payment	PT	BSP Mexico domestic voucher
Domestic payment voucher	RC	BSP Spain domestic voucher
Cards issued by Shinhan	SH	BSP Korea specific
Card issued by HANA	SK	BSP Korea specific
Cards issued by Samsung	SW	BSP Korea specific
Tierra del Fuego	TF	BSP Argentina, domestic card
TarjetaNaranja	TN	BSP Argentina, domestic card
Nativa	NT	BSP Argentina, domestic card
Reserved for future use	HC	BSP Brazil specific

Note: In South Korea, cards are not accepted by merchants on the basis of the card brand but on the basis of the issuer's name. Hence a merchant has to sign a card acceptance agreement with every issuer

Table 6: IATA Approved Payment Instruments, Domestic Usage Only

The penetration of credit cards varies greatly between different countries. Accepting credit cards as the only form of payment can significantly limit an airlines access to a market.

10.4 Co-branded cards

Co-branded credit cards are partnerships between card issuers and merchants. The cards are dominated by the merchant's design but contain the card brand's identification elements (logo, hologram, etc.) as well as those of the issuing bank. The aim of these programs is to increase card usage by rewarding the cardholder for every transaction. "Earn a frequent flyer mile for every $ that you spend" would be a typical airline co-branded reward program. In addition to the increased brand awareness the airline receives income from the miles it sells to the issuing bank who uses them to reward its cardholders. The issuing bank profits from card fees and increased transaction based revenue. Co-branded programs can be a significant revenue component for airlines, balancing the merchant fees they have to pay to the banks.

10.5 Alternative Payment Methods

Alternative payment methods are all those that are typically not covered under the IATA approved FOP codes, such as local debit cards, real-time bank transfers, off-line bank transfers and direct debits, wallets and prepaid cards as well as cash payment options (processed by third parties, not the airline directly).

10.6 Debit Cards

Local debit cards are schemes whose acceptance is limited to a single country or sometimes even to a single bank or banking group, using their proprietary messaging formats. International debit card brands, such as Maestro or Visa Debit work pretty much across the world.

Debit cards usually attract a lower merchant fee than traditional credit cards. Often they are fixed transaction fees, rather than a percentage of the transaction value. The lower costs and a relatively high payment guarantee make them a very attractive alternative to credit cards. Not all brands however can be used for card-not-present transactions over the internet or the phone.

Here is a small sample of domestic card brands: Solo (UK), Laser (Ireland), Carte Bleue (France), Dankort (Denmark), Diners, CartaSi (Italy) Delta, Discover (USA), Isracard (Israel) and UnionPay with about 40 local Chinese debit cards.

Many of these domestic brands however have since been replaced or absorbed by international debit card brands.

10.7 Real-Time Bank Transfers

Real-time bank transfers are an internet payment method based on online banking. To accept a payment the cardholder is redirected to its issuing bank where they confirm the transaction using the on-line banking portal or using their on-line PIN. The payments are non-reversible, allowing the merchant to immediately deliver the goods (issue the ticket). This solution is provided by banks or groups of banks directly. Fees are usually a lot lower than credit card fees.

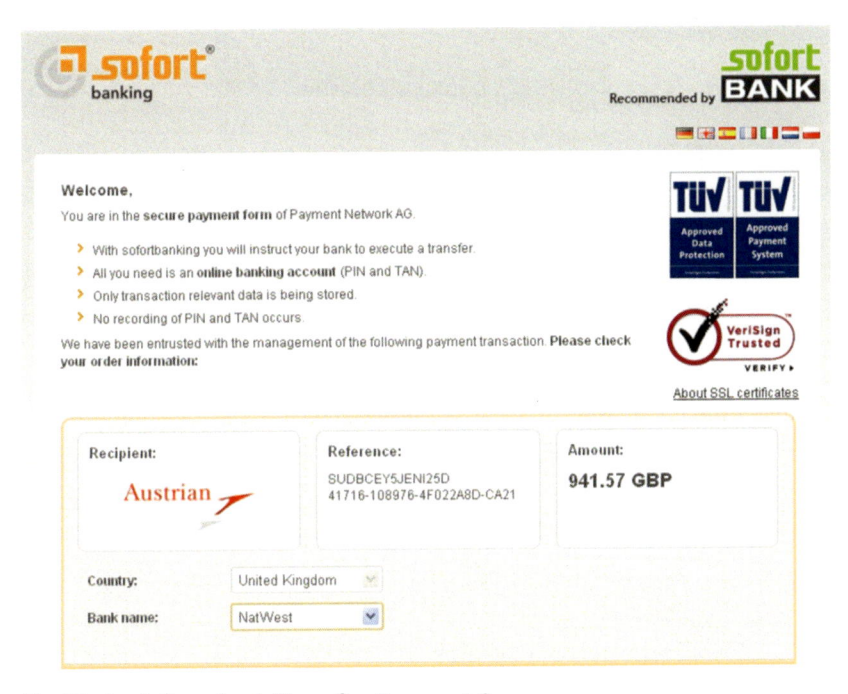

Fig 23: Real-time Bank Transfer Payment Screen

Bank24.ru, money mail (Russia), Débito online (Brazil), Ideal (Holland), GiroPay, SofortÜberweisung (Germany), Nordea (Scandinavia), eNETS (Singapore), EPS (Austria), Interac Online (Canada), Poli (Australia), Safetypay (South America, U.S. and Europe), SecureVault Payments (U.S.) are just some of the real-time bank transfers programs in use today.

10.8 Direct Debit and Bank Transfers

Merchants who use direct debits automatically draw money from consumer bank accounts via an electronic fund transfer. To pay, the account holder simply provides the account details. This process usually takes a few days and the merchant does not have a payment guarantee as the account holder has the right to reverse a payment up to several weeks after it has been taken without giving a reason. It is advisable therefore to use them only in combination with risk management systems that can verify e.g. the address of the account holder.

Direct debit systems are available in Australia, Austria, Belgium, Canada, France, Germany, Ireland, Italy, Japan, Lichtenstein, Malaysia, the Netherlands, Spain, South Africa, Switzerland, United Kingdom, the United States of America and many other countries.

Bank transfers work the other way around – the bank account holder manually initiates the bank transfer. When the funds have been received by the airline (again, usually taking a few days to be processed) the ticket can be issued.

10.9 Cash Payments Options

Cash payment options allow passengers to book on-line and pay later, without the need for a payment card or bank account. For many consumers cash is the only payment option available, especially in emerging markets such as Latin America, the Middle East, Africa and Asia where credit card penetration is low and/or where the bank infrastructure is not yet well established.

The merchant issues the cardholder a payment reference number (or a bar code).That is used to reference the payment either with a post office (e.g. in China), with money transfer bureaus such as Western Union (in over 195 countries), shopping centres (e.g. Oxxo in Mexico), local retailers (such as 7eleven), banks and cash points (e.g. Boleto in Brazil, Santander in Chile, Beeline in Russia) or at ATMs.

The payment scheme informs the airline (usually via the PSP) once it receives a payment (either in real-time or via a batch file once a day). Sometimes the amount and the validity of the payment are verified against the airline's reservation system or the PSP (to ensure that the booking exists and the payment is completed within the ticketing time limit). The carrier can then issue the ticket (either manually or through an automated process).

10.10 Electronic Wallets

There are two types of electronic wallets. They are either virtual accounts that can be preloaded with money, or an access mechanism to one or multiple payment methods (credit cards, bank accounts) that are registered with the wallet. Some are a combination of both.

Most wallets work on the basis of a prepaid account that can be topped up either via a bank transfer, a payment at a cash point or a load transaction using a credit or debit card payment. Funds can also be moved between wallets – another way to top up an account. Once loaded, the funds can then be used for purchases or further transfers between accounts.

Other wallets don't actually hold any funds themselves, but pass the payment request on to one or more payment methods associated with or stored within the wallet. These can be credit cards, debit cards or bank accounts. The wallet becomes the access mechanism, the converter. To authorise a payment the account holder provides their wallet credentials (a user-name and a PIN or password). That triggers a credit card or a debit authorisation, using the account details stored within the wallet.

Fig 24: Example of an Electronic Wallet Payment Screen: CashU

Some wallets have combined both functionalities. They can be loaded with funds or used with any of the cards or accounts associated with the wallet. The success of these schemes is based on the additional confidence factor, as the cardholders don't have to reveal their credit card numbers to on-line merchants to make a purchase. Examples of electronic wallets are PayPal, Google Wallet, CashU, Moneybookers, Toditocard and WebMoney.

10.11 Prepaid Cards

Prepaid cards are an ideal alternative for customers who don't have access to bank accounts or credit cards (e.g. because of age restrictions). They can be purchased against cash at brick-and-mortar locations and then used on-line to pay for goods and services.

Some come in the form of "real" credit cards, carrying the logo of one of the international card schemes. These are usually re-loadable and can be used on-line as well as in the physical world, just like regular credit cards. Others are more like calling cards with an account number and a PIN code, covered by a scratch panel. They are usually not reloadable and come in fixed denominations. More recently the card numbers and PINs are created on demand and printed off at the POS, similar to pay-as-you-go mobile phone talk time (See **Fig 25**).

Paysafecard, CashTicket, Walliecard, and Ukash are typical examples of these prepaid card types. High merchant fees however make those payment methods primarily suitable for digital contents and services, as well as for the on-line gambling industry.

Fig 25: Example of a Prepaid Card: Paysafecard (Courtesy of Paysafecard)

10.12 Mobile Payments

Fig 26: The World of Mobile Payments (Courtesy of Edgar, Dunn & Company – modified)

Pascal Burg from Edgar, Dunn & Company divides the world of mobile payments into physical and remote payment scenarios. In the physical ones the mobile phone can be used as a mechanism to transmit card account data via a contactless interface to a payment terminal (see previous chapters about NFC). Equipped with a magnetic stripe or chip card reader the mobile phone can be converted to POS terminal accepting card payments for goods and services (see **Fig 38**). In an airline scenario this may be used by mobile agents, selling access baggage, upgrades or priority boarding, as well as for on-board retailing.

In the remote scenarios Burg has identified three categories: Mobile money transfers and mobile remote payments, for digital goods as well as for physical goods and services. Mobile money transfer allows users to send money between two phones. The mobile account, identified by the mobile phone number, can be loaded at cash points, ATMs and retail outlets. Once funds are available they can be used for person-to-person transfers as well as for payments to retailers – such as airlines. Kenya Airways was one of the first carriers to accept mobile payments (M-PESA) for tickets (See **Fig 27**).

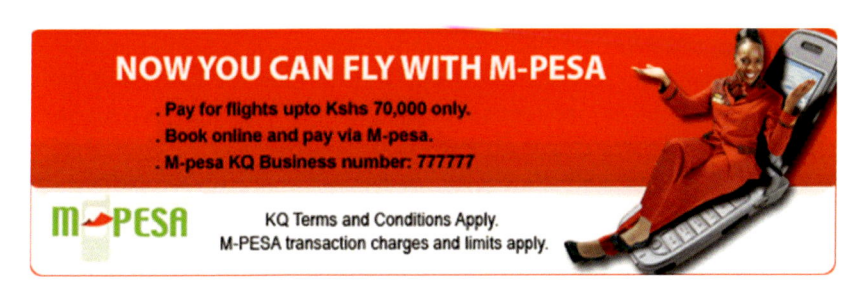

Fig 27: Kenya Airways and Mobile Payments (Courtesy of Kenya Airways)

Mobile remote payments are offered when the mobile phone is used as a shopping portal. The goods (digital and physical) or services are presented to the user either through the phone's web browser or through a native mobile phone application. Payments are taken via a regular credit card or any of the mobile enabled alternative payment methods. Many carriers are already using this process to allow passengers to purchase tickets on their mobile phones and tablets. Digital content is usually charged against the mobile phone bill (operator billing). This however is restricted to low value transactions.

10.13 Frequent Flyer Miles

Frequent flyer reward miles can be seen as a currency in their own right and airlines treat them as such. They can be earned, bought against other currencies, stored, transferred, donated and ultimately used to purchase flights and other goods or services (from flights, hotels, cars to adventure weekends). Frequent flyer programs are issued either by the airline itself or by their loyalty program partner. Similar to the issuing banks, the airline is the guarantor for the value of the miles when they are used inside and outside the airline eco-system (for booking a hotel room for example). The $-value equivalent of all miles needs to be reflected in their books and a certain proportion of that kept in separate, protected accounts.

Mile redemptions are processed in a similar way to regular payments. An "authorisation" message checks the available balance. Once the purchase is completed, the miles are deducted from the account of the cardholder and a financial transaction is initiated. This can be an internal cross charge to reflect the earned revenue (e.g. when the miles are used for an upgrade) or a payment to a third party service provider (e.g. when they are used for a car rental).

10.14 Vouchers and Gift Cards

Vouchers and gift cards, if issued by the airline directly (closed loop system) work in a similar way. When they are sold to a passenger the equivalent currency value is deposited into a pool account. When the voucher is redeemed, the revenue can be recognised. Depending on the local financial regulations, vouchers and gift cards can expire after a given amount of time (six months, a year or several years). Any unused value can then be declared revenue (commonly called "breakage"). This can be a significant contribution to the business case of implementing these programs.

Fig 28: KLM Airline Gift Card (Courtesy of KLM)

Vouchers and gift cards are often issued in fixed denominations and can then be redeemed in combination with other payment methods to cover the total cost of a flight (which may be higher than the value of the voucher). Others can be used for certain routes or flights, regardless of the actual cost of the flight.

Third party issued vouchers and gift cards that can be used across multiple merchants (open loop systems) work similarly to the prepaid cards described in the previous chapters.

Long gone are the times, when cash was king and credit cards were the only way to pay cashless and in card-not-present situations. The variety of payment methods available today is huge, from debit cards, bank transfers, real-time banking, electronic wallets, prepaid cards, mobile and NFC payments. They differentiate themselves by their geographical and demographical reach, their respective costs, the risk profile and the integration and processing requirements.

11 Summary

This part of the book provided an introduction to payments, its origins and evolution over the last 100 years. It looked at the players and their often overlapping roles. It provided a step-by-step guide through the payment transaction and the financial flow including the associated cost and revenue elements for each of the participants. It looked at the risks that are associated with taking payments and outlined the responsibilities each of the players has to assume to reduce fraud to a minimum. The types and cost of fraud were also analysed.

The section about laws, standards and compliance rules took the first step into the specifics of airlines, highlighting the sources of governance that are especially relevant for this industry. A review of airline affiliated payment institutions and payment system integrators together with an overview of the most common payment methods completed this part.

A description of a system however can only ever be a snapshot. Regulations, such as the PCI standards, are constantly evolving, additional payment methods are being introduced on an almost daily basis and new technologies such as NFC have only just surfaced in the airline industry. Part of the challenge is keeping up with the changes.

payments.aero

Part II. Payments in the Airline Industry – Where and How are they Processed?

1   Introduction

This section takes the basics of the payment industry, covered in the previous chapters and applies them to the air transport industry. It looks at all the relevant distribution channels that airlines use today to offer goods and services to their passengers and analyses the payment processes in each of them.

The section begins with an insight into the traditional airline payment flow, where authorisation and capture transactions are processed through the back-office reservation, ticketing and IATA BSP systems. Travel agencies, ticket desks and call centres are rely heavily on this process, but are increasingly using such alternatives as POS devices and IVR systems.

It then takes us through e-commerce and mobile booking engines. For web-based direct distribution channel sit is more common to use a PSP to process the payments. The back-office systems still record these transactions, but are less and less involved in processing the authorisation and the capture.

To capitalise on ancillary revenue opportunities, airlines increasingly adopt additional payment touch points such as check-in desks, self-service kiosks, agent mobile devices and on-board retail. We investigate how payments are taken for excess baggage, priority check-in, upgrades, meals, duty free items, etc. This part also covers the challenges of chip & PIN devices in kiosks, real-time on-board credit card authorisation and taking payments using smart phones and tablets.

This is followed by an analysis of authorisations for on-board telephone calls, payments in staff travel offices, airport lounges and compensation payments, where funds have to be paid out to the passenger.

The section concludes with an overview of the various options airlines have to take payments for 3rd party content such as hotels, insurance and car hire, where the airline is not necessarily the merchant of record.

2 Traditional Airline Authorisation and Settlement Flow

2.1 Overview

Most payments in the airline industry still follow a transaction process unlike that found in any other industry. It is a disjointed authorisation and settlement process -where authorisation is obtained through one channel and the capture message processed through another. The authorisation is done during the booking process through the reservation system or the GDS. The card data is stored in the ticketing system before being forwarded to the airline as part of the sales report. The transaction information is then extracted from the sales report and submitted to the acquiring banks by a variety of means.

This process was originally set up to support a traditional airline workflow:

- The sales agent creates a booking and captures the passenger's card details during the reservation process.
- To validate the card they perform an authorisation request through the relevant card scheme.
- Issuing the ticket is done afterwards, often by another team, and prior to e-tickets involved printing a paper ticket.
- Once the ticket is successfully issued, the card number, expiry date and authorisation code are stored in the ticketing system
- These are then extracted from the sales report and forwarded for transaction submission. Authorisations for cancelled, voided or expired bookings remain unused. Unless they are reversed, they continue to block funds on the card account until they automatically expire after about a week.

Traditional Airline Payment Transaction Flow

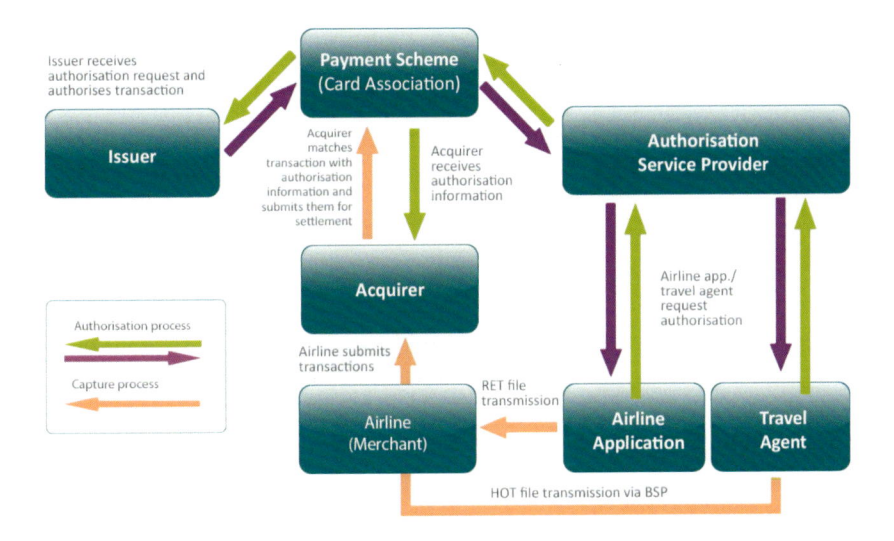

Fig 29: Traditional Airline Payment Transaction Flow

The acquiring banks receive capture messages in a variety of forms and need to match them with the authorisation information before forwarding them to the credit card schemes for settlement. When the airlines receive their funds, they reconcile them in their revenue management and accounting systems against the ticket sales.

Below are the individual steps of the traditional process in more detail.

2.2   Sales Transaction

For every ticket sale transaction the sales agent needs to record the payment method used to purchase it. Valid payment methods range from cash, cheques, credit cards, debit cards, Prepaid Ticket Advices, government warrants, US or UN Transport requests to other miscellaneous payment methods (see page 123 for IATA approved payment methods).

The Form of Payment Identifier (FOP ID) is followed by various additional data elements that allow the back-office systems to process and reconcile the particular payment. This can be the order number for the government warrant or transport request, the budget code for staff travel or the prepaid ticket number.

For credit card transactions, the agent needs to record the following cardholder details: the credit card identifier, the card number, expiry date, the amount and the currency code. Certain card schemes or FOP IDs (e.g. American Express and UATP cards) require the agent to capture additional information, called Descriptive Billing Information (DBI) during the sales/ticketing process.

The most important bit of information that needs to be submitted however is the authorisation code! The authorisation ensures that the cardholder information collected is valid, that the card number relates to a genuine card and that the card is active. It also provides the airline with a certain payment guarantee for the full value of the purchase amount.

2.3 Authorisation Request

Authorisation requests can be obtained in the following way: most GDSs, reservation systems and Local Ticketing Service Providers (LTSP) request credit card authorisations through an IATA defined financial message, the Credit Request ("CRQ") message. They are either green-screen command lines or have been converted into more user-friendly graphical user interfaces.

A CRQ authorisation message contains the agent ID, credit card identifier, card number, card expiry date, CVC, the amount and the currency code.

Authorisation messages are forwarded to a certified Authorisation Service Provider, such as SITA, who in turn pass them on to the particular international credit card schemes (Visa, MasterCard, DinersClub, American Express, JCB and UATP) to whom they are directly linked. (See SITA Credit Card Authorisation, page 115). Some of the airlines and GDSs have established their own direct connections to the card schemes.

The response comes in the Credit Response "CTR" (IATA 2009; Recommended Practice 1791b Attachment "A").

Example for conventional CRQ message:

CRQ
123456/005EA/04CA1234567890123456/0715//99075USD/123

Field	Explanation
Record Type Identifier	3 alphanumeric. "CRQ"
Field Separator	"/" (oblique).
Originator Reference Number	1 to 8 alphanumeric.

Field Separator	"/" (oblique).
Accounting System Code	1 numeric. "0" (zero).
Transaction Type Identifier	2 numeric. "05"
Merchant Identification Number	Maximum 15 alphanumeric
Field Separator	"/" (oblique).
Point of Service Special Condition Code	1 numeric.
	"0" = Normal Transaction;
	"1" = Mail or Phone order;
	"2" = Unattended terminal;
	"3" = Merchant is Suspicious.
	"7" = eCommerce over secure socket (SSL) "8" = eCommerce not secure
Approval Code Response Length	1 numeric "6"
Alphabetic Credit Card Code	2 alphanumeric. E.g. "CA" "VI","TP".
Account Number	Maximum 19 numeric.
Field Separator	"/" (oblique).
Expiration Date	4 numeric – Conditional
	Format is MMYY. For example, "0715" is July, 2015.

Field Separator	"/" (oblique). Conditional, if magnetic stripe data follow
Magnetic Stripe Encoded Data	Maximum 107 alphanumeric. Conditional on the reading of magnetically encoded data.
Field Separator	"/" (oblique).
Address Verification Data	"ZNNNNNNNNNAAAAAAAAAAAAAAAAAAAA"
	Z - Address verification delimiter (must be the letter "Z").
	N..N - New zip code format (nine digits) or old zip code format (five digits, left justified and filled with zeros to the ninth digit)
	A..A - First 20 characters of the cardholder's billing address
Field Separator	"/" (oblique).
Authorisation Amount	Maximum 8 numeric. For example, 99075 is $990.75.
Currency Indicator Code	3 alphanumeric. "USD"
Field Separator	"/" (oblique) – Conditional if CVC2 data field follows.
Card Security Code (CVV2, CVC, CID2)	Format varies per card scheme

Table 7: IATA Defined Authorisation Messaging Format (Source: IATA, SITA)

Authorisation happens in real time and the response message comes back almost instantly. Through the response message (CTR message) the issuing bank either approves or declines the transaction. For an approval, the message contains an approval code (between 4 and 6 digits long). A declined is either a simple – DENY, or an instruction to retain the card, if it has been reported lost or stolen (PKUP).

Approval/Denial Code	Description
0	Approved
1	Link down/please call issuer
5	DENY (Deny)
4, 7	PKUP (Pick up card)
E	ER and two-numeric reject reason

Table 8: IATA Defined Approval/Denial Codes (Source: IATA, SITA)

Note that authorisations through the Authorisation Service Providers are limited to a list of IATA certified credit card schemes. It is very important to be aware that alternative payment methods are not on this list and can therefore not be processed, unless they are converted into one of the approved codes (see UATP and their process for alternative payment methods, page 112). This is one of the reasons for their relatively slow up-take in the airline industry.

All ticket entries created can be changed and voided up until the sales report is run at the end of a shift or day. Initiating the sales report commits all issued tickets and marks them for payment processing. It also allows a sales agent to reconcile his daily sales against the payments that he has taken – most importantly the cash and cheque payments. Credit card transactions are not processed any further at this stage and remain stored in the sales report. The next chapter covers the steps required to settle these transactions.

2.4 Extraction and Submission of Credit Card Transactions

Credit card transactions that originate in the airline's own distribution channels are stored in the sales reports (RET files). Travel agent transactions are reported in BSP files (HOT files). There are multiple ways them to reach an acquiring bank for settlement.

- Where Airlines have processing links to their acquiring banks they extract the payment details from the RET files and submit them directly. In many other cases they use their PSP to converts the RET file into a file format that the banks can process.

- Processing the files originating from BSPs is more challenging, as there is likely to be one file per country that the airline operates in. BSPs use a common file format and are capable of transmitting files directly to the acquiring bank in that format. Not all acquiring banks though can process that format and may require the file to be reformatted. Some acquiring banks have specialised in aggregating and processing files from multiple countries. IATA has set up a service to extract credit card information from BSP files and forward them on behalf of the airline (see IATIA CardClear, page 110). CardAXS, another IATA service, is an example of a bank that can acquire BSP transactions globally (see IATIA CardAXS, page 111).

- Some carriers prefer to collect all BSP files centrally. They then create the billing file and pass it on to the acquiring bank, either directly or through a PSP.

2.5 Settlement and Reporting

Airlines book sales by sales source and currency at the time they are reported to them:

- Bookings through their own reservation system daily through the RET file
- Travel agency sales daily or weekly through the BSP/HOT or ARC files.

To be able to match sales transactions against settlements, settlements need to be broken down in the same way, by sales channel and currency. Airlines anticipate settlements and reporting from the acquiring bank in the same grouping as they submit them. Ideally any fees (merchant fees, transaction fees or account fees) are reported separately to facilitate the transaction matching process.

This reconciliation process enables airlines to identify missing payments and also reduces customer complaints and charge-back requests, as any duplicate payments or payments where no ticket has been issued can be detected and rectified early.

2.6 Implications of Separating the Message Flow

Separating the authorisation message from the transaction submission has significant processing and financial impacts. The simple fact being that as two separate providers process the authorisation and transaction submission the transaction costs are already doubled. A single provider is likely to consider an authorisation and a settlement as a single transaction and charge it as such.

This is not the only implication though. As acquiring banks do not process the authorisation request, they need to ensure that they receive the authorisation information from the relevant payment scheme (MasterCard and Visa provide this service). The banks then need to match up the authorisation and capture requests before submitting them for settlement. Although waiting for this information also adds delays to the process and delays funds getting to the airline, this reconciliation process it is a vital cost saver: unmatched transactions attract a significantly higher interchange fee – particularly relevant in the U.S. region.

In other regions, this process helps to reduce charge-backs, as the information required to defend them is already included in the message. Authorisation matching only works if the correct Merchant Category Code (MCC) has been submitted during the authorisation process (most carriers have their own MCC). However, not all system providers support this and will submit a default MCC for all carriers instead. The Transaction ID that is issued as part of the authorisation response message (and which could be used to match the transactions) is only rarely forwarded with the capture message.

The merchant name transmitted in such settlements is usually limited to the two letter carrier code. This makes it more difficult for the cardholder to recognise the transaction on his statement and increases the Requests for Information and charge-backs. Default values for the Merchant Country Code (indicating where the transaction occurred) complicate the assessment of country-specific fees and may also result in higher merchant fees. Missing or default acquirer ICAs/BINs lead to incorrect billing in the card scheme's systems.

Airlines traditionally follow a very unique way of processing their card transactions. This chapter focused on the generic transaction flow that is used in many of the airlines' distribution channels. The following chapters reference the process described above as they look at each of the channels individually and go into further detail where processes differ for that channel. They also include new, alternative ways of processing payments – where the authorisation and the capture message are processed together, by the same entities.

3   Travel Agency

When you make a booking through a travel agency, whether as an individual or as a corporate customer, you are likely to book more than just a flight. In most cases a holiday or business trip is made up of a flight, a hotel, transfer and add-ons such as excursions. In these scenarios, the travel agent usually takes payment for the entire package using their own merchant agreement and ensures that the down-stream partners, who will eventually provide the services, each receive their share of the revenue. For IATA certified providers the airfares and the revenue for some other journey elements are shared through the BSP system. Quite an astonishing achievement when you think about it – just imagine a three month round-the-world trip…

For airline tickets, the agent has both options, to use their own merchant agreement or to sell flights on behalf of the airline, acting as pure agent for the airline. In this case he would not get involved in collecting the money from the passenger. He does however collect the passenger's payment details and passes them on to the airline.

Both scenarios are possible for bookings through a GDS as well as for bookings made directly with an airline. Here are the two scenarios in detail:

3.1 Bookings through a GDS

When a travel agent makes a booking through a GDS, he can choose between two options:

- Processing the booking and the payment on his own behalf – the travel agent is the Merchant of Record – and paying the airline later, or
- Providing the airline with the passenger's credit card details, so that the airline submits the transaction for payment on their account. For these transactions the airline is the Merchant of Record.

Depending on the sales circumstances, the agent may choose between the two options. Some fare types though require one or the other method to be used. Here are the two options in more details:

3.1.1 Travel Agency as Merchant of Record

In this scenario the travel agency takes responsibility for collecting payment from the passenger. This can be cash, cheque or via a card payment (any domestic or international credit card) processed through a POS terminal. All standard and alternative payment methods are possible in this scenario. Corporate customers usually pay with corporate credit cards or are invoiced at the end of a billing cycle and pay at a later time via bank transfer, direct banking etc. Online travel agencies take internet based payments. Whichever way, the agent is fully responsible for ensuring payment is made and carries the full risk associated with the payment transaction. Any charge-backs will have to be carried by him and he needs to pay his suppliers, regardless of whether he gets paid himself.

Most of these ticket sales are recorded by the GDS and reported to the airline through the BSP systems (see IATA Billing and Settlement Plan, page 106). The total amount of all sales transactions where the agent is the Merchant of Record are debited from his account for a particular reporting period by the BSP. The BSP system shares the amount between all downstream partners. Where applicable, it also settles the commission for the travel agent, netting it out against the transaction amount the agent needs to pay.

Airlines and service providers receive regular sales reports, listing the amounts that they can expect to receive for particular periods.

3.1.2 Airline as Merchant of Record

Where the travel agent acts as a pure sales agent he does not collect the ticket payment from the passenger. Here he acts on behalf of the airline and the airline is the Merchant of Record. The travel agent does however need to collect the passenger's payment card data, and needs to ensure that the cardholder information collected is correct, the card is genuine and active and there are enough funds available. Here are the steps in detail:

- The first step is an authorisation request, usually carried out through the GDS (see above). In some cases the agent uses telephone authorisation services provided by a local call centre on behalf of the card schemes to obtain an authorisation code. A small percentage of transactions are authorised through POS terminals. The cardholder information is stored in the ticketing mask when the ticket is issued. This contains the two letter code of the credit card scheme, the card number, expiry date, amount, currency, the authorisation code etc.

- To help the airline fight possible charge-backs, the travel agent has to request the cardholder to sign the transaction receipt. Wherever possible the agent should perform the usual card verifications: check the signature against the one on the back of the card and the card for its security features. This is not possible for telephone orders or corporate purchases, where the agency has the card number on file (although the agent should have checked the signature when he initially recorded the card number).

- The payment transactions are recorded by the GDS and submitted to the BSP at the end of the specified reporting period. In contrast to the settlement path described in the previous chapter though, these transactions do not get settled through the BSP. As the travel agent has not collected any money, he won't need to forward any funds. He will still receive the commission through the BSP system (where applicable).

The airline, as the Merchant of Record, now needs to ensure that the credit card transactions are forwarded to the relevant acquiring bank, either directly or through various service providers.

Card scheme rules stipulate that "card-present" transactions should be processed at Point of Sale terminals, rather than being keyed in or swiped. This way they can be better validated – via Chip & PIN (in EMV countries) – or at least via a PIN entry. To by-pass these rules and facilitate the transactions in the above scenario, where the card is present, but the card number is entered manually (keyed or swiped) the transactions are submitted with a "card-not-present" identifier – incorrectly. This system is still very much in use on a global scale and credit card schemes are pushing the industry hard change it.

For corporate travel purchases it is common practice for the travel agent to store the customer's credit card details for future booking. This is also viewed critically by the card schemes, unless these details are stored in a PCI compliant storage system. As CSC codes should not be stored under any circumstances, many of these corporate bookings are processed without a CSC – another violation of card scheme rules.

IATA reviews and updates their mandates and best practice manuals on an ongoing basis to respond to these issues as best as possible.

The payment risk for these transactions lies with the airline. In some regions however, it is still common practice for the carriers to keep the agent liable and push any losses resulting from disputed or fraudulent transactions back to them.

The argument being that it is the travel agent's customer, and they should ensure the passenger's credibility. Agencies in turn cover this risk with additional fees (e.g. Money Collection Payments).

3.2 Airline Direct to Agent Sales

GDSs are not the only way for travel agents to access an airline's inventory and sell their tickets. To reduce distribution fees, airlines have set up direct distribution systems, enabling travel agents or corporate customers to book directly through the airline. These systems come in various shapes:

- The easiest way to give a travel agent direct access is through the airline's own reservation system. The agents would be set up in the system with special user rights, allowing them to directly create PNRs and issue tickets.
- Another method provides the agents with a simplified version of the airline's internet booking engine.
- Other airlines have developed specific direct distribution applications.

As all of these systems bypass the GDS and the BSP system, the airline needs to step up and fulfil the responsibilities normally performed by the BSP: the management of the relationship with the agent and even more importantly, the payment process. To do this the airline needs a direct distribution agreement with the travel agent and needs to ensure that the agent pays for the tickets they issue on behalf of the airline.

As with indirect distribution, there are multiple options available to ensure that the airline eventually receives the money for the flights that they provide. Asking the travel agency to enter the passenger's credit card as the form of payment also works in a direct distribution environment, especially if the flight is the only thing the passenger wants.

It does get a bit more complicated when the travel agent is the Merchant of Record and collects the payment from the passenger. As the airline can no longer count on the GDS to record and settle the payments through the BSP, the carrier needs to set up its own recording, invoicing and settlement system.

Rarely does the airline simply invoice the travel agent at the end of a reporting period (weekly or monthly, depending on the transaction volume) for all the tickets that he has sold. Without any additional control, there would be nothing to stop an agent from sell millions worth of tickets and then disappearing (the BSP system protects airlines against such fraud cases). Airlines generally request that the agent pays a deposit that covers the value of all ticket sales the agent is estimated to do in a given time frame. Once the agent has used up his line of credit he has to settle all the ticket sales with the airline – resetting his balance.

Some carriers have automated this process and automatically disable an agent's user access should the ticketed amount exceed the deposit. A bank transfer from the agent automatically resets the balance and re-enables the user, if required. Other carriers manually monitor agency sales and match them against agent payments.

Using electronic wallets (or reloadable gift cards) is another method to automate credit management. Airlines issue them to agents to use for payment of flights using the airline's website or booking systems. The agent can refill the wallet balance by transferring money to a dedicated account. Using a web-based reporting tool they can manage their account, see transactions, download reports or request clarification for disputed transactions. The airline will need to have this wallet or gift card system integrated as an available payment method on their direct distribution channel.

In those payment scenarios, the payment flow for travel agent commissions has to be set up separately. As the fare is now collected directly by the airline, any applicable commissions can no longer be netted out against the amounts that the agent has to pay to the airline. They can be settled via the BSP system. Bank transfers are another commonly used option. There are some high-end direct distribution systems on the market that can manage all these processes for the airline. They are also linked to clearing houses and as a result are better able to trigger the movements of funds between the travel agent and airline as well.

In summary, payments taken at the travel agent are carried out in one of two ways: Either the airline receives the passenger's credit card details along with the ticket information and charge the passenger directly or the passenger pays the travel agent and the travel agent then passes the money on to the airline. In a direct distribution environment the carriers have to manage this process themselves. For bookings through a GDS, or one of the more elaborate direct distribution systems, the settlement of ticket fares and commissions between you and the travel agent is automatically processed through the BSP and the clearing houses.

The next section looks at sales originating from the airline's own ticket desks.

4 Airline Ticket Desk

Airline ticket desks are the airline's retail outlets and are located either at the airport, or at strategically located spots around town. City Ticket Offices (CTO) and Airport Ticket Offices (ATO) is what they are traditionally referred to as. While CTOs are increasingly being replaced by direct distribution channels, such as e-commerce, the ATOs' importance remains strong, and with airlines unbundling their services has probably even increased. Passengers at the airport needing to pay for excess baggage or wanting to buy an upgrade, priority boarding and other ancillary services are usually sent to the airline's airport ticket desk.

ATOs usually accept a wide range of payment methods: from cash and cheques, IATA certified credit cards (through the reservation systems), domestic credit and debit cards (through POS terminals), as well as other miscellaneous payment methods, such as MCOs, budget codes, staff travel codes etc. The following chapters consider the various payment methods and how these are managed in a ticket desk environment.

4.1 Cash and Cheque

Cash and cheque sales are recorded with the appropriate cash/or cheque FOP IDs in the airline's reservation/ticketing system and the money and cheques collected are reconciled against the sales report at the end of a shift or day. Foreign currencies can complicate the reconciliation process a bit, as they need to be converted, the conversion rate can be defined locally or found in the reservation system. The funds are either deposited at a local bank branch, where the airline has an account, or are forwarded to a central location to be deposited with the bank there.

4.2 POS Terminal

In countries or locations where the airline has an established banking relationship, it may decide to set up POS terminals to accept international credit cards and even more importantly, local card types prevalent in that particular country. Transactions processed through a POS terminal are usually recorded as a cash transaction by the reservation system. The local acquiring bank providing the POS terminal to the CTO or ATO processes the authorisation message and the transaction capture. The funds will be settled by payment into the same domestic bank account. All cash, cheque and the POS transactions end up in the same account, allowing the back-office accounting team to reconcile them against the sales reports.

Fig 30: Airline Ticket Desk

Processing cards through POS terminals has multiple advantages. Being able to take payments with local payment cards can be a significant benefit in countries where international card brands are not commonly available. Additionally, local debit card schemes usually attract a significantly lower merchant fee. It is also worth noting too that the fees for international credit card transactions are significantly lower if they are processed on a POS terminal rather than being swiped or keyed in and processed through the BSP system as "card-not-present" transactions.

4.3 Payment Processing through the Reservation System

Where there is no POS terminal available to process a transaction, ticket agents can use the facilities provided by the reservation system to process a payment. As described above, the agent will need to obtain an authorisation code. Then the credit card identifier and the card number are recorded together with the expiry date and the authorisation in the ticketing/reservation system. A back-office process extracts these details at the end of the day for all sales paid for by credit card and forwards them to the relevant acquiring bank.

In both cases, for credit card transactions processed using a POS terminal and those processed through the reservation system, the agent has to perform the standard security procedures – checking the security features of the card and verifying the signature of the card against the signed receipt. If there is any doubt as to the validity of the transaction they should request additional identification from the passenger. Some airlines require staff to take passport or other details to minimise the risk of fraudulent transactions. As the airlines are always the Merchant of Record for those transactions, they take the full risk for any potential fraud cases.

Payments made using miscellaneous payment methods, such as MCOs, budget codes or staff travel codes are recorded with their appropriate FOP ID. They are then reported through the sales report along with all other transactions and follow their own dedicated accounting and settlement processes.

In summary, direct interaction between the passenger and the airline staff allows the airline to accept a wide range of payment methods: cash and cheques for those who may not have access to payment cards and both international and local card schemes for those who do. Card transactions can either be processed locally on a POS system provided by a local acquiring bank, or centrally through the reservation system. Central processing though is limited to the international card schemes.

5 Check-in Desk

The vast majority of airlines do not yet take payments at check-in desks. This means passengers who need to pay for excess luggage or wish to buy additional services, such as upgrades or priority boarding are directed either to the airline's ticket desk, a dedicated service desk or to self-service kiosks.

One of the main reasons for this is that most of today's Departure Control Systems (DCS) do not support sales transactions. They cannot calculate and display a price, process a payment and record ancillary sales. Upgrades have to be done in the reservation systems rather than in the DCS. Check-in agents are not necessarily trained or qualified to process sales, as handling payments is commonly restricted to reservation agents. Cash handling can also be tied to a certain grade. Another concern is that the selling process could slow down the check-in process and increase the waiting time for other passengers.

From a service perspective however it may make sense to allow payments for excess baggage for example right at the check-in desk. Sending a passenger off to another desk for payment is an additional inconvenience on top of incurring extra costs. It is very likely though that next generation DCS are able to process ancillary services and take payments for them. They would be handled similarly to payments at the ticket desk.

Fig 31: Check-in Desk

6   Call Centre

Call centres come with an inherent constraint in that the interaction between the passenger and the agent is limited to voice. This also influences the way payments can be processed in this channel. It restricts the available payment methods to those where all the necessary information can be shared over the phone and excludes those where the cardholder has to identify himself or authorise the transaction with a PIN or password (e.g. for electronic wallets or with 3D Secure). These technical limitations are one of the reasons that call centre transactions are more vulnerable to fraud in comparison to e-commerce transactions. Any payment details, while not strictly confidential, should be handled with the utmost care.

Here are more details about the payment methods that can be accepted in call centres and an analysis into how they are processed to reduce the risk of potential internal and external fraud.

6.1   Cash Collection

For obvious reasons, one would think that cash and cheque are not applicable as payment methods for the call centre transactions. However, carriers in countries with particularly low credit card penetration had to come up with creative ways to enable their cash-based customers to use call centres and accept their payments and as a result have established a cash collection mechanism for call centre booking: some carriers will send out a courier to the passenger to collect the money (Cash on Delivery – COD) in return for the booking confirmation whilst others give their customers a payment reference number for a cash acceptance partner (e.g. Western Union) and a time window, usually 24 - 48 hours, to pay for the ticket. Once the external partner confirms payment, the ticket is issued and mailed to the customer. (See Cash Payment Option, p. 130)

6.2   Credit Cards

Credit cards remain the prevailing payment method for payments in call centres. Their main advantage is that they can be processed without the cardholder having to be present. The card details can be captured over the phone. Here is a list of the most common ways to process them:

6.3 Payment Processing through the Reservation System

As call centre agents are likely to use the same reservation systems as agents in CTOs and ATOs, credit card transactions originating from there are likely to be processed in a very similar way. After processing an authorisation request through the reservation system the card number is stored in the ticketing application, along with the card type identifier, the expiry date and the authorisation code etc. The transaction is recorded in the reservation/ticketing system, extracted and submitted to the acquiring bank.

6.4 POS Terminal

Processing credit card transitions through a POS terminal is a common alternative to processing them through the reservation system. Instead of using the magnetic stripe or the chip of the payment card to initiate the transaction as you would in a regular retail environment, the agent manually initiates the payment. When the customer is happy with the booking, the agent notes the passenger's credit card number, expiry date and CVC code, keys that information into the terminal, confirms the transaction and then issues the ticket. Usually several reservation agents share a POS terminal between them. At the end of the day they have to initiate the transmission of all sales transactions from the POS terminal to the acquiring bank. This also gives them a transaction summary to reconcile against their sales report.

This process allows airlines to accept international credit cards, as well as all local debit and credit card schemes that support cardholder-not-present transactions – where no PIN or password entry is required. It is however obviously particular cumbersome and prone to data entry errors, and more importantly it is known to attract internal fraud. With card numbers noted on pieces of paper and carried back and forth between desks and POS terminals, stealing card numbers and compromising them is not particularly difficult. Further, none of those processes meet PCI compliance standards - card numbers should a) not be accessible to agents and b) never be stored unencrypted – not even on paper notes.

6.5 Virtual POS Terminal

Equipping the reservation agent with a virtual POS terminal improves the situation slightly. A virtual POS terminal is a browser-based application that processes payment transactions on the agent's PC, performing the payment steps virtually, rather than using a physical terminal. The agent enters the cardholder details directly into the web application, receives an authorisation code, issues the ticket and confirms the payment. The authorisation code and the transaction reference number are usually copied into the reservation systems. Some systems also require the credit card number for reference. If the application is integrated with the reservation system, this data is automatically passed across which reduces human data entry errors.

Even though this system eliminates the need to note down card numbers, agents still have easy access to the cardholder information. To further reduce this risk and to comply with PCI regulations airlines have started to introduce voice recognition systems to process the payments without agent intervention.

6.6 Interactive Voice Recognition Systems

Interactive Voice Recognition (IVR) systems are regularly used in call centres to automate call handling. These systems can interpret voice commands and key entries to collect caller information or to help them navigate through menu options. They can also be used to handle payments.

Once the passenger is happy with the itinerary and the price, the reservation agent forwards the call to an IVR system to process the payment. It asks the passenger to either key in or say the card number, the expiry date and CVC code into his phone. The IVR translates the recorded information into an authorisation request, which is forwarded to the acquiring bank. Once the transaction is authorised the call is directed back to the ticket agent who completes the booking and issues the ticket. In circumstances where the transaction is declined, the caller would be prompted to re-enter his information or use an alternative card.

To communicate with the acquiring bank, the IVR system is usually connected to a PSP using a web-service API. For both systems, the virtual POS terminals and the IVR, the PSP can collect the payment confirmations and submit them for settlement to the bank at the end of the day (see Payment Service Provider – Integration Options, page 249).

Using an IVR is the safest way to handle call centre payments for processing as it ensures that the agent has no access to any of the cardholder's information.

6.7 Hybrid Solutions – Separation between Authorisation and Capture Message

Some carriers require all sales transactions to be processed through the back-end systems to comply with accounting and reconciliation processes. They choose a hybrid approach and obtain the authorisation code through one of the options described above but process the capture message traditionally, through the reservation system. Only international credit card schemes can be processed this way.

In a hybrid scenario the agent would perform the card authorisation either through a POS terminal (virtual or physical) or an IVR. Depending on the level of integration, the full cardholder data is either manually or automatically copied into the reservation/ticketing system (for IVR systems this process is always automated). The data is then extracted from the sales report and submitted centrally to the acquiring banks for clearing and settlement.

Interactive Voice Recognition solutions are best suited to handle payments in call centres, as they can process cardholder information in a secure manner. While POS devices, whether physical or virtual, do allow additional payment methods to be accepted, they need tight operational control or significant trust in staff members to keep internal fraud to a minimum.

7   E-Commerce

Direct distribution through the internet has grown significantly over the last decade. An Airline IT Trends Survey indicates that an industry average of 58% of tickets will be sold direct by 2014 (SITA, 2011), the majority of these will still be through e-commerce. For some of the Low Cost Carriers the proportion of directly distributed tickets is well above 90%.

This chapter covers payments in traditional internet-based distribution applications that allow airlines to sell flights, flight related services (excess baggage charges, priority boarding) or other ancillary content (insurance, hotels and car rental) directly to private or corporate customers. It focuses on the airline's web presence that you (as a customer) would access from your desktop or laptop. Applications for mobile phones and tablets such as the iPad, although potentially accessing the application through a web browser, are covered in a separate chapter.

It provides analysis of the technical aspects and their implications on the payment flow, from the moment the passenger is presented with the final price to the payment confirmation.

As previously described, some airlines choose to process the authorisation and capture transactions through their reservation and ticketing systems. The same process can be used for e-commerce applications. Most carriers have decided to break away from this methodology and use a PSP instead to process their payment transactions. This set-up gives airlines the ability to increase the choice of payment methods that can be offered to their passengers. It also gives carriers access to a number of ancillary payment services such as integrated fraud screening and Dynamic Currency Conversion.

7.1   Payment Processing through the Reservation System

When the customer has completed the booking process and gets to the check-out screen the e-commerce application presents the passenger with the payment data entry page. It collects the relevant cardholder information such as card number, expiry date and CVC and checks them for consistency (e.g. Luhn check digit, expiry date is in the future). To obtain the payment authorisation, the web application converts the collected information into a legacy command that is forwarded through the reservation system to the airline's Authorisation Service Providers. If the authorisation is successful the ticket is issued and the card details are stored within the reservation/ticketing system. A back-office process extracts and submits them to the acquiring bank at the end of the day.

As it is consistent with all other distribution channels (ticket desk and call centre) this set-up needs very little or no adjustment to the back-office processes. It does not however make use of the advantages that a PSP can add when used for processing the payments.

7.2 Payment Service Provider (PSP)

E-commerce was the first channel to break away from the legacy way of processing payments through the reservation system. It enables the airline to offer additional payment methods beyond the traditional credit cards: debit cards, electronic wallets (e.g. PayPal), direct debits, bank transfers, and cash payment options (see Payment Methods used in the Airline Industry, page 123). But this is only one of the additional services that a PSP can provide. Many of their systems come with pre-integrated fraud management and charge-back handling solutions as well as currency conversion services.

The main difference to the model describe above is that the PSPs in this scenario can process both parts of the payment transaction: the authorisation and the confirmation message, the first one usually after the creation of the Passenger Name Record (PNR) in the reservation system; and the second one, the confirmation message, after the successful issuing of the ticket. The PSP usually collects all the payment transactions that have occurred during the day and submits them to the appropriate acquiring bank overnight via a file transfer. This replaces the airline's back-end process where the credit card data is extracted from the sales reports and then submitted to the banks.

Some carriers choose a hybrid solution where they obtain the authorisation through the PSP and submit the transactions through the back-end reservation system.

Depending on the payment scheme a PSP can support automated processing of additional transaction types such as transaction reversals (useful in scenarios where the ticket issuing failed, this releases the cardholder's funds held by the authorisation) and refund transactions (required where passengers can perform ticket changes or cancellations through the website).

Being in control of both the authorisation and capture process allows PSPs to offer the airline access to any local or international payment scheme that supports e-commerce transactions. Introducing alternative payment methods can in turn increase the airline's booking conversions ratio and reduce transaction costs.

7.3 PSP Integration Options

There are three main options to integrate a PSP into the e-commerce application:
- Direct integration, where the airline's e-commerce application collects the cardholder information and forwards it to the PSP in a message
- Re-direct integration, where the PSP collects the cardholder information on behalf of the airline and processes them directly
- A combination of the above.

These options are described in more detail below:

7.3.1 Direct Integration – Payment Data is Captured by the Distribution Application

With this option the airline remains in full control of the shopping and payment process, i.e. the e-commerce application prepares the shopping basket (flights and ancillary services), displays the available payment methods based on its internal rules and records the cardholder details that are required by the respective payment method (e.g. card number, expiry date, account number, password). This information is then forwarded to the PSP in an encrypted message using a web service API. When it receives the authorisation response it either issues the ticket or displays the appropriate error message back to the passenger. After the ticket is successfully issued, it sends the capture message to the PSP to confirm the payment.

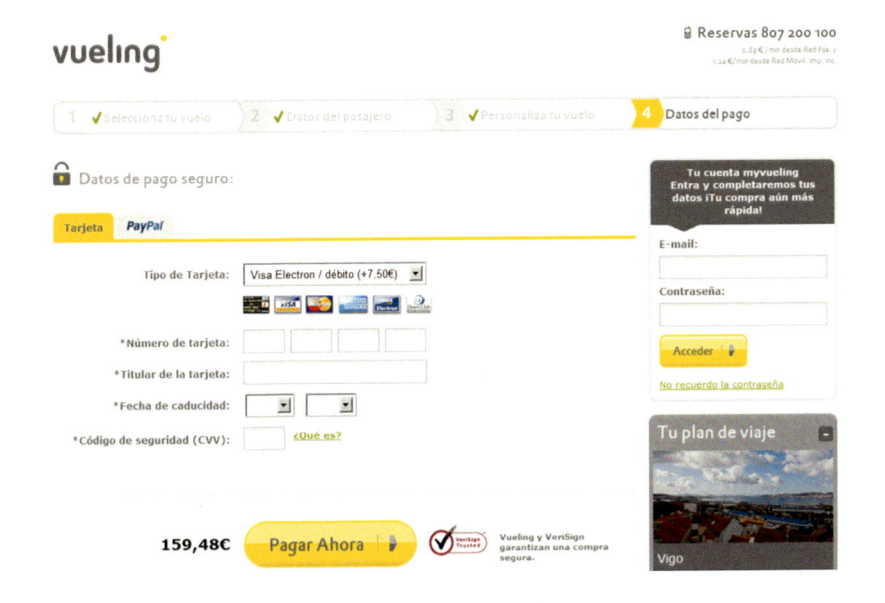

Fig 32: Example of a Directly Integrated Payment Page

As the payment pages remain an integral part of the application, the airline has full control of the booking flow, the design as well as the choice of payment methods that are displayed. This approach also leaves the airline with full access to the cardholder details, which maybe required by some of the downstream reconciliation and service processes.

Having access to the cardholder details however includes e-commerce into the scope of PCI-DSS for which the airline needs to seek certification.

7.3.2 Re-direct Integration – the PSP Captures the Payment Data

An alternative to capturing the payment details within the airline's application is to redirect the passenger to a payment page provided by the PSP to complete the payment there. The PSP records the payment information in its own environment – its own web site (hosted payment pages).

This re-direct can be very obvious to the cardholder, for example if the payment page is opened as a separate window. In the early days of e-commerce, cardholders would trust banks over merchants to take payments over the internet. This has changed and the current trend is to integrate the external PSP page as well as possible into the airline's own website, making the re-direct as transparent as possible to the passenger. Depending on the PSP's systems they are able to totally mimic the look and feel of the airline's pages, adjusting the colours, icons, text style etc. The rules defining the applicable payment methods for a particular situation are managed by the PSP. Adding additional payment methods does not require any changes within the airline application as the PSP adds them within their payment page.

The advantages of this approach are twofold: the e-commerce application itself will never directly process any of the payment details. This reduces the programming complexity and additionally leaves the application out of the scope of PCI-DSS certification. Not having access to, and not passing any cardholder details to the reservation and ticketing system however may require significant adaptations in the back-end service and reconciliation processes. The e-commerce transactions need to be excluded from the batch transaction submission process. The reconciliation and accounting processes need to be adapted to take new transaction reporting and financial flows into account.

Some airlines take a mixed approach. They would integrate the international card schemes directly, whereas for the more complex, alternative payment methods (e.g. PayPal) they chose a re-direct integration and request their PSP to host the payment pages.

RwandAir

Merchant	RwandAir
VAT Registration #	10028613
Reference	IBT00001640
Transaction Date	Thu, 09 Feb 2012 16:24:00 +0200
Amount	$ 478.00 (USD)

Cards Accepted **VISA**

Secured by Othawte
2012-02-09

Card Holder
Card Number
Expiry Date Jan 2012
CVV Digits   what's this?
(3/4 digits on back of card)

E-Mail Address   test@test.com
(for payment confirmation)

[<- Cancel]   [Pay Now ->]

PayGate

Fig 33: Example of a Re-direct Payment Page (Courtesy of PayGate)

7.3.3 Payment Method with Re-direct Requirement

Regardless of the integration type that the airline chooses, some payment methods themselves require a re-direct. In this case the cardholder is directed away from the payment page of the e-commerce application (or the PSP) to a third party website (either the acquiring bank or the payment scheme itself) for an additional transaction authorisation step. This is usually a separate window, where he/she has to enter additional credentials (e.g. a PIN, username or a password). The external entity verifies the data and transfers the cardholder back to the airline's web site, along with a confirmation or a decline indicator.

Examples of such re-direct scenarios are 3D Secure verifications, where the cardholder is re-directed to their issuing bank to enter an internet PIN or a password. The same is required for many bank transfer applications, as well as for electronic wallets such as PayPal, where the payer has to identify himself with their username and password.

Asynchronous re-direct gateways add another level of complexity as the cardholder does not get automatically re-directed back to the airline after having completed the authorisation on the external payment pages. Unless the user gets clear instructions how to progress the booking (i.e. close the payment window, return to the airline page and wait), many of these bookings are likely to remain incomplete. The distribution application (or the PSP) is required to actively check for the outcome of the verification process and continue with the ticket issuing, if successful.

In summary, for airlines wanting to retain tight control of their e-commerce application as well as the design and the process flow within that application, direct integration might be the preferred option. If simplicity is the main strategic driver, then a redirect model, where the PSP takes over the responsibility to processes the payment would win the day.

8   Passenger Mobile Applications

"Mobile is changing everything", and by now everyone agrees with this statement in some form or another. The number of mobile phones in use in the world will soon reach 5 billion. The percentage of U.S. smart phone users is expected to soar 63% by the end of 2015 (CBSNews, 2011). Forrester expects smart phones to emerge as one of travel's two most

important touch points (the other being traditional websites) by 2013 (Harteveldt, 2011). Every airline, big or small is establishing a mobile presence, almost always as an extension of services already available through their web channel. Almost nine out of 10 airlines are already actively selling, or planning to sell, tickets on mobile phones by 2014. In addition, airlines plan to extend mobile distribution services to include ticket modification/upgrades and sales of on-board services (SITA, 2011).

Most airlines though, currently focus on service aspects such as check-in and notification services. Using mobile sites for selling has not yet been broadly embraced, partially due to the added complexity that is involved when taking payments for bookings made this way.

This section covers all distribution applications that are specifically designed for being accessed through a mobile device. Although it focuses on mobile phones and tablet devices, such as the iPad, it could be equally applied to game consoles, e-book readers, and watches etc. which are likely to be used in the not too far distant future to access airline services. It applies to applications that can be accessed using the device's internet browser, as well as applications that are written for specific device operating systems and have to be downloaded from the respective operator's application store.

8.1   Mobile Browser and Mobile Applications

As discussed in the first section of this book, there are two types of mobile payment scenarios: physical (proximity/contact less payments and mobile as a POS) and remote payments. This section looks at remote payments where the mobile phone is used to display an optimised mobile web site where the user can enter their cardholder details. The payment process works in a very similar way to the scenarios described above for e-commerce sites. Due to the nature of mobile devices however, there are some limitations that need to be considered when implementing the payment process:

- Usability: Mobile phone screens can be quite small and the data entry mechanisms very cumbersome, especially when the phone does not provide a full keyboard. It is advisable therefore to limit the data that the customer has to enter to a minimum. Airlines may consider leaving out any data that is not an absolute requirement for the payment process (such as the cardholder's name and address). This however impacts the fraud management process, as it reduces the amount of data elements available to evaluate the transaction risk.

- Limited Re-direct capability: Not all operating systems can support multiple concurrent browser sessions, where the first session remains open while the passenger is re-directed to another page. This excludes the usage of all payment methods that require a redirect such as 3D Secure. Credit card transactions have to be processed on merchant contracts where 3D Secure has been deactivated. On phones where redirects are supported, passengers will face usability issues, as the authentication service providers currently don't offer mobile friendly pages to capture the user's credentials, e.g. online PIN, username or password.

- Integration options: Direct integrations where the application captures the payment details directly and forward them to the PSP through a secure interface (in scope of PCI DSS!). Re-direct integration: Some PSPs already offer mobile optimised payment pages.

Payments against the mobile phone bill (operator billing) are restricted to low value transactions (usually for digital content). This option may be of interest, if an airline wants to sell subscription services such as destination weather information or flight tracking services. Not all mobile phone operators support this service equally, which could lead to service issues especially for customers outside the airline's domestic market, where the service would have been tested.

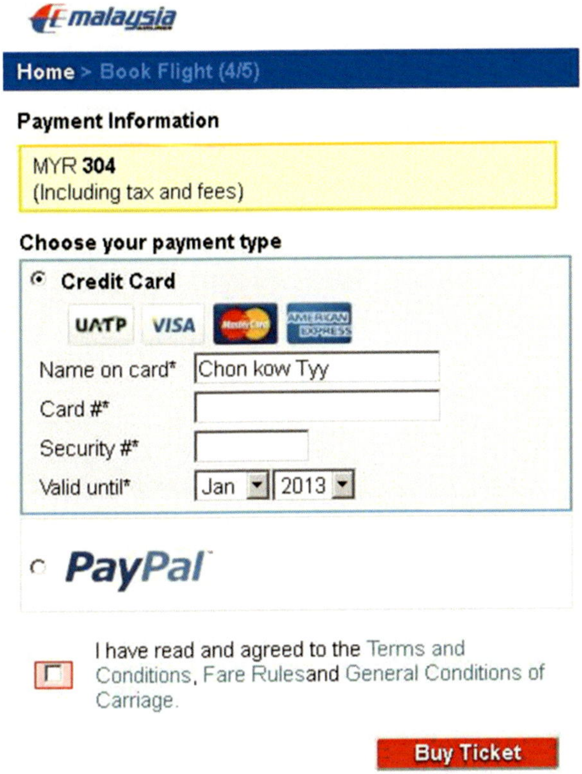

Fig 34: Example of a Mobile Payment Screen (Courtesy of SITA/Malaysia Airlines)

Proximity payments have not yet entered the airline industry. They are more common where speed is crucial in the sales process.

Distribution through mobile applications is still in its infancy – as was e-commerce only a few years ago. It is however growing quickly and will develop into a major channel over the next few years. Smart phones with better user interfaces and bigger screens as well as tablet devices will drive this development. Check with your distribution departments for their product road maps!

9 Self-Service Kiosk

Self-service kiosks are a cornerstone of airline and airport self-service strategies. Today they are used mostly to facilitate the check-in process: to allow a passenger to choose a seat, add their passport details and print a boarding pass. The latest versions even allow self-tagging of bags. To support their ancillary revenue strategies, airlines are increasingly looking to use these kiosks as a sales channel. The 2011 Airline IT Trend Survey revealed that 19% of airlines are already using kiosks as a distribution channel; and another 51% will be distributing services through kiosks by the end of 2014. (SITA, 2011).

Processing a sale and taking payments at a kiosk however is far more complex than in any other channel and as a result many airlines and kiosk providers have not yet tapped into this opportunity. This chapter describes how payments are taken at kiosks today and how they will have to be taken in the future to remain compliant with credit card industry and card scheme standards. It describes the required hardware elements, the integration options and transaction flows.

9.1 Kiosk as Distribution Channel

New airport processes rely heavily on passengers checking themselves in either on-line or through their mobile device before they arrive at the airport, or at the airport using self-service check-in kiosks. Bags need to be dropped at dedicated bag drop counters with check-in desks ideally being used only for service exceptions.

This process works very well for full service carriers as well as for scenarios where the passenger has paid up-front for all the services that they require. It all gets very complicated however, as soon as the airline wants to charge the passengers for extras, such as excess baggage fees, or the passenger wants additional services, such as priority boarding or that special seat with extra leg room, at the time of check-in at the airport.

Fig 35: Ryanair Self Service and Sales Kiosk at Stansted Airport

Most check-in desks today are not equipped to process sales transactions and take payments and hence cannot sell ancillary services. The same applies for self-service kiosks. Most of them do not support sales and payment transactions.

In those scenarios the passenger needs to go to the ticket desk or a dedicated service desk to pay the additional fees. From a passenger's perspective this is quite inconvenient, as they not only have to pay extra, but have to queue again at the ticket or service desk to pay and then come back to complete the check-in. It is definitely a process that you would not voluntarily want to go through as a passenger, just to buy priority boarding.

Enabling kiosks to sell ancillary services and/or to take payment could be the solution to this service dilemma. It has two potential advantages over the current situation. On one hand it automates the process of taking payments for additional fees that would normally have to happen at the ticket or service desk. On the other, it gives airlines an opportunity to generate incremental revenues from their passengers. They are able to up-sell additional services during or after the check-in process: upgrades, priority boarding, seat assignments, meal vouchers, on-board entertainment, lounge access – services that the passenger may not have wanted to buy during the booking process, but may be much more willing to buy now, when they are about to travel.

But selling through a kiosk is not as easy as it may sound. First, there is the issue of pricing, fulfilling and accounting for a sales transaction (not covered by this book). Then there is the challenge of taking payment for it.

The next section focuses on that issue – how to make a payment work at a kiosk. It looks at the various options that are available to an airline to capture the cardholder details and to process the payment through the kiosk: using a magnetic stripe card reader, an EMV compliant chip & PIN terminal or a virtual POS terminal, where the touch screen becomes the payment interface.

9.2 Magnetic Stripe Card Reader

Most kiosks are equipped with a magnetic stripe card reader. They are used in two ways – for identification purposes and for payment transactions.

The most common purpose is to allow a passenger to identify themselves using their frequent flyer card or the credit card that was used to purchase the ticket. Cardholder name and both numbers, the frequent flyer card number, as well as the credit card number can be used as form of identification to retrieve a record from the Passenger Name List (PNL). The card reader reads the track data off the magnetic card stripe and passes it on to the application. The cardholder data is then compared with data stored in the PNL and retrieves the matching flight information. For passengers this process is obviously a lot more convenient than having to type in the booking reference, last name, origin etc. to initiate the check-in process.

For Frequent Flyer cards this process is perfectly okay. Credit card schemes however were never particularly fond of this practice. Misusing the card number for identification purposes is violating their operational regulations that state that "a merchant must not use a card number for any purpose other than as payment for goods and services".

PCI compliance is another issue. IATA is working on a resolution to eliminate the usage of the track data in clear text at all Common Use Self Service (CUSS) compliant kiosks[15]. The primary account numbers of payment cards will have to be truncated by the CUSS platform before they can be passed on to the check-in application for further use. Only the first 6 and last 4 digits of the card number will be readable, the rest will be replaced by "X" (e.g. 1234 56XX XXXX 1234). Frequent Flyer card numbers are excluded from this process and will continue to be passed on fully readable. This rule allows the kiosk application to remain outside the scope of PCI DSS regulations.

Some carriers use the card reader to extract card data and to perform payment transactions, for flights as well as for ancillary services. The transaction process works in a similar way. The passenger inserts their card into the card reader; the card track data is read off the magnetic strip, the name and the card number (Primary Account Number) are passed back to the application. This data is then used to obtain a transaction authorisation through the host systems and the Authorisation Service Provider (see Traditional Authorisation and Settlement Flow, page 142). Once the sales transaction is successfully completed, the card number is stored along with the authorisation code in the sales record. The capture message is generated through the back-office systems at the end of the day (along with all other ticket sales transactions).The cardholder's PIN or signature is, for obvious reasons, not verified during this process. The transactions are submitted as a card-not-present transaction.

---

[15] IATA Recommended Practices RP1706C (CUSS) and RP1797 (CUPPS)

Using existing card readers is definitely the easiest way to process a payment. Although this process has been common practice for many years, it does have two major drawbacks: The fraud risk on these transactions is fairly high and it also puts the kiosk as well as the applications within the scope of the PCI-DSS.

Applications that have access to credit card data in clear text need to comply with PCI-DSS standards, meaning that sensitive data has to be encrypted or truncated before being processed and stored – this is not possible for the way the authorisation is currently obtained. The kiosk and the applications would have to go through a certification process and would have to follow security standards that are, realistically, very hard to achieve for the environments that kiosks operate in. In short: the process of using a magnetic stripe card reader to obtain and process credit card information is no longer compliant with current security standards and will have to be replaced by alternatives as soon as possible.

Ultimately, the only way to process payments at a kiosk in a compliant way is to use a PCI certified POS terminal.

9.3   POS Terminal

POS terminals are available in two main flavours: desktop devices and those for Unattended Payment Terminals. Only the second type should be used for self-service kiosk.

The first type is designed for use at a sales counter – as you would find in a regular retail environment – in your shop around the corner, supermarkets, in restaurants etc. Some airlines have integrated this kind of device with the kiosk, or rather attached the device to the kiosk. Retail POS devices however should only be used in supervised environments.

While one could argue that an airport kiosk is somewhat supervised, only the second type of device really complies with card scheme rules: UPTs that are designed for unattended sales situations, where no sales assistance or supervision is available to facilitate and monitor the payment process. Those devices typically used at automated ticket machines for bus, train, parking or cinema ticket, where you interact with a sales kiosk, rather than a person.

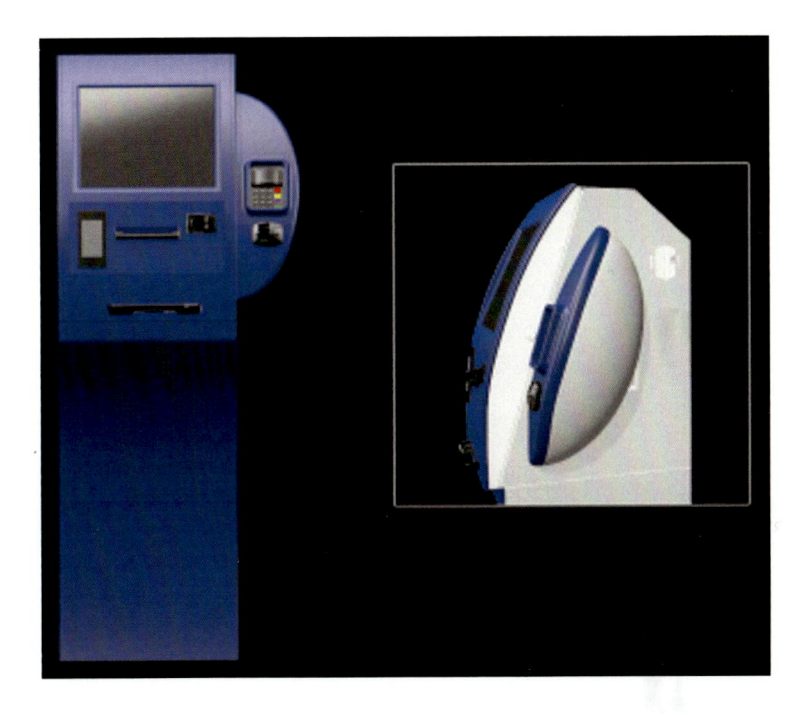

Fig 36: Kiosk with Integrated POS Terminal (Courtesy of SITA)

They have higher security, as the card reader as well as the PIN pad is physically integrated into the frame of sales kiosk (see **Fig 36**). As such they are better protected against manipulation attacks where fraudsters try to gain unauthorised access to cardholder details.

POS devices need certification from the card schemes to be allowed to read their respective cards. EMV Level 1 and Level 2 certification is required to process EMV chip& PIN cards, Carte Bancaire certification to read French domestic bank cards etc. Check with your supplier to ensure that they have the right level of certification for the countries you would like to use the kiosks in.

For debit card schemes that require on-line PIN verification (e.g. U.S. debit schemes), the PIN data has to be encrypted by the POS device before being sent to the acquiring bank. To do that the relevant encryption keys have to be injected into the card reader.

POS devices have multiple interfaces to interact with the outside world: a link connecting it to the kiosk distribution application that needs the payment, a link to the acquiring bank that processes the payment and a terminal management link.

9.3.1 Device Interaction with the Distribution Application

This distribution application orchestrates the sale of the upgrade, excess baggage etc. It presents the passenger with the price and then invokes the payment transaction with the POS device. If the transaction is authorised it issues the relevant documents to the passenger and then confirms the transaction, or initiates a reversal for any situation where the service transaction (e.g. processing the upgrade) failed for any reason.

To initiate the payment transaction a retail application (such as a supermarket cash register) would usually talk directly to the POS terminal. In a kiosk set-up however it is common practice to route the request through the device management platform that not only manages the POS terminal, but other hardware devices, such as printers, scanners or barcode readers (see also Consideration for Common Use Environments, page 184).

9.3.2 Device Interaction with the Acquiring Bank

Through the second interface the POS device connects to the acquiring bank – the interface to perform the actual financial transactions: the authorisation request, the confirmation message, and reversal and credit transactions, where required by the application. The communication between the device and the bank is either through a direct link or through a PSP.

In a regular retail environment POS devices would be supplied by the acquiring bank. They are pre-certified and can be used immediately. In an airline kiosk scenario however, the airline, or their kiosk provider, may choose the POS terminal that best fits the structural and technical requirements of the particular kiosk and then get certification from the acquiring bank to use it. Certification from the bank may be required for the entire set-up, the hardware, the software as well as all parts of the communication infrastructure that links them to the bank. The certification process can differ from country to country and take up to 3 months.

This adds additional complexity to the rollout of such a solution, as airlines typically deploy kiosks not only in one location or one country, but across their entire route network in multiple countries, potentially working with multiple acquiring banks.

In these scenarios it is advisable to use a PSP as an intermediate. This set-up separates the connection between the Kiosk and the PSP, and the connection between the PSP and (potentially) multiple acquiring banks around the world. While each one of the banking integrations would still have to be certified, it moves the complexity of the banking integration away from the kiosk and to the specialist – the PSP.

The PSP would also undertake central collection of the confirmation messages and forward them to the respective acquiring banks at the end of the day.

9.3.3 Terminal Management

One (or multiple) interface(s) are dedicated to terminal management. Terminal management includes the administration of hot card lists (a list of lost and stolen cards that must be declined), the maintenance of terminal parameters (e.g. Terminal ID, merchant name and date format) and the deployment of software updates and security patches from the manufacturer or the software provider.

9.3.4 Certification for Domestic Payment Schemes

The set-up that we have discussed above is applicable to all EMV compliant card schemes (Visa, MasterCard, American Express, Maestro, Visa debit, Discover) as well as those international card schemes that still operate via magnetic stripe transactions (UATP, Diners Club). Local debit and credit card schemes that are not EMV compliant require POS terminals that are specifically programmed and certified. The good news: POS terminals can be certified for EMV as well as for those domestic schemes. So there is no need to make an either/or decision as long as the acquiring bank or the chosen PSP can also support both technologies.

9.3.5 Consideration for Common Use Environments

Taking payments at a check-in kiosk is complex enough, as we have just discussed. Taking payments at a kiosk that is used by multiple airlines is currently a "Gordian Knot" for the airline industry, and has yet to be resolved.

Kiosks at airports are often shared by multiple airlines, commonly referred to as Common Use Self Service (CUSS) kiosks. Depending on the airline logo that the passenger selects when he activates the kiosk, the appropriate application starts up and temporarily turns the kiosk into one for that particular airline. The same would need to apply to the POS terminal that is integrated into the kiosk. Depending on the selected distribution application, the POS device would be temporarily configured to belong to airline X for the first transaction and airline Y for the next one. This would still be somehow manageable, if all airlines that use a particular kiosk use the same acquiring bank in a particular country. In that case the set-up would only have to be certified by one bank and all transactions would go to that bank. The likelihood though that all airlines can agree on a single bank is very small. Kiosk providers are still working on a solution to satisfy such a set-up.

In summary, being able to take payments at kiosks is going to be increasingly important for airlines. Due to the lack of standards and readily available, integrated solutions, only a few airlines (e.g. Ryanair, Air France) have already tapped into this opportunity. Using the magnetic stripe card readers that are available with most kiosks has been the predominant approach to process payments. This however is no longer compliant with EMV and card scheme rules. Fully certified POS terminals are the best way forward. Their integration though is very complex, especially in common use environments. IATA is working on new standards that will help kiosk providers to come up with innovative solutions to this challenge. This will turn the pure check-in kiosks to true sales and service terminals in the near future.

10   Agent Mobile Applications

Mobile agents are an additional way of reducing queues at ticket desks and check-in counters. Equipped with mobile devices and appropriate service applications, they can assist customers who require for example check-in or re-accommodation. But they can equally act as sales agents, offering ancillary services such as priority boarding, upgrades, excess baggage fees, ground transport or lounge access. This can happen at any time during a passenger's journey: at hotels, train stations during check-in, in the departure lounge or in transit areas.

Fig 37: Motorola Handheld Device with Chip & PIN Snap-On Mobile Payment Module for Check-in and taking Payments (Courtesy of Motorola/SITA)

To be able to sell through these devices, similar aspects as with kiosks have to be considered. The application on the device has to be adjusted to take payment. It has to interact with the payment module that is either integrated into the device, attached (clipped) onto it, or completely external (e.g. communicating via Bluetooth) to the application handheld device. The mobile devices are usually designed for heavy duty use (ruggedized). Since it is a controlled environment, the PIN pad and the card reader hardware can be less robust compared to unattended kiosk environment.

Mobile phones, tablets and similar devices have the potential to revolutionise this area. They provide a cheap and easy to use alternative to the typical rugged mobile agent devices.

Fig 38: Apple iPads used as Payment Devices with Integrated PIN Pad (Courtesy of pks services)

In the simplest set-up the internal or external payment unit encrypts the payment message and directly communicates with the acquiring bank (via WiFi or GPRS dial up). If the payment device has received Payment Card Industry – PIN Entry Device (PCI-PED) certification as well as EMV certification the acquiring bank will require very little extra to certify the end-to-end integration. As the retail application does not have access to any sensitive data, it remains out of scope for PCI.

Magnetic stripe cards, chip cards and contact-less cards can be processed with such devices. As with the hardware in kiosks, some countries and local payment methods will require additional certification of the end-to-end set-up.

Should the device need to be CUSS compliant or required to work in multiple geographies, a consolidator may be required – a PSP that receives all transactions first and forwards them on to the appropriate acquiring bank, depending on the carrier, country or payment method.

Sales with agent mobile devices have huge growth potential, but are still far from being common-place. Recording, fulfilling and reconciling these sale transactions is a challenging task, particularly if you are reliant on legacy back-office systems. Payments on these devices can be taken with standard mobile POS devices, clip-on payment devices as well as with more innovative mobile phone and tablet solutions.

11 On-board Retail

Selling duty free products on board a plane has always been an integral part of a flight. The on-board shopping experience has evolved somewhat from the times when cigarettes and perfumes on board a plane were significantly cheaper than at ground level. Today some carriers have converted their planes into almost perfect retail environment - customers pay to come into your "shop", let themselves be locked in for a couple hours during which you can try to sell them any type of goods and/or service. These include not only the obvious items such as food, drinks or duty free products, but extend to lottery tickets, smoke-less cigarettes, telephone cards, insurance policies, ground transport vouchers, events at destinations (e.g. amusement parks, shows) all the way to phone and email access, home shopping catalogue content and chargeable entertainment such as games, videos and gambling (although payment transactions for gambling are not permitted within the Europe region). In addition airlines are selling on board services like upgrades to another cabin class, additional legroom or rental of a mobile in-flight entertainment system. Some carriers have turned the seat-back screens into shopping portals, where the In-flight Entertainment System collects and processes orders that are then fulfilled either by the on-board staff or only later, after the flight by external parties (e.g. Sky Mall).

Taking payment for all those items has, in addition to the inventory management, (re)stocking logistics and revenue management always been the most challenging part of this exercise. The following chapters give some more insight into how the payment process for on-board retail transactions has evolved over time, from cash and credit card imprinters to on-line, real-time authorisations.

FOOD AND BEVERAGE NA SALES SUMMARY (US $)			% Change vs. 2009
	JAN-JUN 2009	JAN-JUN 2010	
Average Sales Per Flight	71	73	2.8
Average Sales per Transactions	9.1	8.6	-5.8
FOOD			
	JAN-JUN 2009	JAN-JUN 2010	
Average Sales Per Flight ($US)	75	69	-8.6
Average Sales per Transactions ($US)	8.8	7.3	-17.0
BEVERAGES			
	JAN-JUN 2009	JAN-JUN 2010	
Average Sales Per Flight ($US)	39	43	10.3
Average Sales per Transactions ($US)	8.4	8.8	4.8

Fig 48: Food and Beverage North American Sales Summary (Onboard Retail Benchmark - Courtesy of Airline Information/GuestLogix)

11.1 Cash and Credit Card Imprinters

Collecting cash has long been the only means of taking payments. This worked well for small value items. But unless passengers carry huge amounts of cash with them – in the right currency, it may have prevented them from purchasing this "a-bit-more-expensive-last-minute-present" for those waiting at home or at the airport. For the carriers, cash provides other challenges. The biggest one is money getting "lost" or remaining "unaccounted for" on the way from the passenger's hand to the airline's bank account where the money ultimately needs to be deposited.

Credit cards were a welcome solution for these situations. They enabled passengers to make spontaneous large item purchases and reduced the cash that airlines needed to handle. Some carriers have completely stopped accepting cash.

At the beginning (and for some carriers until today) card transactions were processed with good old "zip zap" devices, where the card number is imprinted onto a sales slip. This practice however came with a significant administrative overhead. The paper transaction slips had to be collected, accounted for and forwarded to a central office which would then forward them to the acquiring bank for settlement. In addition paper slips tended to get lost and not a few passengers enjoyed their purchase(s) as a freebie.

On-board credit card transactions have another crucial flaw – they do not get authorised by the issuing bank! Flying at 30,000 feet makes obtaining an authorisation code in real-time almost impossible. Needless to say then that card fraud was, and remains the biggest challenge for on-board retailing.

Transactions with lost or stolen cards, or cards with no funds (especially prepaid cards) were the most common causes of fraud. Until a few years ago airline merchants were protected by an off-line floor limit of $500 for magnetic stripe transactions and any fraud up to that limit was covered by the issuing banks. To protect their revenue airlines only allowed one transaction per card and up to exactly $500. This floor limit however was lifted in 2005 and airlines have since become fully liable for all fraud on unauthorised card transactions, which requires an intelligent method of fraud detection since high-yield ticket passengers are also known to spend large amounts on board. After intentional fraud, airlines are also struggling to lower the number of bouncing transactions, which may be caused by a lack of funds in an account.

11.2 On-board POS Devices

The first generation of on-board Point of Sale (POS) retail devices improved the situation significantly. These devices are mounted on the food or duty free trolley and used to process credit card payments, record cash payment and validate voucher payments. They are still in use with many carriers today.

The cardholder data is recorded through the magnetic card reader (card swipe), the transactions are processed and stored digitally, currency conversions are applied where needed with pre-stored exchange rates. The passenger authorises the transactions by signing a printed receipt. Some of these POS devices can carry lists of lost and stolen credit card numbers. In these cases all cards used for payments are compared against that hot-card list before a transaction is completed.

Purchases ordered through seat-back screens are transmitted to the POS device (transaction ID and amount) and payment is then taken by a crew member. Some airlines have implemented card swipe devices at every seat-back to take payments for orders created through the seat-back in-flight entertainment system (these devices however are usually not PCI compliant – they process the magnetic stripe data and card numbers in clear text). Tablets such as the iPad have the potential to replace seat-back screens as in-flight entertainment systems in the near future. They can equally be used to initiate purchases that are then transmitted to a POS retail device for payment with a crew member (See Fig 39).

Fig 39: Using iPads for On-board Retailing (Courtesy of MI Airline)

In addition to the sales report, the POS terminal can generate inventory reports, allowing the crew to reconcile the items in the duty free trolleys at the beginning and at the end of a flight. Once a device reaches its home base after one or more flights, the transactions are downloaded to a central server. This happens either through a docking station, a download cable or by swapping out memory cards. The payment transactions are separated from the inventory transactions and forwarded to the relevant acquiring bank. This process is much faster and less prone to manual errors than the paper-based version (although POS terminals too can break or disappear, or network connections may fail). Where transactions remain in the POS devices for too long this may result in them being rejected by the issuing banks. Speed in sending the transactions to the acquirer is critical.

Some countries and acquiring banks require these transactions to be authorised before they can be submitted for settlement, some accept the submission without a prior authorisation. Transactions that are submitted together with an authorisation code can qualify for a lower merchant fee than those submitted without it. Authorising them however does not reduce the risk of them being fraudulent. Any transactions with lost or stolen cards or cards with insufficient funds would be declined at that stage and cannot be submitted for settlement. It does however reduce the charge-back rate the costs associated with processing them.

11.3 Chip & PIN Devices with GSM Communication Capability

The latest generation of on-board retail devices further improves the process flow and reduces the risk of fraud: First, they are equipped with a chip card reader and a PIN entry device (pin pad). For all EMV cards, this reduces the risk of counterfeit and stolen cards being used for an on-board payment. Payment transactions require the passenger to enter his PIN. Transactions up to certain limits can be authorised off-line by the chip card itself– these transactions are then guaranteed by the issuing banks. Card swipe and cash transactions are handled as described in the chapter above. In the Europe region EMV certified POS terminals are mandatory as of 2013.

The devices are further equipped with a mobile communication device (GSM module) to facilitate the data exchange with the back-office management system. As soon as the POS device reaches GSM coverage, just after the plane has landed, a crew member initiates the sequence for the device to dial the back-office through the mobile phone module. Once the connection is established the payment transactions as well as inventory information are transmitted. In addition to the sales data exchange, the device receives an updated hot-card list (which may contain up to several million card numbers). Chip-based transactions are stored encrypted within the POS device and have to be sent directly to the acquiring bank for further processing (through a separate call). Magnetic stripe transactions can either be submitted along with the off-line authorised chip & PIN transactions or are separated out and collected at the airline's back office, submitted for authorisation where required and subsequently sent for settlement to the acquiring bank. The inventory information is used for reporting and accounting purposes as well as to trigger correct replenishment of the trolley.

Chip & PIN devices supported by GSM technology can further reduce the fraud risk and significantly improve the administrative and inventory processes. But it still does not really tackle the core issue– getting a real time transaction authorisation. As airlines make progress in creating a "connected" aircraft they will be able to move towards real-time authorisation and settling.

11.4 Real-time Authorisations through Satellite Communication

Real-time on-line authorisations do not only greatly reduce the risk of fraud, but would also allow higher value (and hence more profitable) goods and services to be sold during a flight – think expensive watches, jewellery etc.

Fig 50: On-board Retail Device with GMS and Bluetooth Connectivity (Courtesy of Initium Onboard)

One of the first attempts to achieve on-line authorisations used the on-board telephone systems available on many long-haul flights. The crew members dialled a dedicated number, using a corporate payment card. After establishing a connection, they keyed in the card number, expiry date and the value of the transaction. The system would request an authorisation with the respective card scheme then respond either with an authorisation code or a decline message. As calls from on-board a plane are very costly, these authorisations were only justifiable for high value or suspicious transactions. The costs must have outweighed the benefits, as this system has not really gained traction with carriers.

Some airlines are using ACARS (a cockpit system mostly resembling SMS functionality) to indirectly authorise amounts above a spending level. In addition to being costly, this process is cumbersome as the card data needs to be typed in by the flight deck crew, the message needs to be processed by a ground department and mostly authorised manually. For the passenger this is also not a user-friendly experience.

The introduction of WiFi, Bluetooth and GSM telephone services for passengers on board the latest generation of aircrafts has given new hope to airlines and the providers of on-board retail systems. Linking to a ground station for an on-line transaction authorisation and reduction of lost transactions seems to be much more achievable with the help of these technologies. This is how it works:

For aircrafts to be able to provide passenger communication services they need to be equipped with the appropriate satellite communication systems (very expensive!). These then need to be linked to the internal infrastructure inside the plane (as provided by OnAir or Aeromobile for example), enabling the WiFi, Bluetooth and GSM communication with the passenger's mobile phones, laptops, as well as with POS retail and payment devices.

To comply with PCI-DSS standards, communication of the credit card data needs to be encrypted. This can happen either in multiple stages between the POS device and the satellite system then between the satellite system and the ground station and between that and the PSP/acquiring bank. Alternatively the POS device can encrypt the message at time of processing with the keys of the PSP or the airline's acquiring bank. At no stage must any of the transmitting entities store any of this data. The acquiring bank is likely to want to evaluate the entire set-up, from the aircraft to the interface with the bank before they agree to accept transactions.

Rules within the POS terminal could decide to either accept a transaction without authorisation or to establish an on-line connection. This allows the airline to balance the telecommunication costs with the costs of rejected transactions and charge-backs. EMV transactions up to a certain amount can be authorised off-line by the chip. The transaction confirmation (capture) messages are transmitted to the back-office or directly to the acquiring bank after the flight via the mobile phone module. Transactions that have not been authorised on-line can now be authorised or directly submitted for settlement without any prior authorisation.

The newest generation of retail software will be developed for mobile devices like smart phones and tablets. The payment functionality will be completely separated using WiFi or Bluetooth to communicate with each other. It will integrate passenger data (e.g. Passenger Name List or flight manifest) enabling additional sales and service functionalities (e.g. upgrade offers based on customer value). Combining passenger data with payment date also allows authorisation decisions to consider passenger specific information (e.g. frequent flyers are known and trusted passenger and allowed to buy higher value goods without on-line authorisation). Together with this payment reconciled with passenger data can be beneficial to the post-sale and revenue analysis processes. Real-time authorisation will also enable the processing pseudo-monetary payments (i.e. frequent flyer miles, vouchers) and inventory bases sales (car rental, hotel beds, theatre tickets).

Pilots for these integrated systems that communicate in real-time are ongoing and it won't be too long until they will be available on a wider commercial scale.

In conclusion, on-board retail is already a major contribution to airline revenue. Streamlining the on-board payment process can significantly improve the bottom line results. High-tech POS devices with Chip & PIN and GSM, WiFi and Bluetooth communication functionality can increase the security and facilitate the administration process. Widely available real-time authorisation capabilities via satellite communication systems will be a real break-through for this industry, although offline operation will never disappear. It will further reduce the fraud risk and open up opportunities for additional, higher value goods and services to be sold on-board.

12 On-board Telephone Systems

Many of the medium- to long-haul flights offer facilities to make telephone calls on-board the plane. The phone handsets are usually integrated into the in-flight entertainment control units or alternatively carriers have a small number of "public" phones located around the galley areas.

Swiping a credit card activates the system. It establishes a connection through the satellite system of the plane to the ground station. The credit card information is forwarded to one of the Authorisation Service Providers (e.g. SITA), who send them on for pre-authorisation to the credit card scheme. Once they receive a confirmation, they establish the phone connection (dial tone) for the passenger. When the passenger has completed the call, the total cost of the call is calculated and submitted for authorisation and settlement. Where SITA provides the service, they are the Merchant of Record for all transactions, regardless of the originating carrier. They collect all revenues and share them back out between the individual carriers.

The system was established long before PCI standards were introduces. The card readers don't have chip card units, the data may or may not get encrypted... This set-up would need a lot of technical upgrading to remain fully compliant. As it will become redundant with "connected aircraft", allowing passengers to use their own mobile phones, airlines are likely to push any upgrade of the current system out as far as possible.

13 Staff Travel Office

Staff travel applications usually follow either the ticket office, or the e-commerce distribution model. Payments are taken accordingly and are processed either through the reservation system, or through an external PSP.

14 Lounge Access

Lounge access is no longer only available to those who have booked Business or First or are qualifying members of a Frequent Flyer schemes. For many airlines it has become an ancillary revenue item that can be purchased either along with a ticket, on-line, at a self-service kiosk or at the lounge reception.

Payments taken on entry are usually accepted in cash or as a card payment through a local POS terminal. When sold along with a ticket, the price is added to the ticket price and processed as a single payment.

Some credit card schemes offer lounge access as part of their premium product incentives. The entrance fee is often charged to the card and then refunded by the issuing bank.

15 Compensation Payments – Service Recovery Payments

There are various situations that require payment to be made to the passenger, rather than the other way around. The most common situations are compensation payments for passengers who have been inconvenienced in one way or another: for downgrades (where they can no longer fly in the class they booked), off-loads (where they cannot fly at all on the flight they have booked), for flight delays and cancellations, for delayed or missing bags as well as for other discretionary compensation situations (e.g. coffee spilt over a suit).

The following sections discuss the various options available to an airline to process these compensation payments. Cash and cash vouchers in the form of MCOs are the most common ways to process such compensation payments, but alternatives, such as prepaid cards are becoming a preferred alternative.

15.1 Cash, Cash Vouchers and MCOs

MCO and vouchers are usually the airline's preferred options for any pay out situations, as they can only be redeemed with the airline, against other flights or services.

The benefit is that the funds, although "paid out", remain within the airline. The issuing of an MCO is recorded in the reservation/ticketing system and reconciled along with all other ticket sales in the sales report.

Most passengers though would prefer to receive cash instead of vouchers, if given the choice. In circumstances where passengers are legally entitled to cash, airlines need to put cash payout processes in place.

Cash payouts are easy enough to administer, when they are required rarely and in small amounts. The incoming cash received through ticket sales at the ATO usually provides enough funds for the odd compensation payment. There are however scenarios that make cash handling at airport offices a very challenging task. Take for example the cancellation of a flight where 200 passengers are legally entitled to a compensation of $100 each. For this and other emergency cases, they do need access to large amounts of cash.

Stacking emergency cash in safes at the airport is one way to deal with those situations. This puts a lot of responsibility and accountability on the staff and brings with it the risk of fraud and theft (ticket offices known to store cash are attractive targets for robberies). The cost of storing and insuring the cash in addition to the lost interest on those funds adds to the unattractiveness and has pushed airlines to seek alternative solutions.

Some have eased the situation through agreements with local banks or currency exchange bureaus to provide the extra cash in emergency situations. But this only works where the bureaus are large enough, hold enough funds themselves and only during their opening hours – so not an ideal solution either. Carriers needed another alternative.

15.2 Card Based Solutions – Chip and Prepaid Cards

In 1999 British Airways (BA) introduced one of the first chip card based compensation scheme called "ChipCash". Instead of giving passengers cash, BA gave them a payment card that could be converted into cash, outsourcing the cash handling all together.

BA check-in and baggage handling desks were equipped with chip card readers/writers and had a stock of "empty" payment cards. To make a payout a staff member uploaded the amount owed to the passenger onto the card. The passenger could then redeem the card at any of the partner currency exchange bureaus at airports around the world.

The currency exchange bureaus had similar POS terminals to read the amount on the chip, converted the amount into local currency (if required) and paid out the amount to the passenger. Both transactions (load and redemption) were transmitted to a processing centre for reconciliation and initiation of the bank transfers to the bureaus.

Fig 40: Two Generations of British Airways Compensation Cards: ChipCash and Cash Passport (Private; Courtesy of AccessPrepaid Worldwide)

This solution was a first step to outsource the cash handling to an entity much better equipped to deal with cash. It did however require a dedicated load and un-load infrastructure as well as dedicated communication lines to transfer the transactions. Both these were hard to maintain. The invention of pre-paid cards, that replaced this scheme, resolved some of these issues (Travelex, 2011).

Prepaid cards from international card schemes such as Mastercard, Visa or American Express have two main advantages over the proprietary solution described above. First of all, they can be loaded without a dedicated POS infrastructure and secondly they can be redeemed for cash at ATMs and used for payments. Merchants accepting payments with these cards for food, "first needs" items or accommodation can use their standard POS terminals and existing merchant agreements.

The airport offices have a stock of card carriers with deactivated cards. The card carriers also contain the card's PIN (covered of course). To activate a card, the airline agent loads the card with the required amount. This happens through an administration screen that is either integrated in the reservation or DCS application or a stand-alone web-based application. To avoid internal fraud, the loading process is controlled by individual load limits that can be overridden only by supervisors. Once activated, the passenger can use the card like any regular bank card, up to the amount it has been loaded with.

The issuing bank that is providing the prepaid scheme records all the load transactions and invoices the airline with the daily total load. It authorises cash withdrawal and payment transactions, manages the card balances and the funds on all the cards and supports the cardholder with any payment related queries including charge-back requests.

The passenger usually has between 3 and 6 months to use the funds before they expire. Local legal regulations control what can be done with any unused funds remaining on the cards after their expiry date. In some cases they can be refunded to the airline, in others they have to be donated to charitable organisations or kept in a deposit account by the issuing bank. BA, KLM, TAP, SWISS and AUA are examples of carriers which have been using this system for several years.

Next page:

Fig 41: AUA Compensation Card with Card Carrier (Courtesy of Paylife Bank)

Austrian

000033

1798025000239957

Zahlen und Bargeld weltweit! – mit Ihrer Prepaid Card
Worldwide payment and cash! – with your Prepaid Card

- Akzeptanz in über 120 Ländern der Welt
  Acceptance in over 120 countries worldwide
- Zahlen bei mehr als 7 Mio. Vertragspartnern
  Payment at more than 7 mio. contracting partners
- Bargeld an mehr als 950.000 Geldausgabeautomaten weltweit
  Cash at more than 950.000 cash dispensers worldwide

... überall wo Sie dieses Zeichen sehen
... everywhere you see this sign

Maestro

Bitte unterschreiben Sie Ihre Karte!
Die Geschäftsbedingungen zur Benützung Ihrer Prepaid Card sind beigelegt!
Please sign your card!
Terms and conditions for the usage of your Prepaid Card are attached!

Ihr persönlicher Code:
Your personal code:

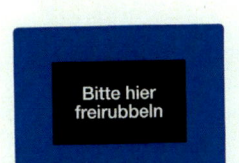

Bitte hier freirubbeln

Internetzugangsnummer:
Internet access number: 16165

Austrian

Card-Nº
8025 0002 39957
Karten-Nr.

Bitte merken Sie sich Ihren persönlichen Code und notieren Sie ihn nirgendwo! Sollte die Karte gemeinsam mit dem Code abhanden kommen, würde das für den unehrlichen Finder oder Dieb bares Geld bedeuten! Bei Verlust oder Diebstahl wird weder eine Ersatzkarte ausgestellt noch ist es möglich die Karte sperren zu lassen!

Please memorize your personal code and do not write it down! Should your card get lost together with the code the dishonest finder could withdraw or pay with the loaded amount! In case of loss or pilferage no replacement card will be issued and it is not possible to block transactions on the card!

Den Code brauchen Sie / *You will need this code*
- für den Bargeldbezug am Bankomaten
  to withdraw cash at the cash dispenser
- zum Bezahlen an der Bankomat-Kasse
  for payment at the cash point
- als Zugangsberechtigung zur automatischen Umsatzabfrage über Telefon
  to attain access for automated balance query per telephone

Empfangsbestätigung / Receipt

Hiermit bestätige ich den Erhalt der Prepaid Card, geladen in der Höhe von/ *I hereby confirm having received the Prepaid Card loaded with the amount of*

€   Kartennummer / *Card No.*   7717980250002

Grund / *Reason*	Passagierdaten / *Passenger data*
[A] Nichtvereinbarungsgemäß erfolgte Beförderung auf / *Denial of confirmed passage as negotiated on*	TicketNr / *Ticket No.*
Wegen / *Due to* ☐ Überbuchung / *Overbooking* ☐ Stornierung / *Canx*	Vorname / *First Name*
☐ Freiwillig (Enthaftungserklärung erforderlich / *Voluntary (Release mandatory)* ☐ Unfreiwillig / *Involuntary*	Familienname / *Surname*
	Straße / *Street*
[B] Nichtbeförderung in der gebuchten Business-Klasse auf / *Downgrading to Economy Class on*	PLZ, Stadt / *ZIP, City*
FlugNr / *Flight No.* Datum / *Date*	Land / *Country*
Von / *From* Nach / *To*	Emailadresse / *Email address*
Ort / *Place* Datum / *Date*	
Validator, name and/or ID of the issuing agent	Unterschrift Kunde / *Signature Customer*
	Zu Lasten von / *Debit to*
	3 letter code / *Agent ID No.*

Apart from compensation situations, prepaid cards can also be used to replenish the petty cash in airport offices and in emergency payment situations (e.g. buying spare plane parts, fuel etc.).

The processing of compensation payments should not be overlooked in an airline's overall payment strategy. Cash is the most obvious solution, but its disadvantages have pushed many carriers to look for alternatives, the best available being prepaid cards from one of the international credit card schemes.

16   Taking Payments for 3rd Party Ancillary Services

This section covers payments situations where the airline distributes third party content - ancillary products and services that are provided by parties other than the airline itself, such as insurance, ground transportation, car-rental or hotel rooms. It applies to many of the distribution channels mentioned above.

There are three ways a passenger can be charged for these products and services:

- The airline adds them to the price of the ticket and charges everything together in one payment transaction. In transactions in these scenarios the airline receives the funds and needs to forward them on to the third party.
- The airline uses the payment card details for multiple payment transactions. One for the ticket with the airline as the Merchant of Record and one or more transitions for the other service with the third party's merchant ID).
- Alternatively the third party provider processes the payment on its own behalf as a separate transaction.

Here are the details:

16.1 Airline takes Payment for the Entire Shopping Basket

From a user-experience perspective the first option seems easiest and best - paying for the ticket and all ancillary items in one transaction. From an airline perspective however, this has implications that should be assessed on a product by product basis:

- First, the airline needs to create a mechanism to separate the revenue payable to the third party provider and pass it on.

- Then, the airline needs to consider the risk taken on, when accepting payment for goods or services. The entity taking the payment (the Merchant of Record) becomes liable for the delivery of the service. If the airline accepts the payment, it becomes responsible for ensuring that the hotel or car rental provider etc. fulfil their promises. Any complaint (and charge-back if required) would initially have to be resolved by the airline.

- Thirdly, bundling flights with hotel and car content is a business model that requires a travel agency licence in many countries. Airlines need to verify whether this applies to the countries and products they are planning to combine into a single transaction.

It is common for airlines to take payments for insurance policies or ground transportation, where no inventory needs to be held and the transaction value, as well as the risk of the service not being provided is relatively low. For all other content however, airlines prefer to follow different models.

16.2 Airline Charges Deposit or Booking Fee

An easy way around the issue of bundling services is to charge the passenger only for the deposit or booking fee for a hotel room or hire car. The remaining fee needs to be paid directly to the hotel or car rental company at the time of check-in or check-out. The initial fee usually remains with the airline and is often non-refundable for the passenger, regardless of whether the service is provided or not. Any transaction dispute about the actual service needs to be resolved by the third party provider.

If the entire transaction fee needs to be charged at the time of booking there are two options available to make the third party provider the Merchant of Record.

16.3 Payment Details are used for Two or More Transactions

In this scenario, the payment details that are captured during the payment process are used for two or more transactions: The first one for the flight and the ancillary services provided by the airline with the airline's Merchant Identifier (ID) and any subsequent ones using the third party provider(s) Merchant ID (for all additional goods or services). This process used to be transparent to the cardholder and worked reasonably well for credit card transactions. The introduction of 3D Secure though requires the cardholder to enter an internet password to authorise a transaction. A similar requirement applies to many other alternative payment methods, where additional transaction validation is required from the cardholder. In those cases it is impossible to re-use cardholder details for a further transaction in the background, unseen by the cardholder. The cardholder has to authorise every individual transaction separately – not the best user experience.

As a result, splitting payments between multiple merchants is nowadays fully visible to the customer. The payments are processed in multiple steps, indicating individual amounts and the respective responsible merchant. This also reduces support queries from passengers who would have been confused about multiple transactions on their credit card statements when they were expecting only one from the airline itself.

This model also applies for travel agency transactions where the agent charges the air fare on the airline's merchant agreement and the service fee on their own.

16.4 3rd Party Provider takes Payment

The easier alternative for an airline is to complete the payment process for their own services and then forward the passenger to the third party provider's site to pay for any additional charges. In those scenarios the hotel or car providers manage the sales and payment process on their own web site. The passenger is fully aware they are now with a different provider. For any disputes they would automatically contact them rather than involving the airline, who simply acted as a point of referral.

In summary, integrating third party content into an airline's booking process is a balancing act between being in control of the customer and the shopping process on one hand and the financial risk and complexity on the other hand. The more content the airline sells on its own behalf, the bigger the possible financial reward. This however has to be balanced with the legal implications, the management overhead associated with forwarding the revenue shares and possible customer service complaints.

17   Summary

This section looked at all the relevant distribution channels that airlines use today to offer goods and services to their passengers and analysed the payment processes in each of them. The payment scenarios vary greatly from one distribution channel to the other (e.g. ticket desk and mobile) and each one has its own specific challenges (e.g. connectivity for on-board transactions). This makes processing payments in the airline industry especially complex.

Common infrastructures (like the BSP) and the need to keep systems interoperable between participants (governed by IATA) add a further layer of complexity. The back-office systems (e.g. reservation and ticketing systems) that the distribution channels rely on are not always geared up to handle new payment methods and alternative ways of paying. They often require a work-around to support next generation technologies. Changes in laws and compliance requirements challenge the way airlines have been taken payments for many years and require a fundamental process rethink (e.g. using credit cards for identification purposes). Technological enhancements (e.g. Chip & PIN) further contribute to the need for constant evolution of airline distribution channels.

The requirement to take payments for ancillary revenue drives the introduction of additional payment channels and scenarios (e.g. taking payments during check-in or at the boarding gate). For some of them (e.g. Chip & PIN payments at CUSS kiosks or real-time authorisations for on-board transactions) the industry is still looking for viable technical solutions.

payments
.aero

Part III. Back-office Support Processes

The previous section described how payments are processed in various airline distribution channels. This section looks at the back-office processes airlines need to set up to support the end-to-end payment process.

It starts with the order screening process required to minimise the risk of accepting fraudulent transactions as well as the process to defend charge-backs, predominantly resulting from payment fraud. It then covers the transaction reconciliation process that ensures there is a confirmed payment transaction for every sale, and lists transaction correction processes, such as refunds, reversals and credit transactions. Credit transactions may be required due to reconciliation discrepancies or as a result of a passenger changing their mind and requesting a refund.

Different airlines have automated these processes to various degrees. Some handle them manually, some have them fully automated and integrated into the reservation, accounting and ERP systems. Here are the processes in detail.

1   Order screening

Order screening helps to minimise the risk of accepting fraudulent orders and rejecting legitimate purchases. It usually combines an automated order screening process, using automated fraud detection tools, and a manual review process.

The automated process screens transactions in real time for indications of fraud and provides a risk score based on multiple risk evaluation criteria (see Vendor Selection – Fraud Screening Tools, page 254). Depending on the result the system either:

- accepts the transaction and sends it for payment authorisation
- accepts the transaction, sends it for authorisation but flags it as "high risk", or
- rejects it.

In the first two cases the ticket is issued after the payment is completed. During the manual review process a risk analyst further investigates transactions that were accepted but rated risky. Common procedures are for the analyst to:

- Analyse and validate the results of the automated scoring system
- Analyse the transaction data for suspicious elements
- Contact the cardholder's issuing bank to validate the payment information
- Analyse the passenger's transaction history
- Contact the passenger and validate the information provided
- Contact the cardholder (if different from the passenger) to confirm the purchase authorisation
- Decide whether to accept or reject the order.

If the analyst decides the transaction is fraudulent or too risky to accept, he has to take corrective actions, such as cancelling the PNR, refunding the transaction amount, notifying the passenger and searching the database for any other transactions that may relate to the order. If this is not done quickly enough the passenger may already have travelled.

Some airlines re-screen their orders multiple times after the original purchase (e.g. two days and a week). This enables them to react to instances where card numbers or passenger details have only later been associated with fraud and black-listed by the card schemes or other merchants.

E-commerce Merchant Order Screening Process

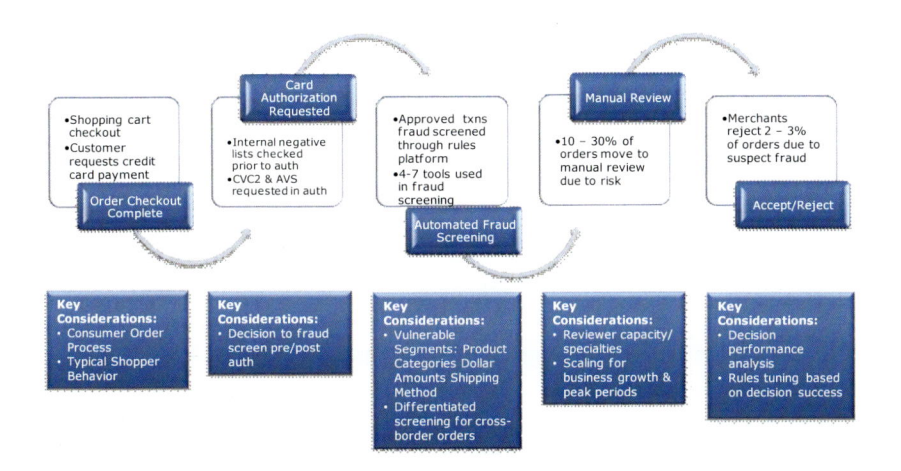

Fig 42: Typical Order Screening Process for E-commerce Transactions (Courtesy of DataCash)

If relevant, the automated tools need to be updated with the conclusions. The passenger and payment information need to be added to either the black or the white list and the rules modified to take the particular fraud case into consideration.

An alternative to completing the booking and flagging the transaction for a later manual review is to delay ticket issue until the review is complete (which may require changes to the existing sales process). Either way there is a significant operational impact to fraud scoring if it is to be managed correctly with maximum value derived from the service.

212   Back-office Support Processes

To increase productivity and effectiveness of the manual review process, airlines are implementing case management systems. These present all relevant information in one screen and allow the risk analyst to initiate subsequent workflows from it.

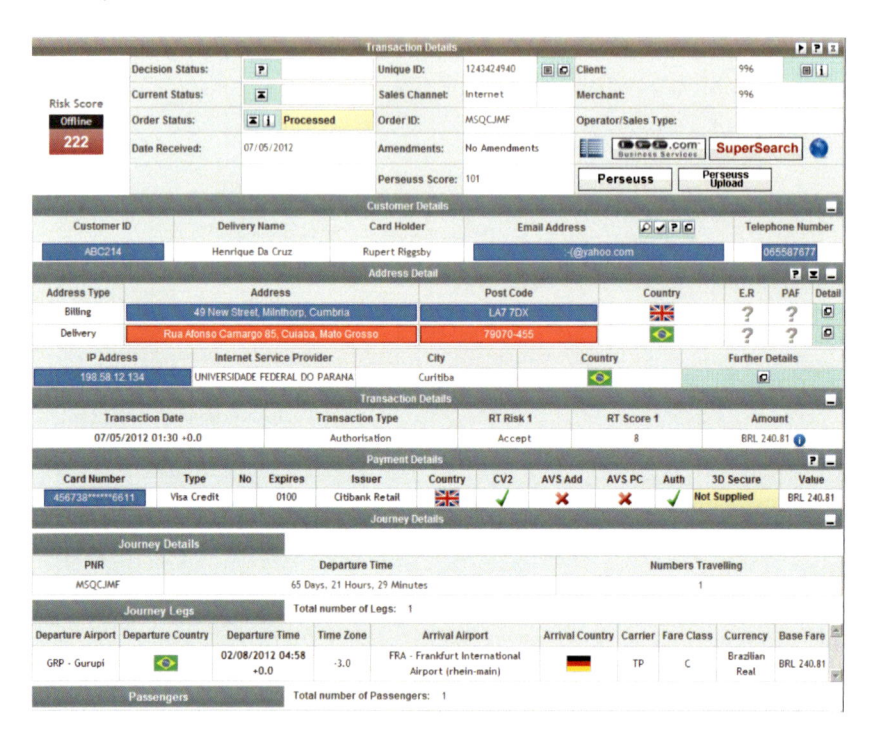

Fig 43: Example of a Case Management Screen (Courtesy of DataCash)

Larger carriers usually have an in-house fraud analysis team who conduct reviews on a part- or full-time basis. Where no in-house team is available the process can be outsourced to external providers (see Supplier and Partner Selection, page 253).

2 Transaction Reconciliation

Transaction reconciliation is the process of matching sales transactions with payment transactions. As airlines add more payment methods, serve more markets and use more processors the reconciliation operation become increasingly complex.

Reconciling happens at two levels, at the transaction level and the remittance level.

The transaction level reconciliation matches the PSP/acquiring bank transaction reports against the sales reports, using the unique payment transaction ID to tie them up. It ensures that there is an acknowledged payment transaction for every ticket sale, ticket cancellation or refund recorded in the sales report. Payment corrections performed through the management consoles of the PSPs may not be captured by the sales report and have to be separately accounted for.

For all confirmed and reconciled transactions the accounting department creates an open position in general ledger system against the PSP or acquiring bank. Any discrepancies need immediate manual intervention and correction. Ticket sales without a payment transaction need to be clarified with the distribution channel as well as the PSP to find out why and at what stage the payment information has gone missing. Where the transaction information cannot be recovered the passenger has to be contacted for another payment or to confirm cancellation of the ticket.

Failures in the ticket issuing process can lead to cases where the passenger has been charged, but not been issued a ticket. When the passenger retries the booking he may be charged twice. In both cases it is equally important to contact the cardholder, validate the requirement for the booking, confirm the ticket status and initiate a transaction refund if required.

The next reconciliation happens at the transaction summary or remittance level. The accounting team compares the financial statements that they receive from the PSP or acquiring bank along with an actual payment against the open position that they have previously created for all confirmed purchases. It ensures that the airline receives the funds that they are expecting. This monitoring process is particularly complex when the acquiring bank delays payout of funds by up to several weeks to cover their acquiring risk.

The typical reconciliation operation involves pulling reports from multiple PSPs or acquiring banks and comparing them against internal sales reports. In many cases this is done manually, supported by Excel spread sheets. It is slow-going and difficult to tie payment amounts to the original transaction, since reports often lack common reference data and reporting formats.
More and more airlines are automating these reconciliation processes, either within their ERP systems or through dedicated reconciliation systems. This reduces their administration costs and allows them a more centralised view of their payment data.

3 Card Operations – Transaction Correction Processes

Corrective payment transactions such as manual payment reversals, refunds and credit transactions are required to correct missing or incorrect payments detected during the reconciliation process as well as to resolve sales issues. Very often they are not initiated by the ticketing agent directly, but referred to a specialist back-office department – the card operations team (sometimes part of the accounting team or referred to as the credit card department).

Passengers can change their minds about their bookings and want to be refunded for changed or cancel tickets, ticket agents do make mistakes and need payment transactions to be changed or cancelled. Service disruption situations may require a passenger to be compensated or refunded towards his original purchase transaction. System errors are another source of passenger complaints that need investigation and possible transaction corrections. All of them are resolved and processed by this team.

The agents on this team have access to the payment reporting systems, as well as to the management consoles of the PSPs and acquiring banks to investigate transaction histories and to perform the necessary correction transactions. To ensure that they are associated with the relevant booking they should, wherever possible be initiated within the airline's back-office systems. Transactions performed in the PSP management consoles directly do not get accounted for in the sales report and will therefore trigger a reconciliation mismatch.

Some alternative payment methods though, such as direct banking and bank transfers, can only be adjusted within the systems of the PSP or the acquiring bank. Certain forms of payment, such as cash payment options, cannot be corrected or reversed at all. For those situations the passenger needs to be contacted and an alternative compensation payment agreed (e.g. cheque, bank transfer). To avoid this manual administration some carriers would rather not add payment methods that do not support automated refunds.

4 Collection – Charge-back Processing

Challenging charge-backs is a critical process to protect the airline's revenue. Research shows that, on average, merchants win 40% of the fraud-related charge-backs they challenge, resulting in net recovery of 28% of all fraud-related charge-backs received (CyberSource, 2011).

216 Back-office Support Processes

One out of four change-backs can be recovered

Win rate

40%
Re-present-
ments won

On average, merchants win 40%
of charge-backs challenged

Net Recovery Rate

28%
Chargebacks
Recovered

* Net Recovery Rate is expressed as a
% of all fraud-coded chargebacks received

Source: CyberSource Online Fraud Report

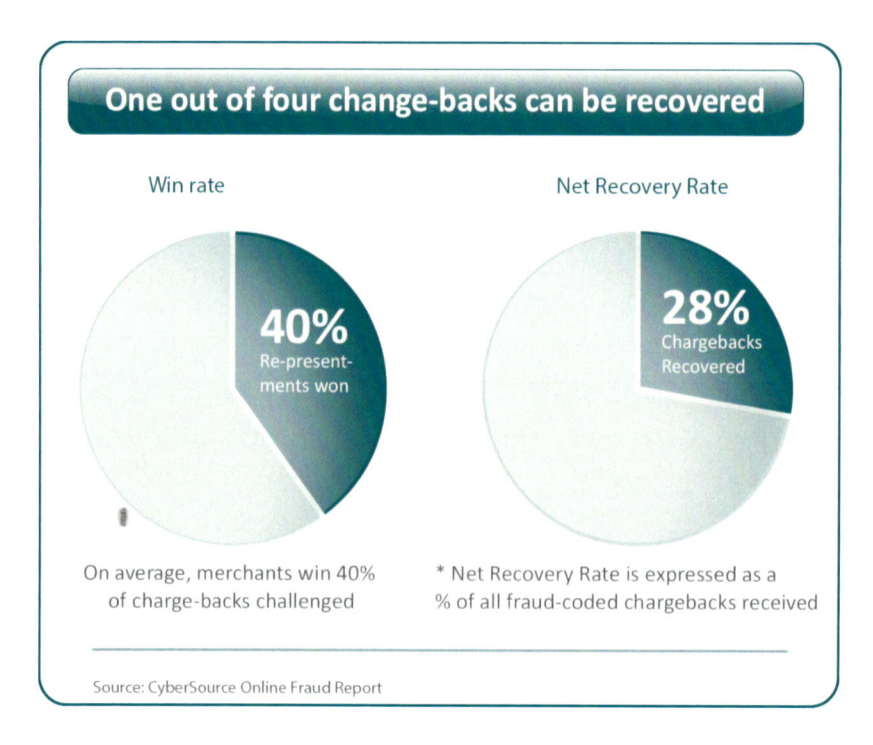

Fig 44: Typical Charge-back Recovery Rate (Source: CyberSource, "*Insider's Guide to ePayment Management*", 2011)

The card operation team often handles the collection process in addition to the operational payment support. They receive requests for copy and charge-backs through the daily PSP or acquiring bank reconciliation files as well as directly through the transaction management consoles. These consoles support the airline agents in defending the claim. After an internal transaction investigation the agent collates and uploads all relevant documentation to support the claim (booking and payment confirmations, delivery confirmations, PNR, boarding confirmations etc.). From there it is forwards to the issuing bank for further review (see Transaction Dispute Process, page 68). The collection team needs to work closely with the order screening team to ensure a coherent defence approach.

5   Credit Card Validation before Check-in

One way to reduce the payment fraud risk is to ensure that the person travelling is actually in possession of the credit card that has been used to pay for the flight. Where this rule is enforced the passenger has to present the relevant credit card at the check-in desk before check-in can be completed.

For third-party bookings, where the person flying is not the person who has paid for the flight, the passenger is requested to bring or to submit ahead of their trip a photocopy of the payment card, signed by the cardholder (e.g. Oman Air). To avoid having to turn passengers away during the check-in process, they need to be made aware of this procedure well in advance; during the booking process as well as multiple email reminders in the run up to the departure day.

If the passenger cannot supply either the card itself or the confirmation letter of the cardholder they may be requested to pay again, using a new payment card. The original payment transaction would then be refunded. In rare cases they may be refused to fly.

These rules need to be applied with certain flexibility. Children travelling, where their parents have paid for the ticket or passengers where their partner has paid for the ticket, both with the same last names, should be treated differently from situations where the passenger does not even know the cardholder.

Some carriers apply this process to all their passengers. This avoids passengers feeling they are being treated differently to other passengers who are not being checked. It does however create a lot of extra work and increases check-in times. Alternatively it can be restricted to third party bookings where the cardholder is not flying himself or to selected PNRs that have been flagged as "suspicious" or risky by the order screening department.

Authorization letter from Cardholder

I ...., holder of .... (Name of issuing bank) credit/debit card bearing No.................................... expiring on .... do hereby authorise Oman Air to process the payment for .... against tickets issued on booking reference (PNR)..........................

I acknowledge the purchase of Oman Air tickets against the PNR reference as mentioned and/or coupons for related charges described above and I am aware of applicable restrictions and/or penalties as shown on such tickets and/or coupons.

Signature of Card Holder
Date:
Contact Number:
Address:

Note: For card payment verification, we will require:

1. A clear copy of both sides of the credit card (blank out the ccv number).
2. Copy of the cardholder's passport.
3. Above authorisation letter duly signed by card holder.

You can e-mail documents to cca.verification@omanair.com or fax to 968-24153300. If you require any assistance, call us 24 X7 on +968-24531111.

Fig 45: Example of an Authorisation Letter from the Cardholder (Courtesy of Oman Air)

An entry in the PNR/PNL notifies the check-in agent of a required check. Self-check-in would be disabled for such passengers. Only when the indicator has been removed from the record can the passenger be checked it (not supported by all reservation/DCS systems).

Different payment methods have different risk levels associated with the payment. For 3DSecure transactions for example, where the airline has a payment guarantee, such extra checks may be redundant.

These are some of the most prominent processes that are required to allow a secure and smooth payment processing environment. Later chapter about the deployment of a payment project (see Internal Process Adaptation, page 277) will highlight additional areas within an airline that need to be engaged to support an airline's payment processing business.

Part IV. Planning Your Payment Project – a Step by Step Guide

1 Introduction – How to use this Guide

The first part of the book introduced the payment basics, the second and third part applied them to the airline industry. This section applies both aspects to YOUR payment project – whether implementing or changing the way payments are taken and processed by your airline. It is a guide to support you – the person responsible for, working with or interested in such a project – through all the project stages – developing a strategy, selecting suppliers, implementation and process adaptation through to the final go-live.

It starts with a discovery exercise – a review of your airline's current payment infrastructure and support processes. It then analyses current payment channels and payment markets, the suppliers currently used as well as all costs related to the payment process.

Understanding the current set-up supports the goal-setting and strategy development phase outlined in the next section. It will ask what drives your payment strategy: Is it reducing costs? Is it improving conversion rates and market reach?

Do you need to improve the system's reliability and stability? What about the back-end support processes? Which one of those goals is the most important? How would you rank them? The chapter gives examples of common goals for airline payment projects and outlines some strategic approaches to achieve them.

The section that follows focuses on external partners whose services you are likely to need to support your payment strategy: acquiring banks, Payment Service Providers, system integrators and ancillary services providers, such as fraud management solutions or currency exchange providers. It looks at selection criteria to evaluate existing providers or choose new ones. It describes standard product and service offerings and common pricing models. An outline of the implementation processes and implementation options will further help you to plan your engagement with these partners.

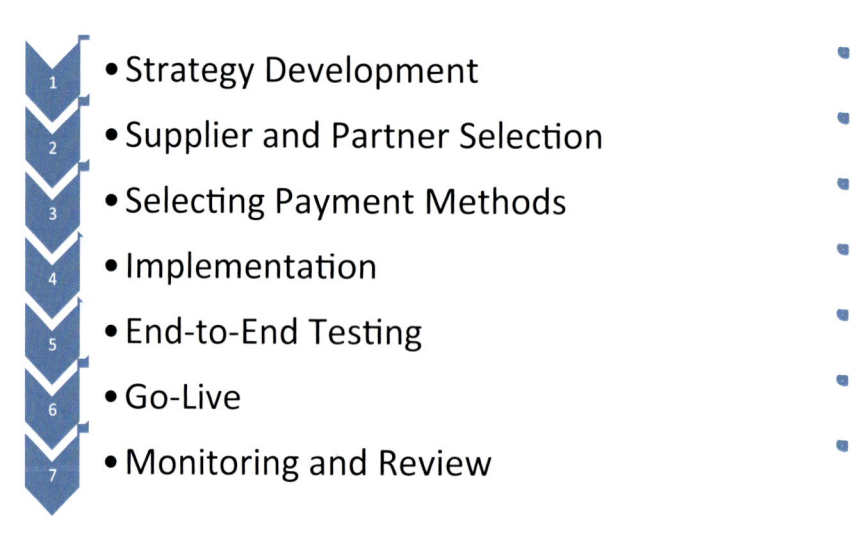

1. • Strategy Development
2. • Supplier and Partner Selection
3. • Selecting Payment Methods
4. • Implementation
5. • End-to-End Testing
6. • Go-Live
7. • Monitoring and Review

Fig 46: Sample Flow Chart for a Payment Project

The last chapters of this section guide you through the actual implementation phase: The adaptation of the distribution software and the back-end systems as well as the adjustments to the related back-end service processes (financial reconciliation, reporting, customer service, etc.) to ensure an end-to-end payment transaction life cycle support. Setting up a monitoring process provides means of correcting any issues and ensures an on-going success after the go-live date.

2 Strategy Development

Unless you are working for a start-up airline, it is likely you are not starting with a blank sheet, but that your payment project is a change or an improvement to the current situation. As taking payments is a vital part of every airline's processes, any changes to the payment environment need to be well thought through, well prepared and implemented without any operational impact. This chapter will guide you through the thinking and preparation process. It takes you through the environment evaluation and gives you guidance for the goal and strategy setting – all you need to lead up to the actual execution of the project.

2.1 Evaluation of Current Set-up

Before changing any system or infrastructure it is good practice to take some time to evaluate the current set-up. Whether you are starting from a green field or improving and existing system, the questions below will help you to find out more about the environment you will be operating in. Documenting the outcome will give you a good base-line for your project. Here are some areas and questions that may help:

Current payment set-up
- What distribution channels are currently accepting payments?
- How are payments being taken?
- What infrastructure is used?
- How stable is the payment process (payment issues in % of booking failures and aborted sales transactions)?
- Are there any known service and support issues caused by the payment process?
- Who controls the infrastructure/software/hardware?
- Who is responsible for its development?
- How flexible is it?
- How reliable/resilient is it?

Existing markets and those you are planning to enter
- What are the prevailing payment methods in those markets?
- What payment methods are accessible to your target customers?
- What payment methods do you already accept?
- Are there any specific financial regulations in those markets that may influence your payment strategy?
- How is surcharging viewed?

Payment costs
- What are end-to-end payment transaction costs?
- Where do they occur – in what parts of the process?

Payment process
- What is the end-to-end transaction flow?
- What entities are involved?
- What departments are involved?
- What systems are used?

Evaluation of service providers
- Who are the external providers currently involved in processing payments?
- What channels/countries are covered by each?
- How do they charge? What commercial models do they follow?
- What contracts are in place, what are the conditions, what are the termination clauses?
- What services do those providers offer that you are not using today?

Fraud and risk management
- What does your current risk and fraud management system look like?
- What are the processes around fraud prevention and risk management?
- What are your total costs of fraud?
- What are the channels/markets with the highest fraud?

Service and support infrastructure
- Which departments are involved?
- What works well, what does not work well?
- Where are the "pain points"?

Back-office payment processing infrastructure
- What are the system components, what is the system architecture?
- What technology is used?
- How flexible is it?
- Is it compliant with current security standards?

Going through this exercise may already highlight some of the pain points that need addressing. Articulating and quantifying them provides vital input for the next step – setting goals and developing a strategy.

2.2 Goal Setting and Strategy Development

Clear goals and a defined strategy are crucial to any project. This section discusses some of the motives that may have initiated your payment project and how to document them before you start your project.

Whether you are in the fortunate situation of being able to decide the payment strategy yourself, or you are being tasked to execute a strategy, make sure that the goals are clearly stated and you have Key Performance Indicators (KPIs) to measure your success against. If there is more than one driver for your project, you may need to prioritise them as part of your strategy development exercise.

Ensure that there is a prioritisation for conflicting goals ahead of project start. Maximising the number of payment methods for example may be the best strategy from a distribution perspective – more customers will be able to complete a purchase. Every additional payment method however, increases the complexity of support and reconciliation required. Risk management is another example. The fraud team's success is measured by a low fraud rate. They would more likely decline a risky transaction while the sales team – measured by the amount of sales – would risk "anything" for an additional booking.

Here is a sample of goals commonly found for in airline payment projects: Increase conversion; increase revenue; reduce costs and security and compliance concerns. For each of the objectives you will find a list of possible strategic approaches to achieve them.

Increase conversion– to improve the 'look to book' ratio and reduce payment failures during the sales process you can:
- Add additional payment methods
- Optimise the sales and payment process
- Improve the processing infrastructure to increase reliability
- Improve the service level of external providers/change suppliers /use multiple suppliers

Increase revenue – the payments team can support this by:
- Adding payment functionality to additional distribution channels
- Supporting payments in additional markets
- Allowing payments for additional goods or services
- Generating payment related revenue through surcharging and Dynamic Currency Conversion

Reduce Cost – There are four main cost areas where an optimisation of the payment process can address and reduce costs:
Transaction costs:
- Review suppliers (PSPs, acquiring banks, other service providers)
- Optimise merchant fees (interchange fees)
- Consolidate suppliers
- Replace integrators with direct connections

Fraud and fraud related costs
- Improve fraud management systems
- Improve and automate processes
- Increase fraud management competence within the organisation

Support and maintenance costs
- Simplify/-refresh infrastructure and technology
- Review and improve payment support processes
- Increase system performance, reliability and resilience

Cost of money (funds held up by the payment process)
- Reduce the time between the customer payment and the settlement of that revenue into your accounts

Security and compliance – Reduce the risk of security breaches and gain or retain compliance with card scheme and security standards:
- Launch a risk assessment project
- Initiate a certification process (e.g. PCI-DSS compliance)

Try to quantify the benefits of the goals that you have identified relevant to your situation and estimate the effort to achieve them. A high level business case will support your case for one or other strategy. Ensure that all stake holders are involved in the strategy definition process and that you get their buy-in before you go through the final approval and sign-off process.

2.3 Project Set-up and Kick-off

There is not much payment-specific to be said in this chapter. Ensure that you have a project manager and team members assigned from each of the relevant stake holder areas, equipped with the right authorities to make decisions (or at least bring them about). Congratulations and welcome to the project – if you are one of them ☺!

Break your strategy down into a high level project plan. Give yourself enough contingency for things that may come up as you go along. Secure funds to get you to the next decision stage (assuming that your project follows some sort of multi-stage project life cycle). Ensure that everybody is familiar with the goals of the project - and kick it off.

3 Supplier and Partner Selection

This part of the book will help you to engage with and evaluate external partners and service providers you are likely to need to support your payment strategy: acquiring banks, Payment Service Providers, consolidators, fraud and currency exchange providers and token storage systems.

It can be used to re-evaluate existing providers as well as to find new ones. Each chapter starts with a review of the provider's role in the process as well as a break-down and description of its major service components. It further describes common cost models, outlines engagement stages and explains implementation options. A list with selection criteria and questions will help you to find the provider that best supports your payment strategy.

3.1 Acquiring Bank

As discussed in earlier chapters, the (merchant) acquiring bank is the airline's legal gateway to one or multiple card schemes. As they are or will be managing a large part of your revenue, it is very important to choose that partner carefully. This section will highlight some of the criteria that you can use to compare different banks against each other and to ensure you pick the right one – if you are in the lucky position to have a choice. Acquiring banks do take on a significant amount of risk for every airline that they agree to acquire (see Participant's Risks and Responsibilities – Acquiring Bank, page 89). They don't make that decision light-heartedly or without completing a rigorous risk assessment process.

3.1.1 Why do I need an Acquiring Bank?

Summarising previous chapters, you need an acquiring bank to:
- Give you access to one or more card schemes
- Receive and manage the funds from all transactions that they have acquired on your behalf
- Provide a guarantee for your business towards the other participants of the card schemes (i.e. compensate cardholders for all un-flown tickets, should your airline go out of business)

3.1.2 What to Consider when Choosing an Acquiring Bank?

If you are looking for an acquiring agreement for the first time, then the banks that you have an existing relationship with may be a good first port of call. Building on an established relationship may reduce a lot of legal and commercial overhead on both sides that comes along with any new partnership. Only if they cannot or do not want to provide you with an acceptable contract or their license does not cover the payment methods and regions that you require, will you need to look for other options.

3.1.3 Market Reach

Market reach will probably be very high up on your evaluation criteria list. The bank needs to be allowed to operate in the countries where you want to take payments. Just having subsidiaries in those geographies may not actually be enough. It is the countries that the bank is licensed to take payment in, that will determine whether a bank is suitable for your needs or not. As previously discussed card schemes issue national, regional and global acquiring licences. Banks can decide what licenses they want to apply for, depending on their needs and target market. Not every bank has necessarily bought a licence beyond their domestic market.

Local banking regulations further restrict the ability of banks to operate in countries other than their home one. And even if they have international licenses for some schemes, they may not necessarily have them for all the payment methods that you may need.

3.1.4 Forms of Payment

Accepting international card brands such as Visa or MasterCard is fairly straightforward and most banks would support those. Acquiring alternative payment methods is a lot more difficult for a bank to implement outside their own country. National debit cards schemes and all forms of direct banking applications for example usually require you to work with an acquiring bank in that particular country.

3.1.5   Currencies

Working across multiple countries normally means working with multiple currencies. The bank that you want to work with needs to be able to fulfil your requirements for multiple currencies. In this context it is important to differentiate between the transaction currency and settlement currency. The transaction currency is the one that the customer pays in. It usually correlates with the currency the departure country. The settlement currency is the one that you receive your funds in from the acquiring bank.

Where the transaction currency is different from the settlement currency, the bank performs a currency conversion. Conversions of course incur a fee. Ensure that you agree upfront on the source of the exchange rate that will be used as well as the mark-up that the bank will apply. For some currencies the bank may not be able to support a direct conversion from the transaction currency to the settlement currency. For those a double conversion via a base currency will be required, incurring a double conversion fee of course.

To avoid some of the conversion costs it may be advantageous to operate multiple settlement accounts in multiple currencies. This of course is only relevant if you have expenses and can reuse the funds in that currency.

Ensure that the bank you choose can fulfil your need in terms of the number of currencies that you are planning to accept as well as the currencies that you want to your funds to be managed in. This needs to be arranged for everyone of the payment methods that you are planning to use. Ensure that your currency strategy is aligned with your organisations' overall operational, tax and legal requirement for various currencies and countries.

3.1.6   Ability to "Domesticate" Transactions

Acquiring international transactions attracts a higher merchant fee than processing a domestic transaction. If you do have a local subsidiary or a registered sales office in a specific country, you may want to process the transactions locally. Some acquiring banks are able to use a network of own subsidiaries and partner banks across multiple counties to be able to process many of your international transactions as domestic ones at a domestic rate. This process is called "domestication of transactions" and may help you to reduce your transaction costs drastically without the need to have multiple acquiring bank agreements in multiple countries. If you do have a large proportion of your transactions coming from one or two foreign countries you may want to ensure that your acquiring bank can support this process. Choosing an additional local acquiring bank in those specific markets would have the same effect but comes with the overhead of having to manage an additional partner.

3.1.7 Service and Operational Support

Good customer service and support is not always a given. As a relationship with an acquiring bank extends beyond the contracting and the implementation phase it may be worthwhile to look at your potential partners' approach to this subject. Accepting card payments will require an almost daily interaction between your operation teams and the bank's service teams. It is important that your working hours, to some extent at least, overlap with those of the bank and that both teams can communicate in a common language.

Your internal support teams will want to have the following questions answered before going live, you may want to keep them in mind while evaluating the bank:

- Who can they contact for a transaction investigation/resolution situation (when you either over-charged a cardholder or transactions are missing)? How much support will the bank provide in investigating those transactions and helping to correcting them?
- How does the bank help you with defending charge-backs? Are there automated processes in place?
- How can they support you in validating suspicious payments and fighting fraud– will they follow up with the respective issuing banks to ensure that a transaction is genuine?

Ask for support manuals and engagement structures to find out about the acquirers support set-up.

3.1.8   POS Terminals

If you require POS terminals from that acquiring bank to process card-present payments at ticket desks or call centres, ask for
- The commercial model (buy or rental agreement)
- The communication infrastructure that is required between terminal and the bank (via phone lines or IP). Ensure that the communication costs are included in the business case.
- The support infrastructure (technical and operational). Take the support of POS terminals in restricted air-side areas into consideration.
- Security and compliance aspects (e.g. are the terminals PCI compliant)
- Integration options. How do they connect and communicate with your distribution applications?
- Payment methods and geographical reach. In what countries can you deploy the POS terminals (which countries does the bank have a licence for) and what payment methods can they accept?

3.1.9   Licence and Compliance Check

The acquiring bank will be going through a risk and compliance evaluation of your organisation and your business model, so should you with the bank. Check that the bank is financially stable, has the required legal certificates and licences and complies with the financial regulations of the markets that they are active in. Banks are regulated and regularly monitored by the local Financial Authorities. They ensure that the funds that the bank will hold on your behalf (for the time between when they are received from the card scheme until they are pad out to you) are properly managed and secured. These controls however greatly vary from country to country. You may want to find out where the bank is headquartered, what financial jurisdiction it falls under and the implications on its financial controls.

3.1.10   Financial Regulations

You are probably familiar with the financial regulations in your home market. Working with an acquiring bank and taking payments outside your own country may create additional legal and fiscal challenges for your airline. Many countries for example require you to have a local subsidiary set up within that country if you want to open a bank account with an acquiring bank. Some local payment methods (such as direct debits and bank transfers) often require the same, or may be provided at lower cost to you if you are domiciled in that country. Other countries have restrictions on exporting funds outside the country where the transactions have been acquired. Ensure that you have included these aspects in your evaluation process.

You hopefully still have a list of more than one potential acquiring partner left after going through this first set of selection criteria. By now you are likely to have already established a good relationship with your assigned account managers at the different banks. The next step is usually are quest for a commercial proposal. Do not expect this to be a straight forward process, as the merchant fees and other conditions very much depend on your airline's business parameters, such as volumes, countries, currencies, transaction types and business risk. With each acquiring bank that you would like to work with, you will have to go through an evaluation process that allows the bank to analyse your business and the business opportunity. Ensure that you leave yourself plenty of time for this process. It is not uncommon that it takes several weeks to be completed.

3.1.11 The Acquirer's Risk and its Implications

One would expect that a sizable transaction volume and a healthy growth potential should be a welcome business opportunity for an acquiring bank. In theory, the higher your volume, the more attractive your business should be for the bank and the smaller you would expect the merchant fees be. This however is only one side of the coin and not necessarily true for the airline industry. As discussed in previous chapters (see Participant's Risks and Responsibilities – Acquiring Bank, page 89), banks do carry the financial risk for all un-flown tickets, should the airline that they acquire go out of business. The higher the volume and the lower the perceived financial stability of the airline, the higher is the risk that the bank is taking on, by signing it up.

The evaluation process, usually carried out by the risk and compliance department, helps the bank to evaluate this risk and take a decision on the merchant fees and the required insurances you will need to provide them to cover, or at least reduce their potential financial exposure.

3.1.12 How does an Acquiring Bank Evaluate my Business?

Banks have standard processes in place to capture the information that they need to allow their risk management teams evaluating your business. The information and documentation that you will have to submit usually comprise of:
- Company details
- Ownership structure
- Details of the management team
- Annual reports (audited, if available)
- Financial health information (balance sheet, Profit & Loss and cash-flow report for the current year)
- Current business volume and expected growth; by channel, origin (domestic, regional, global)
- Average transaction volume and transaction amount
- Average number of days between the purchase of a ticket and the departure(un-flown flight liability analysis)
- General environment (industry outlook, fuel costs, potential labour issues)

If you have processed credit card transactions previously, acquiring banks will look at your previous
- Charge-back rates
- Reasons for charge-backs

Although working for the same bank, these risk and compliance teams are acting independently and may not always share the same opinion on an opportunity as the sales team who is more likely to be very keen on your business.

It makes things easier and it may work in your favour if you have an existing commercial relationship with the bank. If you are doing other business with them already they know your organisation and have general visibility of your overall financial situation. This can help to reduce the perceived risk and may result in lower merchant fees and less securities that they require.

A local acquiring bank has also got greater flexibility to take local market situations into consideration. Take a national flag carrier for example whose financial health may not look good but who enjoys strong governmental support and financial backing. A bank close to or in this market may assess the situation very differently than a larger international acquiring bank that has less or no understanding of that particular market and that carrier's relative position.

For an international acquiring bank it may be easier to work and contract with one of your subsidiaries located in the country or region the bank is based in. It may help to reduce the perceived business risk, as the bank is familiar with the legal context. In some countries and for some payment methods it is a legal requirement for the airline to have a domestic presence to be able to sign an acquiring contract.

The acquiring banks that you ultimately contract with will want an on-going review of these business parameters. Any changes may have an impact on the merchant fees or required risk deposits. Ensure you negotiate and agree the process of any changes to the terms of your contract.

Merchant Acquiring Information Request Form

Merchant Information	Details
Company Business Name	
Contact Name / Title	
Contact Number(s)	
E-mail Address	
Opportunity details	
In which Countries will Acquiring services be required?	
Estimated Card Turnover, in USD (Annualised) by country	
Estimated Number of transactions	
Sales Channels up for bid in this process, plus channel % split	
Percentage of each Card usage (breakdown by card type)	• VISA = • MasterCard = • Maestro = • Other =
Credit vs Debit % split	• Credit = • Debit = • Other =
Corporate / Consumer Card % Split	
Cardholder Origination by sales channel	• Domestic • US / Canada • European • Central Asia • Asia Pac • Latam • Africa / Middle East
Please provide signed accounts for the last 2 years	

Fig 47: Example of a Merchant Acquiring Information Request Form

Sometimes the Payment Service Provider you are using to connect to an acquiring bank will perform these checks and ask for those assurances. This will be the case where the Payment Service Provider is offering you Treasury services (they receive and manage the incoming funds on your behalf). These PSPs share some of the financial risk described above with the acquiring bank (see the chapter below for more about this topic) and hence take over some of the assessment tasks.

It is very likely that one or other potential acquiring bank drops off the list during this process. They will either indicate politely that they are not really interested in your business, or offer credit terms that are no longer commercially viable for your business.

Hopefully you still have a choice between multiple banks with whom you can go through to the next step – a commercial proposal.

3.1.13 Commercial Proposal

The commercial proposal will contain two main elements: The fees and the risk mitigation requirements. The fee components will include:

- Account set-up and implementation
- On-going account management
- Transaction fees (independent of the payment method)
- Merchant fees per payment method (transaction based, percentage based or a combination)
- Risk management fees (CVC and address validation, 3D Secure, hotlist management)
- Currency conversion rates (where the transaction currency differs from the settlement currency)
- Administration fees for report generation, fund transfers and charge-back handling

Some banks will require you to guarantee minimum monthly fees. Ensure that there is a termination clause in the contract that suits your business needs and allows you to switch providers, should you want or need to.

Depending on the outcome of the risk evaluation process, the acquiring bank will require different level of guarantees to cover their commercial exposure for the value of the un-flown tickets in case the airline ceases or curtails business. Here are some of the options available to banks to cover this risk. The proposal from the acquiring bank will contain at least one of them:

- Deposit
- Bank guarantee
- Hold back period – delayed settlement: this delays the transfer of your revenue into your accounts closer to the time that the passenger consumes the service (is flying). This can be anything from 7 to 28 days, sometimes even longer.
- Rolling or staged deposits that increase and decrease with the volumes the bank is processing for you. This also allows adjusting the deposits for seasonal changes
- Registered rights on assets (hanger, aircrafts etc.)

Any sort of deposit and hold back period is likely to be a very contentious topic within your organisation, as cash flow is vital to your business. Ensure that you engage the right departments within your organisation to get to a solution that best fits both your internal requirements as well as those of the bank.

The commercial proposal, of course, is the key component in your selection process. Ensure that you get good internal support (e.g. purchasing department, legal) during the selection and negotiation process. A base percentage more or less in this contract will have a significant impact on the bottom line of your organisation.

3.1.14 Technical Integration

This section is only relevant, if you choose to directly integrate with an acquiring bank. In most cases you would use a PSP to connect to the bank.

There are two main scenarios where you would establish a direct connection: one to transmit and process credit card transactions generated out of your reservation/ticketing systems (RET files). The other one is if your volume is large enough to justify the relatively more complex acquiring bank integration process versus a more straight forward PSP integration. POS-terminals also link directly to the acquiring bank, and usually don't need any additional technical integration and certification.

Credit card information from ARC, BSPs and internal sales reports are usually transmitted as files as opposed to real-time transactions. Some acquiring banks are able to process them without conversion (they can input the RET and HOT file and extract the card information). Some need you to extract the credit card information and submit them in a format defined by the bank. As those files are likely to need a secured transmission method, ensure that an appropriate communication infrastructure is in place (e.g. sFTP).

Integrating direct distribution channels such as e-commerce with a bank is usually quite complex, expensive and requires long and elaborate certification processes. Normally banks prefer to push such integrations to their partner PSPs or their own PSP subsidiaries. If your credit card transaction volume is large enough– for your domestic market for example, the acquiring bank may be willing to open their systems and allow you to integrate with them directly to process on-line authorisation and settlement transactions.

Ensure that the bank can provide you with sufficient interface documentation and integration support. Ideally they can give your development team access to a test environment. The certification process can take anything from a few weeks to several months. The better they are organised and the more attractive your business the less time this process is likely to take.

Most airlines would however avoid the effort of going through the process of a direct integration and use a PSP.

3.2 Payment Service Provider

Payment Service Providers (PSP) predominantly facilitate the connection between an airline's direct distribution application and the world of payments. As described above, a direct integration with an acquiring bank can be a complex and lengthy process. PSPs have gone through that process on behalf of their customers – usually with more than just one acquiring bank and are hence able offer a wide range of payment methods across multiple countries through a single interface.

They complement this with payment transaction administration and management tools as well as facilities for consolidated reporting. Integrated ancillary payment services, such as fraud management tools, DCC and credit card storage services can further optimise an airline's payment processing, often far beyond what an individual acquiring bank would be able provide.

Some PSPs also engage in card-present transactions and are able to provide Point of Sale (POS), kiosk and agent mobile payment services.

3.2.1 What comes first – PSP or Acquiring Bank?

There is no clear answer to the debate as to whether an airline should first select the PSP or an acquiring bank. Some argue that it is easier to find a PSP than it is to find an acquiring bank. As a result one should first agree on an acquiring bank and then a PSP already linked to that bank, or who be willing to integrate with that bank. Others argue that PSPs can support your search process for an acquiring bank in markets you want to go to.

Your particular requirements, target markets and the financial stability of your airline may determine your choice. If you are restricted to working with a particular acquiring bank, you may want to use a PSP that is already integrated with the bank. If finding an acquiring bank is less of a worry for you, then choosing a PSP with the right market reach, service level and commercial proposal should be your first step.

IS YOUR PAYMENT SET-UP READY FOR TAKE OFF?

Changes in the way that passengers want to book and pay for flights mean that the airline industry needs to react quickly to meet this new demand - without compromising on security or accuracy.

When it comes to consumer payments, it can be hard for even the most sophisticated business to keep up. Rapid developments in technology offer customers a host of new ways to buy and pay for goods and services, meaning that everyone from retailers to restauranteurs need to cater for this demand or risk losing custom to faster, more agile competitors.

The airlines industry is no different. In fact, flight operators are under greater pressure than businesses in most other sectors, needing to react to changing payment trends without losing their tight grip on security when taking bookings from passengers.

A quick glance at some statistics from the sector helps to explain why this task is particularly difficult within the aviation sector. Between May 2010 and May 2011 alone for instance, the number of international air passengers grew by seven percent [1]. And findings from a recent survey by KPMG reveal that people are more likely to book flights online (70 percent) than they are to buy luxury goods (65 percent)[2].

Keeping up with demand

Faced with an increasingly complex payments picture, airlines need a solution that can meet the specific and intensive needs of the sector.

WorldPay's dedicated approach is the result of decades of tailoring, shaped and honed by feedback by customers that include some of the aviation industry's biggest names.

With its all-in-one package, WorldPay allows airlines to offer alternative payments alongside international credit cards across all sales channels.

WorldPay helps airlines to offer their customers the widest range of payment choices, without compromising on security:

- **The broadest reach:** able to accept more than 150 international currencies, WorldPay processes millions of payments across the world every day

- **Accountability and visibility:** full itinerary data and passenger records are included in credit card processing

- **Seamlessly integrated:** WorldPay can be introduced into booking and reservation systems for internet and call centre transactions with ease

- **Works world over:** WorldPay offers full international capabilities, providing multi-currency, multi-lingual cross-border trading and settlement

- **The highest standards of fraud prevention:** WorldPay's risk management solutions tackle the threat of fraud head on. Sophisticated fraud-detection algorithms blend with age and identity checking and a range of other features.

With years of experience working with the aviation sector, WorldPay offers airline operators one of the most inclusive and advanced solutions on the market today.

For further information, contact:

Email: airlines@worldpay.com
Phone: +44 (0)203 246 5582

1. http://articles.economictimes.indiatimes.com/2011-06-30/news/29721873_1_passenger-traffic-iata-freight-traffic
2. http://www.kpmg.com/global/en/issuesandinsights/articlespublications/consumers-and-convergence/pages/default.aspx

www.worldpay.com

WorldPay

3.2.2 Categories of Payment Service Provider

Depending on their level of involvement in the handling of your funds we can differentiate three groups of PSPs:

- **Pure system integrators** – These PSPs concentrate on the technical components of payment processing and do not get involved in either, the financial flow and the contractual relationship that you have with your acquiring bank. The revenues are transferred directly from the acquiring bank to your airline's accounts.

- **Collecting PSPs or Full Service Provider**– This group of PSPs is able to collect payments from different acquiring banks on your behalf, consolidate them and transfer them to your account as one amount. This simplifies the reconciliation and accounting processes and reduces the overhead related to the management of multiple suppliers and multiple revenue streams. Although you still have to sign contracts with the respective acquiring banks, they are usually pre-negotiated and prepared by the PSP. In many cases they are three party contracts between the airline, the bank and the PSP.

    This is particularly important for those payment methods, where you need to be legally domiciled and/or have a bank account in the respective country (e.g. for direct debits and bank transfers). These PSPs can manage that on your behalf. The same applies, if you want to qualify for local or regional interchange rates. The PSP may be able to represent you locally.

    Handling merchant's money was for a long time restricted to institutions with a banking licence. These restrictions have been lifted in some countries. In Europe for example PSPs can be certified as "Payment Institutions" under the European Payment Service Directive (PSD). This allows them to acquire and manage funds on behalf of their merchants – without the need to apply for a full banking licence.

PSPs who do get involved in the financial settlement process share some of the risks and responsibilities that usually reside with the acquiring banks. As such they themselves perform a lot of the risk assessment, normally associated with applying for an acquiring agreement. The additional service is likely to be reflected in slightly higher transaction fees.

- **PSPs with a banking license/Banks with integrated PSPs** – These PSPs have either a banking licence or - the other way around - the bank with the banking licence provides its own internal PSP service. Such PSPs have an additional advantage over PSP that only collect funds; they can provide you with a fully integrated acquiring and PSP services, reducing the amount of entities that you have to negotiate and contract with to one. Providing both elements of the service also gives them more flexibility with their pricing models.

Most PSPs will be able to provide you with the standard international credit card brands plus a limited number of local cards. The more payment methods you want to offer, the more useful a PSP that can collect and consolidate various payment streams becomes. Full-service PSPs with a banking license (still a minority) can further simplify the life of a merchant during the sign-up phase as well as on-going throughout the life span of the contract.

3.2.3 Market Reach

Regardless of the type of PSP, one of the most important selection criteria will be the market reach. The prospect PSP needs to cover the reach of your airline's network as much as possible. Ask for a list of the countries the PSP already operates in. The merchants supported there should preferably be travel related, as every industry has its own specific needs. Also have a look at the size of the merchants that they support. Being a lot larger or smaller than the average merchant brings its own challenges. Having offices near where you are based indicates their dedication to that particular global region and ensures that you will have local support, in the time zone(s) you require. The number of acquiring banks the PSP is integrated with may be relevant to you if you have not yet selected one, or need multiple banks across multiple target markets.

3.2.4 Relevant Payment Methods

If increasing alternative payment methods is high on your agenda, ensure that the PSP can cover those you would like to offer to your passengers. PSPs can be a good source of information about prevailing payment methods and habits in a particular country and will be more than happy to support your research and decision process.

If a PSP does not currently support a payment method you would like to use, ask if it is on their road map, or if they are prepared to add it. Get an estimate for the standard integration cost and time for an additional payment method. In some cases a PSP may be prepared to contribute to, or cover the entire cost of a new integration as they can reuse it across their merchant base.

3.2.5 Supported Currencies and Currency Conversion

Ensure that the selected PSP does support all the transaction currencies that you would like to accept for your ticket sales. If your provider does get involved in the management of your funds, check out in what currencies they are able to hold them for you (account currency).

Where the transaction or settlement currency differs from the account currency, the amount needs to be converted. Agree on the source of the exchange rate that will be applied and the mark-up that the provider will charge you. For some more exotic currencies, a conversion through a base currency may be required, incurring a double conversion and possibly double charges.

3.2.6 Fees and Fee Structure

PSPs structure their fees in various ways. That can make it quite difficult to compare one provider against another. Here is a breakdown of the most common fee elements, categorised in three groups:

Set-up and administration fees
- Implementation and system integration and fees (some PSPs charge for the integration with your distribution system)
- Account set-up fees
- Monthly account maintenance fees
- Charge-back, reversal and refund fees
- Report generation (and statement) fees
- Manual intervention fees
- Operational fees (e.g. for changing a parameters)
-

Transaction and processing fees
These are independent of the payment method that has been used for a particular transaction. They include:
- Transaction fees (regardless of the transaction type)
- Settlement fees (for captured transactions)
- Remittance fees (when the funds are transferred to your accounts)
- Value added service fees (e.g. fraud screening, currency conversion)

Full Service PSP fees
PSPs that have an acquiring agreement with an acquiring bank can also give you payment method specific pricing (Merchant fees)

- Transaction fees (independent of the transaction amount)
- Volume base fees (in % of the transaction amount)
- Some payment methods attract a combination of both of the above fee types

To cover their fixed costs, suppliers usually require minimum monthly payment guarantees, regardless of the actual business volume (which can be quite small at the beginning of a project).

Ensure you know the reason for and frequency of each fee element. Try to apply them to your expected volume and projected usage of each payment method to get a comparable result.

3.2.7 Financial Regulations and Compliance Considerations

When dealing with suppliers abroad it is advisable to seek local legal help. Financial regulations in the countries you are planning to work in may restrict your ability to do business the way you are used to in your domestic market (e.g. exporting revenue from countries such as India, South Africa or China). Taxes, stamp duties etc. can turn a good looking deal with a supplier into a financial nightmare. Keep these things in mind when comparing suppliers from different countries.

Ensuring the PSP complies with local regulations is good practice. As with every supplier, you would want to run through some basic vetting before entering a contractual agreement. Here are some of the areas that you may want to verify:

- Is the PSP registered to do this type of business?
- Is the PSP registered to do business in the countries they operate in?
- Do they have the relevant compliance certifications (e.g. ISO27001, SAS 70)
- Are they PCI-DSS compliant? Are their suppliers compliant (for an organisation to remain compliant, all their suppliers dealing with payment data need to be compliant as well)?
- Financial stability – ask for annual reports. How long has the PSP been operating?
- How are the funds managed (if involved in the financial flow)? Ensure that they are kept in trust accounts, separate from the PSPs own funds.

3.2.8 Transaction Management Tools and Reporting Infrastructure

This area is relevant for your fraud, operations, accounting and service teams. They will need 24/7 access to information about all payment transactions that have been processed by the respective PSP. This can be either through real-time access to the PSP's system as well as through off-line reports.

Ideally the PSP has a web-based transaction management facility allowing your agents to view, search and download transaction information, using standard and tailored transaction reports. An infrastructure to perform transaction corrections, reversals and refunds can be very helpful. Some providers have automated dispute processes in place to support your teams in handling challenged payments and defending charge-backs (see fraud screening tools in chapter 3.3.3)

Here is a list of the most relevant elements of functionality that you may want to include in your PSP evaluation:
- Consolidated reporting – can the PSP consolidate all transactions from multiple acquiring banks and payment schemes into one reporting infrastructure?
- Standard transaction reports – format, frequency; How are they transmitted? How can they be accessed? Can they be modified to your needs?
- Access to ad-hoc reports – how you can define the search criteria, which ones are available and can you download the result?
- Transaction search facility
- Analytical tools and graphical statistics
- Manual transaction correction– Manual payments, reversals, refunds, credits
- Dispute processing support– "Request for information" and charge-back processing

Ask for either screen shots, user guides or a demo account to understand the quality, user friendliness and flexibility of the systems.

3.2.9 IT and Infrastructure Set-up

Taking payment is a mission critical operation. Any disruption in your supplier's systems can have a huge impact on your revenues. You want to ensure that these systems are available 24/7/365, without interruptions or deterioration of quality. Request some of the following information from your potential suppliers to evaluate and ensure the likelihood of a wrinkle free service:

- Robustness of the infrastructure – Where is the application hosted? Does the data centre run on a redundant infrastructure? What monitoring systems are used?
- Availability – What up-time is the provider willing to commit to? Don't accept anything less than 99.9X%! (99.0% equates to an outage of almost 7 ½ hours per month, 99.9% equates to about 45 minutes per month, 99.99% to about 5 minutes)
- Transactions per Second (TPS) – How many transactions per second can the system handle? How many in parallel? Is that for the total volume of all of the customers or for you only? How does that relate to your requirements? Is the system scalable?
- Response times – How quickly does the system respond to an authorisation request? Is that including ancillary services, such as fraud checks etc.? (this is usually measured excluding the time it takes for a transaction to be routed between your and the provider's systems)
- Disaster recovery infrastructure – Is it available? Where is it? What are their disaster recovery procedures? How long does it take to get it on-line?
- Maintenance procedures – Are there service windows? How often and how long are they? What is the impact on operations?
- Service Level Agreement (SLA) – How quickly does the supplier respond to faults, defects and service requests?

Penalties in the form of service credits are a common method of ensuring up-time remains within the agreed service levels. If you have any doubts about the service quality of your potential provider it is always recommended to ask for feedback from reference customers.

3.2.10 Implementation Support

Implementing a PSP into your distribution environment can take anything from three days to three months. Although half of the implementation responsibility and work lies on your side, an experienced project team with the right infrastructure and processes in place within the PSP can significantly contribute to a successful and timely integration. This is especially true if it is the first time your organisation is implementing a PSP.

Discuss with your potential supplier(s) some of the following areas upfront and you will get a good feeling of the likely complexity and how well they will be able to support you.

- Standard on-boarding plan – recommended time for implementation
- Structure of the project team
- Do they provide consulting prior to, during and after the implementation phase?
- Are the technical interfaces well documented?
- Does the implementation need to be certified?
- Are development and test environments available (to support your team with the integration work)?

3.2.11 Service and Support

A good working relationship between your own support teams and those of the PSP is vital to ensure a smooth operation. As with the relationship with the acquiring bank, find out how the support team can be contacted (call centre, email, management portal), ensure that there is a common working language and your support hours overlap. The support should cover areas such as:

- Financial reporting and transaction reconciliation
- Investigating missing or un-matched transactions
- Technical support (changes to the interface, system interruptions)
- Managing payment methods (adding, changing)

3.2.12 Integration Options

As discussed in Part II (Channel integrations), there are different options when integrating a PSP into the booking process. The airline either collects the cardholder information within their distribution application or forwards it to the PSP via a secure interface or the airline embeds the PSP's payment page into the check-out process. In this scenario the PSP collects the payment details and processes them directly. A batch integration, where the airline submits transactions in files, is the third option.

Here are some additional considerations to keep in mind for the evaluation of these three options:

The direct integration: this type of integration is usually fairly straight forward as long as
- The interface is clearly defined and
- All the transactions types you require are supported

Ensure that your application is hosted in a PCI-compliant environment.

Re-direct integration: To ensure that the PSP's payment pages can be seamlessly integrated into your distribution application, your PSP should be able to provide:
- Language support for the countries that you wish to operate in
- Customisable look and feel to ensure that the payment page looks like one of your own pages (colours, navigation buttons, fonts)

Batch file processing: If you need to process BSP files (HOT files) for your travel agency transactions or settlement files from your own reservation system (RET files), ensure that the PSP is able to directly import and process them. Some PSPs will require to the airline to convert the files into a specific format before submitting them.

If your payment strategy includes distribution channels, such as call centre and ticket desk applications, you may want to investigate further integration options, such as:
- Virtual POS terminals – see Part II., chapter 6.5
- Payments through Interactive Voice Recognition systems – see Part II., chapter 6.6
- Processing card-present transactions - see Part II.

Ensure that you are clear about type of integration that you require and that the PSP can support it.

3.2.13 When are Multiple PSPs Required?

Once you have completed the process of pre-selecting acquiring banks and PSPs you may find that none of the suppliers can quite fulfil all your needs to your full satisfaction. Don't be alarmed. It is quite common for airlines to choose more than one provider to realise their payment strategy.

Using a domestic PSP for the home market and one for the international market is a common set-up. The domestic provider usually has the widest range of local payment methods and can optimise your transaction costs benefitting from domestic processing rates. The global provider on the other hand will bring the benefit of covering many countries even though sometimes at a slightly higher cost.

Some airlines don't want to rely on a single provider and choose a second one as a backup. This ensures operational continuity, should one supplier's systems not respond. It also puts the airline in a better commercial position, as they can easier negotiate conditions between two competing suppliers.

Legal restrictions may not allow your preferred PSP to operate in one of your destinations (e.g. embargoed countries like Iran, Syria, North Korea). For those countries you would also need an additional local provider. Some countries may simply be commercially not attractive enough to your main provider to work and operate in.

3.2.14 Ancillary Payment Services

PSPs can usually provide you with some or all of the following additional services, mostly fully integrated into the rest of their management and support infrastructure:

- Fraud screening
- Dynamic Currency Conversion
- Secure Credit Number Storage – Token services

Some PSPs provide these services as in-house solutions. Most PSPs though have integrated external specialists of their respective areas. The following chapters give you some guidance to evaluate those systems, regardless of whether they are provided internally by the PSP or by a third party. If you buy these services separately from your PSP, you would need to ensure that they can be directly integrated to your distribution channel and embedded into the payment transaction flow.

3.3   Fraud Management Solution Provider

Fraud management solutions should not be missed out in your payment strategy. Accepting credit card transactions in a card-not-present environment, such as e-commerce, call centres and mobile channels inherently attracts a certain amount of fraud. Fraud management systems help to reduce and keep fraud and the cost of fraud at an acceptable level.

Most solution providers emphasise four different strategies to reduce the impact of fraud to your business:

- Detecting possible fraud up-front – prevention is always better than after-the-fact resolution

- Reducing "false positives" rates – turning less legitimate customers away and processing good orders without interruption, resulting in better customer service

- Reducing fraud-related personnel and operating costs – eliminating manual review effort through automation

- Improving confidence in on-line distribution channels – fear of fraud should not be a roadblock to entering new markets

Before implementing fraud management solutions, you will want to determine the level of effort that you want to put into detecting and rejecting suspicious orders. If you want to completely eliminate fraud and the related charge-backs, you are likely to incur significant operational expense and probably reject a large amount of legitimate passengers' orders due to suspicions of fraud. On the other hand, not having any systems in place and simply accepting every booking received without some level of review is not recommendable either. Only you can determine the level of fraud that is acceptable within your organisation. It is likely to be a compromise between the targets of your sales teams and those of your fraud management teams.

3.3.1   Market Specialisation and Reach

Ensure that the supplier you choose has a good track record in the airline industry. The airline business model differs significantly from other on-line businesses, such as gambling, selling digital content or physical goods. It has its own distinct requirements. Knowledge of your markets (does the supplier have other customers there) can be a further advantage, as you may be able to share some of the fraud data with your fellow merchants in the same region.

3.3.2   Resource Management

Airlines can choose to manage their fraud operation internally, or outsource it partially or completely to the fraud solution provider.

Self managed:
In this scenario, you have your own risk management and order screening team within your organisation. The provider gives you access to the fraud management systems, where you can set the fraud screening rules and parameters, monitor the transaction screening results and review suspicious transactions yourself.

Managed service:
Providers can support your internal fraud management operation in two ways:
- **Performance Monitoring:** They can supply you with fraud experts that either for you or together with you monitor the effectiveness of the automated screening processes. They will refine the rules and parameters on a regular basis to improve the fraud detection rate and to reduce the decline rate of false positives.

They also set up new rules for changing business requirements (e.g. new routes). When the system detects new fraud patterns they help you develop and implement new fraud strategies to counter these attacks.

- **Manual Review:** Some of the providers can also support your manual screening process. They can provide you with resources to review the orders the system has flagged as risky or suspicious. You can either completely outsource this process or supplement your existing internal team with temporary or full-time fraud analysts.

- **Collection – Charge-back processing:** The processing of "Requests for Information" and defending charge-backs can equally be partially or fully outsourced to external service provider.

Automated fraud solutions generally help you to reduce the manual effort you may currently require to manage your sales. They should also allow you to scale your business without significantly increasing these resources.

3.3.3 Fraud Screening Tools

Fighting fraud is an ever evolving "game" with fraudsters inventing new ways of abusing the system and fraud solution providers developing new strategies to protect your business against them. Over the years they have developed an arsenal of fraud screening tools to support that effort. They either work on a transaction level, where each payment transaction is analysed individually and in real-time for indications of fraud, or on a customer level, where the personal details of the passenger are checked (such as address, telephone number). Bear in mind that none of these tools will be able to stop fraud. They can only work as detectors for potentially fraudulent transactions.

Here is a list of the most common fraud screening tools:

Fraud Screening Tool:	Description:	Comments:
Lost and stolen card databases	Verifies card numbers against proprietary or shared, domestic and international screening databases	It takes quite some time for a compromised card to appear on these lists
Address Verification Service (AVS)	Validates the numeric portion of the billing addresses provided by customers with the card-issuing bank's records. Works for some of the major card schemes but only in the US and the UK	Not reliable, as matching logic can result in high rejection of valid order
3D-Secure	On-line PIN verification service provided by major card schemes: Verified by Visa, MasterCard SecureCode, JCB J/Secure, Amex SafeKey	Provided by most PSPs as part of standard service. Does extend the check-out process by one step
Black lists Negative data sharing between merchants	Databases containing e-mail addresses, IP addresses, physical addresses, names, usernames, passwords and other data variables that have been related to previous fraud cases; helps to reduce future fraudulent attempts by the same fraudster or others associated with the fraudster	These can be the airline's own historical lists as well as lists shared across multiple merchants or industries (e.g. IATA Perseuss or Ethoca)

White lists	Databases containing e-mail addresses, IP addresses, physical addresses, names or usernames of good customers.	These lists protect regular customers from being rejected due to strict rule sets; reduces "false positive" rates
Rule engines	Screen transactions for patterns common with fraudulent activity, Create risk scores for each rule or parameter	Allow assessment of the overall risk associated with a transaction based on the accumulated risk score
Velocity checks	Record daily/weekly/monthly transaction attempts from the same credit card, user, e-mail or IP address within a certain period	Can detect fraudsters working with a block of card numbers to find one or more that will work on a purchase
Advanced address and phone number verification	Validates names, addresses, phone numbers and phone number structures against directory data; uses credit bureau data and public record information	Reliable, but limited to only a few countries where official registration databases are available
BIN Information	Identifies the issuing country of the payment card	Detects discrepancies between departure airport, billing address and card issuing country

IP Geo-localisation	A way to identify the customer's geographical location; allows comparison of geographical location of the IP address with the billing address/ origin of the flight	Needs to be combined with systems that can detect IP swapping and IP masking,
Google Maps and Google Street view	Help to verify delivery addresses	Used during the manual review process
Device identification (Device fingerprint)	Creates a unique profile ("digital fingerprint") of the device that is being used to make a booking; the profile is based on browser settings, memory size, processor speed etc.	Used to expose multiple payment attempts from the same device; Can be subverted by changing browser settings and using botnets
IP Packet inspection	Detects IP anonymisers and botnet fraud. Verifies IP packet signatures	Detects true purchasing device; supports device identification
Pattern recognition & Transaction link analysis Neural Technologies	Detects fraud by comparing transaction profiles to previously fraudulent transactions; incorporates statistical modelling of historical data to identify fraud trends and patterns	Can detect more complex fraud patterns than simple rules-based systems
Statistical Algorithms	Calculates the likelihood of a certain transaction to happen and derives a risk factor	Can be complex and expensive to manage

Table 9: List of Fraud Screening Tools

Tools that can respond within fractions of a second can be integrated into the payment flow prior or after to the financial transaction authorisation. They build up a risk score based on which you can decide to either approve, decline or refer a transaction to a manual review process. All of them can be used as a secondary evaluation tool to manually screen orders after they have initially been accepted or to re-screen some time later.

The providers differentiate themselves by the
- amount and variety of tools that they can support you with,
- speed and accuracy of the various tools (can they be used within the payment flow?),
- amount of input parameters they can utilise to drive these tools,
- relevance of their data sources to your markets,
- effectiveness of the fraud algorithms (especially for the transaction link analysis and neural technologies),
- level of integration between the tools and the flexibility that they give you to operate and manage them, and
- cost

3.3.4 Integration Options

Fraud solutions can either be installed in your premises or hosted at the provider's facilities. Either way, they need to be tightly integrated within the payment process of your distribution and back-office applications. Availability of the relevant data elements is key to fraud management tools. You may have to adapt your distribution software to provide the additional information that is required (e.g. IP address or device finger print would be data elements that are usually not readily available during a payment process).

If you are using a PSP, it is likely that they can provide you with pre-integrated fraud solutions. In those instances the additional technical integration work within your systems may be less.

If manual review is required you will either have to delay ticket issue until the evaluation has been completed (which may require changes to their existing sales process) or delay the review and cancel the ticket if found to be fraudulent. To streamline the manual order screening and chargeback handling process you may want to integrate your provider's tools with your ERP systems.

3.3.5   Implementation Support

A fraud management tool is only as good as the rules and parameters set up within it to support your specific business needs. The implementation of a new fraud system needs to go beyond pure technical integration. It should comprise the definition of the risk management strategy and set-up of the rules. Here are the basic steps of this process:

- Review current processes and historic data
- Define target fraud levels for different target markets
- Analyse fraud detectors and fraud indicators
- Configure systems (up to several hundred rules and parameter settings)
- Perform testing and training

The amount of customisation required depends on the implementation package you choose. The basic package is likely to give you a system with a generic airline fraud model. If you are prepared to pay a bit extra, the provider will help you to customise it to meet your specific needs. Including the analysis of historical data may incur additional costs.

3.3.6   Management Console

The management console is a vital component of your fraud system and can be another differentiator between the vendors. It usually consists of the following components: the rule console, a case management console and reporting tools.

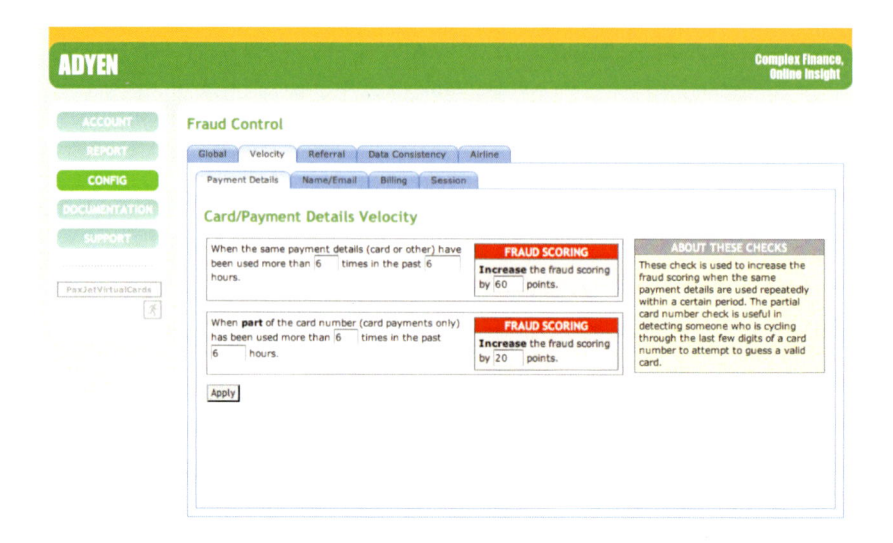

Fig 48: Example of a Risk Management Console (Courtesy of Adyen)

The Rule Console is used to create and modify rules on-demand, deploy transaction filters and to administrate black and white lists. Some tools will allow you to analyse the impact of a new rule, before you switch it live. The interfaces should be intuitive enough to enable your fraud teams to perform the changes without needing to get your IT department involved.

Case Management tools are used by the order screening team to review bookings that have been authorised but flagged as "potentially fraudulent" by the automated risk analysis tools. The manual review process will either confirm the legitimacy of the transaction (by performing additional risk checks, calling the passenger, checking with the bank etc.) or trigger cancellation of the booking. The tools should also where possible support the risk analysis agent in this decision process. Some systems will automatically filter and prioritise the backlog (e.g. by transaction value, time to departure or risky routes).

Both tools, the rule and the case management console, need to have good reporting facilities with standard and customisable reports and the ability to download the information for further analysis.

3.3.7 Additional Services

Some suppliers include regular performance monitoring and reviews in their service packages. This typically comprises a review of your fraud strategies, your fraud screening rules, a charge-back analysis and an update on the latest fraud and fraud prevention trends. Most vendors would be happy to provide you with internal or external staff training sessions.

3.3.8 Fees and Fee Structure

Fraud solution providers structure their fees in various ways. They may be part of a package with your PSP. Here is a breakdown of the most common fee elements:

Set-up and administration fees
- Implementation and system integration and fees (some provider charge for integration with your distribution system)
- Account set-up fees
- Rule set-up and customisation fees (depending on the level of customisation)
- Historic data analysis
- Monthly account maintenance fees
- Report generation (and statement) fees
- Manual intervention fees
- Operational fees (e.g. for changing a parameters)

Transaction and processing fees
These depend on the tool and services that you are subscribing to:
- Transaction fees (some tools may be included in the basic PSP transaction price, others will incur additional fees)
- Service fees – should you required a managed service

Suppliers regularly require minimum monthly payment guarantees, regardless of the actual business volume (which can be quite small at the beginning of a project) to ensure that their base costs are covered.

Ensure you know the reason for, and frequency of each fee element. Try to apply them to your expected volume and projected use of each payment method to get a comparable result.

3.4 Currency Exchange Service Provider

Currency conversions are needed in many parts of an airline's distribution and operational processes. Flights are always quoted in the currency of the departure airport/country[16]. The price for all foreign countries hence requires a conversion at some stage. Some carriers are giving their passengers the choice to pay in a variety of additional currencies (Multi Currency Pricing). Alternatively passengers are offered a currency conversion calculator to give them an indication of the final price in the currency that they are familiar with.

Carriers usually task their payment division to integrate the appropriate currency conversion services for the above scenarios. They can range from the delivery of a daily file with the current conversion rates between your base currency and all the other currencies that you trade in, access to real-time currency conversion service to Dynamic Currency Conversion (where the transaction currency is converted into the currency of the payment card during the payment process). Some supplierscan complement these solutions with treasury and cash management. Currency services can be made available through your PSP who will either supply the service himself or by various integrated specialists. Here are the services in detail:

3.4.1 Foreign Exchange Rate Look-up

Exchange rates can either be retrieved from static files or dynamically accessed through a web service call to the service provider. Static files updated daily or weekly are sometimes easier to integrate but strong

---

[16] With the exception of some soft currency countries where the flights are quoted in USD

currency fluctuations may require you to have a more dynamic view of the current exchange rate. In those circumstances a real time access through a web service would be preferable. Ensure to receive a service for your base currency or the currencies that you operate in. Alternatively you have to calculate the required exchange rate through a reference currency (convert the amount e.g. into USD first and then into the currency that you need).

3.4.2 Dynamic Currency Conversion

DCC services can be integrated into your web based distribution applications as well as into call centre application, POS devices at ticket desks, travel agents, on-board or even at kiosks.

For web based distribution applications the DCC functionality can either be embedded directly into the application (through a web service) or through a re-direct service where the conversion dialogue with the passenger happens on a web site of the DCC (or PSP) provider. The option you choose will largely depend on the payment integration option you have selected. If your PSP manages the payment pages within their systems then the PSP will need to process the DCC transaction as well. Call centre and ticket desk applications are more likely to require DCC through a web-service API. POS devices have the DCC functionality pre-loaded by the acquiring bank.

The service uses the first six digits of the card number to verify if a particular card is applicable for DCC. To increase the accuracy some providers use an additional three digits to detect the currency of payment cards that were issued in currencies other than the home currency of the bank.

Converting the fare into the passenger's currency of choice is only one part of the DCC service. Your accounting system is not necessarily aware of this conversion during the payment process and still expects the revenue to arrive in the quoted currency. To allow your back-office systems to reconcile the incoming payments with the sales report you will want the revenue converted back into the currency that you were originally quoting before it arrives in your accounts.

For this to happen, the DCC provider will need a daily summary file of all transactions that were actually completed using the proposed currency conversion. He then purchases the relevant currencies and trades them with your acquiring bank – so you receive them as expected. To mitigate the risk of high exchange rate fluctuations of soft currencies you may wish to receive your funds in a different currency to the one you quoted the passenger (you will have to adjust your accounting/revenue management systems though). Ensure that the DCC process does not delay the payout of your funds.

Global DCC providers will be able to support a wide range of supported currencies and countries. Ensure that they match with your main markets. (See page 82 for more information about DCC).

3.4.3 Fees, Fee Structure and Revenue Opportunity

Basic currency conversion services are usually provided for a fee. Here is a breakdown of the most common fee elements:

Set-up and administration fees
Currency conversion services usually attract:
- Implementation and system integration and fees (some provider charge for integration with your distribution application)
- Account set-up fees
- Monthly account maintenance fees
- Operational fees (e.g. for changing a parameters)

Transaction and processing fees
Currency conversion services are either offered for a
- Transaction fee or a
- Subscription fee

DCC – a revenue opportunity
There are usually no direct costs for the airline associated with this service. Instead the service provider (and in some cases the technical integrator) is expecting a share of the revenue that is generated from using DCC.

CASE STUDY

continuumcommerce
the payments people

About Etihad Airways

Etihad Airways is the national airline of the United Arab Emirates, and has - in just eight years - established itself as the leading premium airline brand in the world. Etihad was nominated as 'World's Leading Airline' at the World Travel Awards for the last three years in a row (2009-2011).

With a fleet of 63 aircraft operating more than 1000 flights per week, serving an international network of 84 passenger and cargo destinations in 52 countries Etihad has become the fastest growing airline in the history of commercial aviation.

About Continuum

Continuum is the acknowledged market leader in the provision of Dynamic Currency Conversion (DCC) and Multicurrency Pricing (MCP) solutions to the airline and travel industry with more airlines live in production than all other DCC and MCP providers combined.

Working with Continuum we can help you to make more money on a DCC transaction than you will make on the underlying ticket.

For a no-fee business case outlying how you too can generate margin from existing payment transactions, contact us at:

info@continuumcommerce.com

Telephone: +353 66 7100 700

www.continuumcommerce.com

90% of airlines are losing money on-payment transactions – the other 10% are working with Continuum:

The Challenge
As a service to its guests Etihad Airways wanted to offer the ability to pay in the currency of guests' credit or debit cards. As a business goal Etihad wanted to leverage the opportunity to generate a new ancillary revenue stream with minimal disruption to existing business practices.

The Solution
Etihad engaged Continuum's specialist DCC travel and payments team to deliver Etihad's joint objectives of guest service and a new revenue stream.

The Outcome
With the deployment of Continuum's DCC service Etihad is now re-claiming the foreign exchange margin otherwise taken by issuing banks. In addition its guests are guaranteed price certainty at the time of purchase in their local currency.

"We undertook a very comprehensive search to find a DCC provider that ticked all the boxes. Specifically the vendor had to have deep knowledge of GDSs and Reservation Systems; proven experience of innovation in the wider payments and acquiring space; have a dedicated DCC travel platform, development, and support team; a compliant risk managed DCC solution; and a commitment to genuine partnership. Our choice in selecting Continuum was an inspired one; the solution has worked extremely well for us and has generated very significant revenue for the airline; it has evolved and grown with us from launch and continues to offer our Etihad guests the ability to pay in the currency of their own card with the price guaranteed at the time and point of purchase."

Ricky Thirion, Vice President Treasury, Etihad Airways

Airline Reservation System

1 PAX fare priced in EUR

mobile

call centre

3 Real-time DCC offer request & response

web

6 PAX choice of Opt-in or Opt-out of DCC

IVR

9 DCC revenue reporting & MIS data extracts for reconciliation and business intelligence

PoS

FX exchange rate sources

2

DCC Provider

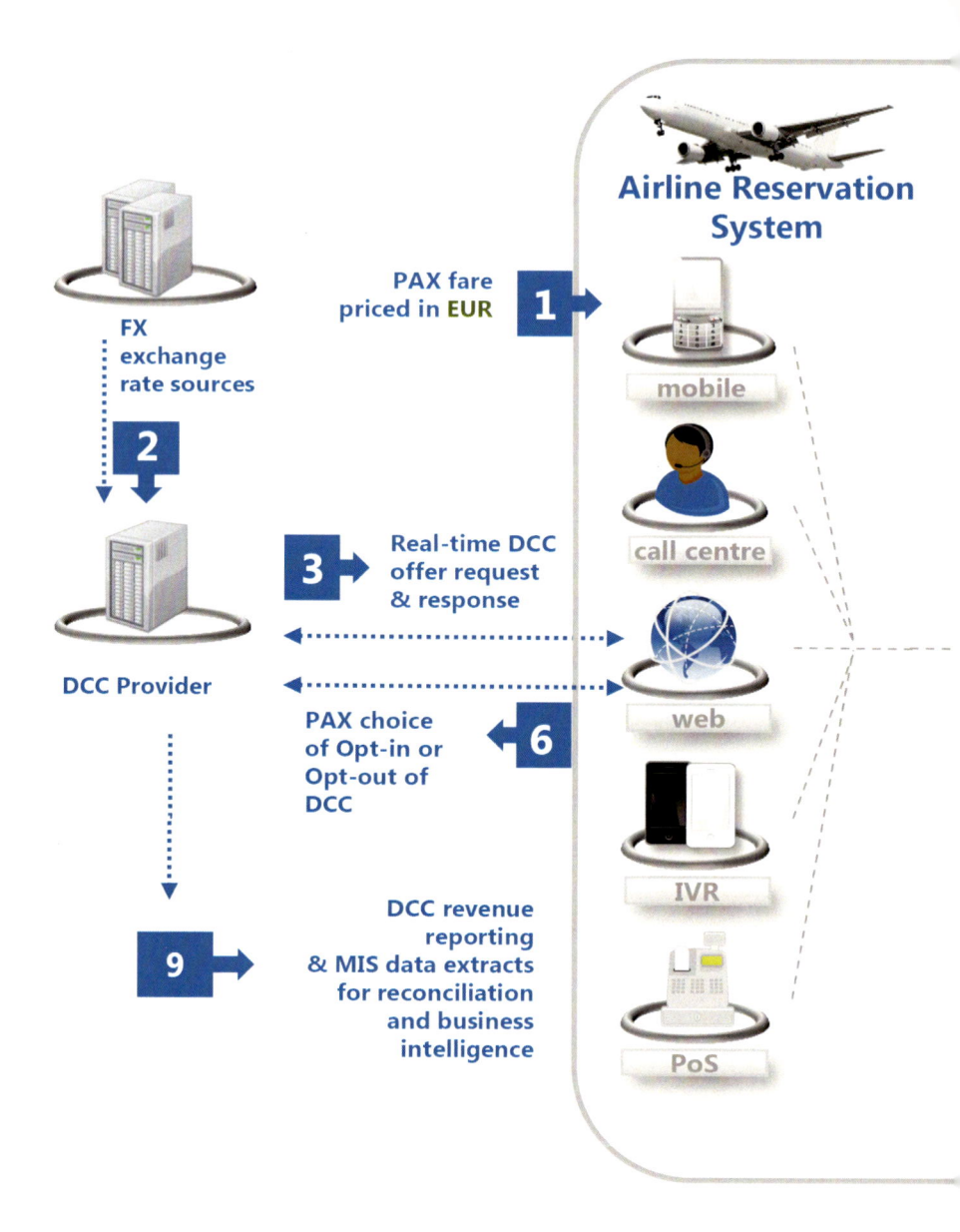

Example DCC flows showing a USD card holder purchasing an airline ticket priced in EUR.

Diagram is courtesy of Continuum Commerce Solutions
www.continuumcommerce.com

For further information, please contact info@continuumcommerce.com

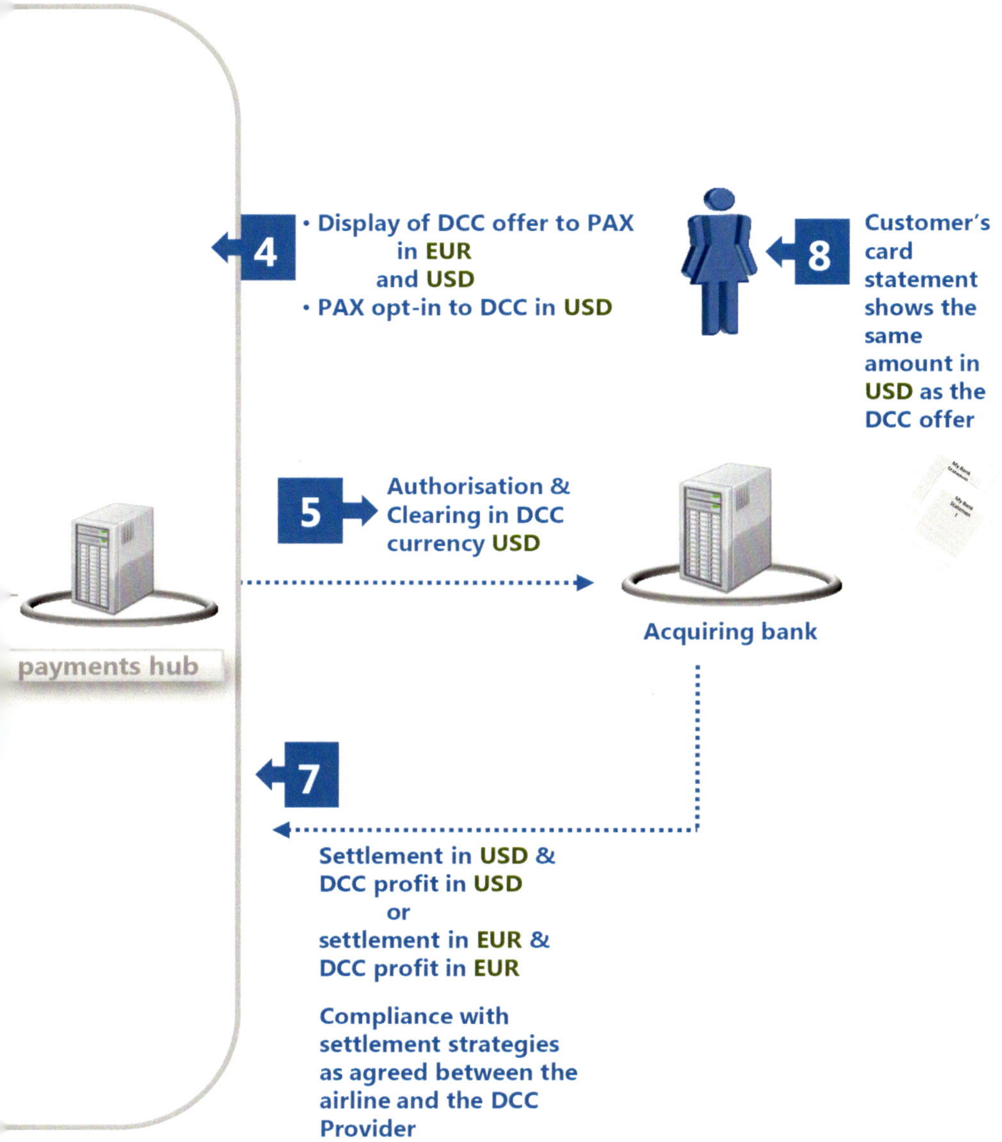

4
- Display of DCC offer to PAX in **EUR** and **USD**
- PAX opt-in to DCC in **USD**

8 Customer's card statement shows the same amount in **USD** as the DCC offer

5 Authorisation & Clearing in DCC currency **USD**

Acquiring bank

payments hub

7

Settlement in **USD** & DCC profit in **USD**
or
settlement in **EUR** & DCC profit in **EUR**

Compliance with settlement strategies as agreed between the airline and the DCC Provider

3.4.4 Support

The DCC solution should come along with management tools where you can set the exchange rate mark-up for the different currencies, view all data in relation to the transactions and download them for further analysis. Request that your staff get continuous training and support as part of the service package.

3.5 Secure Card Number Storage - Token Solutions

This service allows you to "store" cardholder data (credit card numbers) in your customer databases and ticketing systems as well as in your ERP systems, without having to worry about PCI compliance. It does this by replacing the original card number (PAN) with a reference number or token. To process a subsequent payment transaction with the same card (either for a new purchase, a refund or reversal) the application retrieves the token number (either from the customer's profile or a previous transaction). It forwards this number to the token service provider who converts it back into the real card number. Most PSPs have this functionality included in their service package, taking on the responsibility of storing the real card data securely for you.

When choosing a service like this, ensure that the token format matches the format that is required by your ticketing and accounting systems (especially in legacy environments). Most token solutions keep the format of the original credit card number (e.g. 16 digits). They replace first 12 digits with the token number and keep the last 4 digits the same. Some systems retain the first 6 and last 4 digits and replace the rest of the card number with numeric or alpha numeric characters. Customer service representatives and airline agents use the retained numbers to verify customers against their credit cards (e.g. during check-in) or to respond to payment queries.

Previous page:
Fig 49: DCC Transaction Flow (Courtesy of Continuum Commerce)

Some providers will actively manage the card data. They will delete lost and stolen cards and automatically update expiring cards with new "valid to" dates (where supported by the card schemes and issuing banks)

The services can be accessed through a web service API, either as part of the PSP interface or as separate service if you are using another third party provider. Ensure that the provider stores the card numbers in a PCI compliant data centre.

Costs are usually calculated on a "per token" basis (so ensure that the system checks if a card is already stored before issuing a new token ID). The price sometimes depends on the length of time that you need the information to be stored for.

3.6 Passenger Service Systems Providers and Payment Integrators

If your distribution software is developed internally within your organisation, then your development team will be tasked to implement the service providers' solutions mentioned above. If you are using a Passenger Service Systems (PSS) provider for your distribution applications, then they will have a vital role to play in the integration exercise and need to be engaged in the vendor selection process as early as possible.

Some of the PSS providers have their own payment platforms, some work with partners and subsidiaries to cover this aspect. Ask them about their payment infrastructure and the suppliers they already work with. Choosing and using a PSP or an acquiring bank which is already pre-integrated into the relevant distribution application can save your organisation not only cost but also cuts down implementation time to a great extent. They may also be able to give you access to lower rates with those vendors (through volume discounts across all their airlines).

If you want, or need to work with a supplier which is not yet integrated, ensure you cover the following points off as part of the selection and planning process:

- Discuss with your PSS provider the supplier and the payment methods you would like to use
- Provide your PSS with the relevant contact person/people and interface documentation
- Agree on implementation costs and time-lines
- Set-up an engagement model (e.g. do you want your PSS provider to talk directly to your PSP?)
- Agree on a testing strategy

If you are developing your distribution software in-house, you may still want to use the services of a PSS provider or payment integrators to cover the payment aspects. They can give you access to multiple pre-integrated PSPs, acquiring banks and ancillary payment services through a consolidated interface. This saves you from having to integrate and manage multiple third party entities yourself, freeing up internal resources. They also take over the certification process and ensure on-going compliance with industry standards.

Whenever you provide payment integrations internally, ensure they are set up centrally as a service (Service Oriented Architecture), available for any of the distribution applications that require a payment.

4 Selecting Payment Methods

Once you have selected your acquiring bank and your PSP and know who will link your distribution application(s) to them you may want to revisit the list of payment methods that those suppliers will be able to support. Decide on those that you want to implement first. Each additional one may increase your potential market reach and your sales conversion. At the same time however, they may increase the risk, cost and complexity of your payment processing. Below are some criteria to help you find an optimal balance.

4.1 Penetration and Reach

Probably one of the most important selection criteria for a payment option is its relative popularity in a particular market. What percentage of your target group (social demographic, region, age etc.) are using it and for what types of purchases (frequent, low value vs. infrequent, high value transactions)?

4.2 Potential Additional Sales

Combining this figure with the capacity that you are planning to sell in a particular market will give you an indication of how many additional sales you could be making – or losing, if you did not offer this particular payment method, due to the lack of alternatives for a particular target group. Adding a domestic debit card scheme in your home market is very likely to make more additional sales than adding one in a country that you fly to twice a day.

76% of consumers are looking for a choice of payment methods when booking online

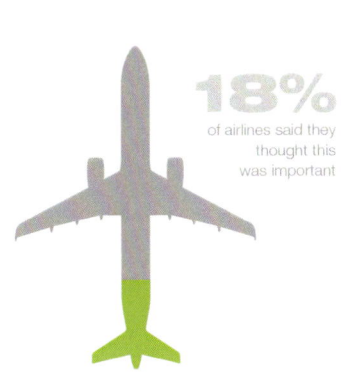

18% of airlines said they thought this was important

Fig 50: Why a better Payment Selection needs to be on every Airline's Radar (Perfect Passenger Payments - Courtesy of WorldPay)

4.3 Costs

Just because a lot of people use a particular form of payment in a specific country does not necessarily make it a viable option for your business. Some are specifically designed for digital on-line content, where merchant fees in excess of 15% are totally acceptable. This is an absolute no-go for an airline and its products. Other payment methods may have particularly low transaction fees but have no, or limited payment guarantees. Again, these may not be particularly suitable for the airline market. In some cases accepting a certain payment method may be the only way to get into a market, even if it is relatively costly. Ensure you understand the complete costs of an end-to-end transaction, including the costs of transferring the funds into your accounts, in the currency and country that you need them in.

4.4 Strategic Value

Look at possible strategic value in accepting a scheme. Especially the younger ones are often interested in cooperating with airlines to promote their card's usage and acceptance. These partnerships may provide additional benefits above and beyond pure additional sales volume.

They may offer you sharing of advertising and promotion costs, if you agree to add them to your payment portfolio. If your airline participates in a co-branded credit card program, ensure that scheme this is accepted as well.

4.5 Liability for Bad Transactions and Fraud

As airline sales tend to be high value transactions the security aspect is particularly relevant. Find out about the payment process and the risks that are associated with it – either through your payment suppliers or through other merchants in the market. What are the rules around fraudulent transactions? Who takes the risk? What are the charge-back and re-presentation processes? Take a market specific approach to the risk evaluation. The same payment method may attract different levels of fraud in different countries and regions. The costs of fraud need to be added to the total payment costs.

Fig 51: Selecting Payment Methods (Courtesy of DataCash)

4.6 Costs for Risk Mitigation, Fraud Prevention and Monitoring

The same applies to fraud prevention and risk mitigation costs. Some payment methods can be de-risked by introducing (or adjusting your) automated monitoring and fraud management tools as well as manual review processes. The acceptable level of risk and its mitigation costs are very much dependent on the airline's strategy. While some consider credit cards as too risky, others build their entire business model on direct sales through them. Yes, it may be risky and the risk mitigation systems costly, but it enables a direct distribution model that would not have been possible without them.

4.7 Regulatory Requirements

Domestic payment methods like local debit cards, cash payment options or direct debits are governed and regulated by the national financial authorities. The rules and regulations set out by these institutions are different in almost every country and can be quite challenging to understand, especially when it is not your home market. The requirement to have a domestic bank account or a domestic subsidiary, to pay special local taxes, to hold funds with the central bank or to join local financial organisations etc. can make a potentially interesting payment method too complex to deal with. Your PSP can usually help with some of the bureaucracy, but it may still not be worth the effort.

4.8 Transaction Processes and Integration Consideration

Some airlines will not accept payment methods that cannot be automatically reversed and refunded. These transaction types occur relatively frequently in an airline's day-to-day operations and generate a substantial back-office workload if they have to be queued for manual processing.

Payment methods that do not follow the standard authorisation – confirmation process flow require additional integration work within your distribution application. Some may even require manual processing steps (e.g. manually issuing tickets when cash payments arrive). Redirect payment methods need to be linked to external web sites – a process that is not suitable for every distribution application (e.g. mobile).
Verify the payment methods and their integration requirements with your PSS provider or with your own internal development team to identify and estimate any potential development costs.

4.9 Operational Impact

Every card scheme has its own payment cycle, reporting format and reporting frequency. Unless your PSP consolidates the information and the funds for you, your support and accounting teams will have to adapt their processes accordingly. If any additional contractual relationships are required the legal and purchasing teams have to get involved – adding administrative overhead to your payment set-up.
An airline's marketing, distribution and sales teams are likely to push for as many payment methods as possible. These have to be carefully weighed up against the additional risks and costs associated with them. Scoring them against these criteria will give you a good starting point for a prioritisation exercise.

5 Implementation

By this point you will have chosen your suppliers, signed the contracts, agreed on the initial set of payment methods and lined up your implementation resources. The next section of the book covers the project implementation phase: the adaptation of the distribution software comprising a business process analysis, design considerations and system configurations as well as the back-office processes that need to be adjusted.

5.1 Adaptation of Distribution Software

One of the major steps is the integration of these new external services into the distribution application. This can be a PSP, a payment method or a new value-added service. For your (internal or external) development team it will be important to receive a detailed service and service interface description. This will enable them to evaluate, estimate and plan the integration work. Development and testing times can be greatly reduced if the external provider has test environments, test cards and test scenarios available. Establishing direct contacts between your own and your supplier's technical teams will shorten the clarification process for ad-hoc implementation questions.

5.1.1 Business Process Considerations

There following areas and processes need to be carefully analysed as part of the evaluation, estimation and planning process:

- How are the various external service accessed?
- In what sequence are they used? (E.g. fraud checking before the authorisation request, then DCC?)
- Definition of the payment flow (at what stage does the authorisation happen, what triggers the capture message?)
- Are split payment transactions required? How are partial payments handled?
- What happens in error scenarios? E.g. automated reversals/ refunds processes when ticket issuing or partial payments fail.

- How are redirect payment methods displayed? Does the application/distribution channel support redirects? Take pop-up blocker and security certificates into consideration.
- How are "pending payments" handled? (e.g. bank transfers and cash payment options) What triggers the issuing of the ticket when the payment is confirmed? Automated PNR cancellations for uncompleted, "pending payment" transactions?
- Is asynchronous transaction processing required? These transactions require the application to actively query the external system for the outcome of an authorisation request, rather than waiting for an instant transaction response.
- At what stage are available payment methods displayed (at the beginning of the booking process or only at the payment page)?
- What parts of the process need to be encrypted between the website and the application host – e.g. Secure Socket Layer (SSL) certification or Extended Validation Secure Socket Layer (EV SSL)?

5.1.2 Design Considerations

The end user experience has a big influence on the success of a booking web-site. Optimising the page can significantly reduce drop-out rates, especially during the payment process. Here are some of the design parameters that need to be considered:

- Horizontal versus vertical display of payment methods
- Display order of payment methods (e.g. the one with the lowest cost first or the most relevant first)
- How many are displayed – which ones are displayed under what circumstances?
- Logos or only the names of the payment method
- Page flow for re-direct windows
- Inclusion of clear user instructions, help and FAQ sections

For re-direct payment gateways, the PSP hosting the payment page will provide design guidelines with similar questions.

5.1.3 System Configuration

Once the system is integrated, it needs to be configured to your specific business rules. This will be required in both domains, in your own distribution systems, as well as in your suppliers' systems. Here are some of the areas to be considered:

- Available payment methods (which ones will be enabled), based on payment method rules (channel type, origin, destination, currency, value, time to fly)
- Time to fly cut-off for last minute bookings (disable/don't show payment methods that are not applicable for these bookings)
- Merchant IDs and/or PSP reference numbers
- Available currencies
- Processor rules (what processers will be used for what channels/locations)
- Form of Payment ID (FOPID) per payment method (required for ticketing, needs to be defined and agreed with the fulfilment and accounting team)
- Surcharging amounts and logic
- Fraud screening and order processing rules
- DCC rules and currency exchange mark-up settings
- Automated reports (what reports, frequency, format, recipients).
- User and access management (who has access to what data ad who can do what?)

5.2 Internal Process Adaptation

Implementing or changing payment processes in the distribution application is not something that can be done in isolation without the involvement and support of many of the back-office support teams. Whether you introduce payments to a new channel, add a new service provider or include a new payment method, the following departments within your organisation need to be taken into consideration and their processes adapted if required:

5.2.1 Airline Staff

If the changes affect the interaction between the distribution software and your reservation, ticketing or any service agents, they may need to be re-trained or at least informed about these modifications. Manuals and user guides will need to be updated, work processes modified and their descriptions changed.

5.2.2 Customer Support

If the changes are customer-facing, the customer support team needs to be engaged. They may need to create new or update existing customer support processes and service guidelines (e.g. refund policies)

5.2.3 Product Management, Marketing and Sales

Any changes that affect the way the customer engages with the airline may also need to be run by the product and distribution teams. They may need to update marketing collateral and sales brochures. The addition of a new payment method may even qualify for its own promotion or press release.

5.2.4 Order Screening and Risk Management Teams

The risk management team needs to create new sets of rules for any changes in distribution channels, payment methods, destinations or currencies. They need to understand the new risk profile and adjust the automated systems as well as the manual order screening procedures accordingly. If you are implementing new risk management tools then engagement with these teams is likely to be a project in its own right.

5.2.5 Collection Team

Changes to the payment process (like adding 3D secure or adding additional data elements) may change the rules that are applicable to a certain payment transaction. The collection team needs to be aware of any modifications to be able to appropriately defend charge-back claims. New payment methods introduce new sets of rules all together. These need to be fully understood and the collection processes adjusted accordingly.

5.2.6 Card Operations

For each new payment method the card operations team needs suitable tools to process transaction corrections (i.e. manual payments, reversals, refunds). Workflows, manuals and sometimes the support software need to be adapted.

5.2.7 Reconciliation, Accounting & Treasury

The accounting team may have to set up new accounts and reports to support new forms of payment, channels, markets as well as new PSP and acquiring relationships. The reporting files from new suppliers and changes within the files for new payment methods need to be mirrored in the airline's reporting and reconciliation systems. The treasury department will want to have visibility of the different currency flows.

5.2.8 Purchasing/Procurement

The purchasing department may have supported you already during the supplier selection process. At project cut-over the on-going relationship management with the supplier is likely to be taken over by them.

5.2.9 Legal

Apart from the contract negotiations with the external suppliers the legal team may have to get involved when changes to the "Transport terms and conditions" are required for new ways of taking payments (e.g. new channels) or new payment methods.

5.2.10 IT Support Infrastructure

Once developed, the additional or modified software, hardware and interfaces to external partners need to be handed over to the support team to be embedded within their support infrastructure and procedures. This includes the set-up of operational monitoring pages (to ensure that applications are constantly available and the connectivity to the external partners maintained). Internal processes, manuals and escalation procedures need to be updated, the contact detail of external providers shared with the internal support teams. The service levels need to be measured and compared against the SLA.

6 End-to-End Testing

Integration testing will have happened against your test environment and the test systems of the various external service providers. The final test cases for your new systems, before promoting them into the live environment, should always be real, live transactions with live cards that are then refunded through the customer support process. This not only verifies the new set-up, but also builds confidence that the back-end processes, including the reconciliation and accounting systems are all set-up correctly. Here are some further tips for your final end to end testing:

6.1 Transaction Flow

Ensure that the testing covers the following scenarios:

- Full transaction life cycle with real cards: Perform at least one live transaction with every new payment method. Don't just reverse it before it is processed by the PSP. Allow the transaction to be captured and forwarded to the acquiring bank for processing and then refund it afterwards.

- Negative testing: Use incorrect card numbers, expiry dates and passwords to ensure that there are no default authorisation parameters left turned on. Try to trigger at least some of the fraud parameters to ensure they are working correctly (e.g. try multiple incorrect card numbers from the same PC, before you use a real card).

- Financial flow: Ensure the funds reach the right accounts. You may need to reach an agreement with your acquiring bank to expedite the settlement of the test transactions, if you have agreed to a delayed settlement for regular transactions.

- Customer support/card operations: If possible, initiate the transaction refund through the customer support/card operations group to ensure that all the support processes are in place. Process the transaction refund a day later to allow both parts of the financial flows (the credit and the reversal) to happen, ensuring they do not net themselves out in the same reporting period.

- Reporting and reconciliation: Performing a payment and a refund transaction will allow your accounting team to compare the reports against actual incoming and out-going funds.

6.2 Support Processes

Ensure your IT support team is confident about supporting the new systems and processes. You may want to create a test incident to confirm the right steps are being followed and the incident gets resolved within the agreed time frames.

7 Go-live

When all your tests have been successfully completed and you are confident that the support operation is running smoothly, you can schedule migration into the live environment. Once the system is live, you may want to repeat some of the end-to-end tests, or at least closely monitor transactions that are initiated by genuine customers with genuine cards. Ensure you monitor your fraud management systems closely. Fraudsters are quick to discover and exploit loopholes in newly setup systems.

8 Monitoring and Review

If you still own the project after go-live, you may want to monitor it against the KPIs, which you will have set out and agreed at the start of the project. These may include aspects such as:

- Are you achieving the savings that you have anticipated?
- Has it reduced the fraud to the expected levels?
- Are the payment methods that you have introduced being used at the expected levels?
- What are the conversion rates? What are the drop-out rates?
- Does the new system allow you to grow, without increasing the payment processing resources?
- Have the changes reduced the complexity of your operations?
- What are the issues that you have introduced with the new set-up?

282 Planning Your Payment Project

- Are there any technical or operational issues that would need to be resolved?
- Are the suppliers performing as promised?

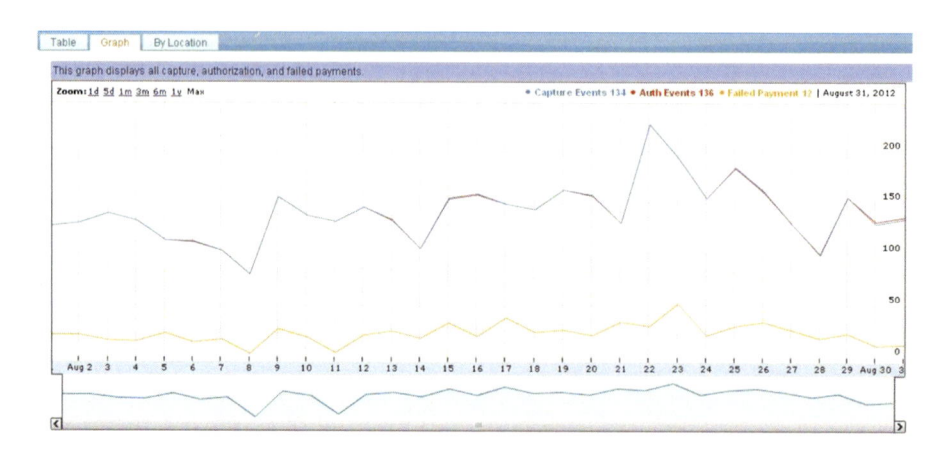

Fig 52: Transaction Monitoring Page (Courtesy of SITA/Malaysia Airlines)

9 Summary

Implementing a payment project is a complex undertaking that involves a large number of external and internal entities. As with every project, a structured approach makes a successful outcome much more likely. Having clear goals and a clear strategy is a good start and helps throughout the implementation phase of the project.

Depending on the scope of the project you are likely to have to integrate one or multiple payment processing partners from acquiring banks and PSPs to fraud solution and ancillary service providers. This chapter provided tools to evaluate them and to understand their service and pricing components.

Selecting and integrating payment methods is likely to be another key component of your payment strategy. This section highlighted the parameters that have to be taken into consideration and outlined criteria to pick out the payment methods most suitable for your organisation.

It concluded with the implementation phase, looking at the adaptation of the distribution software as well as the required modifications of the back-office processes. It lists a set of internal stakeholders that are likely to need to be engaged.

Final end-to-end tests will ensure that all the changes and the implementation have been successfully applied. On-going monitoring and measuring against the Key Performance Indicators outlined in the strategy will give you a good indication of the success of your project.

If they have all been met it is a good time to set new goals for further improving your operation – and to start all over again from the beginning of Part IV.

Part V. Supplier Directory

This section contains a listing of suppliers with a strong focus on the airline industry. It is divided into the following categories:

- Acquiring Banks   p 286
- Currency Conversion Solutions   p 292
- Consulting & Research   p 297
- Fraud Management Solutions   p 398
- Gift Cards / Prepaid Cards   p 302
- Payment Technology & Integrators   p 304
- Media and Publications   p 307
- On-board Retail Solutions   p 309
- Payment Conferences & Courses   p 310
- Global Payment Schemes   p 311
- Payment Service Providers   p 314
- POS & Hardware Providers   p 322
- Processors   p 324
- Recruitment Companies   p 324

Please visit our web-site for more up-to-date information:
www.payments.aero

First Data Merchant Solutions

www.firstdatams.com

Location	Basildon, UK
About	First Data Merchant Solutions is part of First Data Corporation, a global leader in the payments industry. First Data Merchant Solutions leverages the global scale of First Data to deliver complete and bespoke payment acceptance solutions to the airline sector. First Data has developed specialist expertise enabling it to better understand and serve the airline industry with a worldwide cross border payments system.
Regions	Global
Sample list of Airline customers	N/A - confidential
Contact	Brian Geary Director, Large Corporate Sales +44 (0)1268 296338

First Data.

Electronic Payments Without Borders

Global – Flexible – Market-leading

First Data Merchant Solutions, part of First Data Corporation, is a leading independent global expert in electronic payments. We go beyond the transaction to offer airlines a complete card payment acceptance solution including:

- → A worldwide cross border payments system to suit airline needs
- → An innovative and flexible approach to risk, tailored to the airline industry
- → Enhanced MI and payment reporting giving you a daily view of your business online
- → Pro-active chargeback management with the aim of reducing costs

For more information call us on

+44 (0)800 652 5808[†]

quoting reference AL
Monday to Friday, 8.30am to 5.30pm (GMT)

Alternatively, email us on
customer.enquiry@firstdatacorp.co.uk

> **Merchant Solutions**

Merchant Solutions are provided by FDR Limited, trading as First Data Merchant Solutions, as agents for Bank of Scotland plc, as the registering member under the relevant Card Schemes.
[†]Telephone calls may be recorded for security purposes and monitored under quality control process.

Acquiring Banks

Elavon Merchant Services

www.elavon.com

Location	Watford, UK
About	Elavon provides end-to-end payment processing services to airline merchants globally. Our payment products are supported by the most reliable network in the industry and include credit and debit card processing, dynamic currency conversion, multi-currency support, cross-border acquiring, fraud prevention and other consultancy services. We are: #1 airline processor by processed volume #2 hospitality processor
Regions	Global Platform for airline processing, with additional local capabilities in USA, Canada, Puerto Rico, Mexico, Brazil and Europe
Sample list of Airline customers	We would be delighted to put airlines in touch with our existing airline customers on a case by case basis.
Contact	Meridien House, 69-71 Clarendon Road, Watford, Herts, WD17 1DS, UK Jeremy Dyball International Corporate Sales Manager +44 (0) 7867 781 043 jeremy.dyball@elavon.com

SEB Euroline

www.seb.se

EUROLINE
REMOVING THE BOUNDARIES TO YOUR BUSINESS

Location	Stockholm, Sweden (HQ)
About	Euroline, a wholly-owned subsidiary of the SEB group, banks on superior knowledge to offer strategic card acquiring solutions to the airline industry. We work in close partnership with clients to develop solutions relevant to their businesses. Plus, we ensure simplified business processes are established through a sophisticated infrastructure complete with services like multi-currency platforms, management reports and risk management support.
Regions	Global
Sample list of Airline customers	Aeroflot, Air China, Air France, Air Transat, Copa, Ethiopian Airlines, Finnair, Kenya Airways, KLM, Scandinavian Airlines, TAM
Contact	Lars Göran Bergvind Head of International Sales larsgoran.bergvind@seb.se + 46 70 518 69 17 + 46 8 14 69 00

Worldpay

www.worldpay.com

Location	London, UK
About	No other business combines our scale, global reach and capability in acquiring merchants, capturing and processing payments. Our gateway, acquiring, alternative payments and risk management services are used by the world's leading international and domestic airlines. Working with our customers we have tailored our solution to suit the special needs of the airline sector.
Regions	Global
Sample list of Airline customers	81 airlines, including British Airways, Emirates, South African Airways
Contact	The Walbrook Building, 25 Walbrook, London EC4N 8AF Michael E Parkinson (VP Airline) Telephone: +44 (0)7776 147 384 Email: airlines@worldpay.com

WORLDPAY. A LANDMARK SOLUTION FOR GLOBAL PAYMENTS

WorldPay makes getting paid faster and easier. With a network of 200 banking connections, accepting more than 110 payment methods in 115 currencies, we bring your customers closer.

Email: sales@worldpay.com
Phone: +44 (0) 800 321 3932

WorldPay™

www.worldpay.com/globalsolutions

Currency Conversion Solutions

Continuum Commerce

www.continuumcommerce.com

Location	Tralee, Ireland
About	Continuum Commerce (formerly GCX - Global Currency Exchange) is a wholly owned independent Irish based international payments company providing a comprehensive suite of multi currency card payment optimization solutions which provide airlines worldwide with new revenue streams and reduce operating costs at minimal investment. Continuum is proud to be the first and the leading provider of DCC (Dynamic Currency Conversion) services to the airline industry worldwide. Continuum is the acknowledged market leader in the provision of Dynamic Currency Conversion (DCC) and Multicurrency Pricing (MCP) solutions to the airline and travel industry with more airlines live in production than all other DCC and MCP providers combined. Working with Continuum we can help you to make more money on a DCC transaction than you will make on the underlying ticket.
Regions	Europe, North America, Latin America, Middle-East, Asia Pacific, Africa
Sample list of Airline customers	Continuum works with a large number of low-cost and full-service airlines across both GDS and Reservation platforms. Continuum also provides its services to Online Travel Agents.
Contact	Head Office: InnovationWorks2, Kerry Technology Park, Tralee, Co. Kerry, Ireland. Tel: +353 (0)66 7100 700 Fax: +353 (0)66 7100 750 info@continuumcommerce.com Eoin McGillycuddy Vice President Sales +353 87 243 9344 emcgillycuddy@continuumcommerce.com

continuum
The Payments People

Proudly providing Dynamic Currency Conversion and Multicurrency Pricing Services to airlines since 2001

www.continuumcommerce.com

CEBU PACIFIC "Working with the Continuum team was quick and easy. Now, using the DCC application, our passengers can choose convenient payment in their own currency when they book online." Liezel Tagle Director of E-Commerce

Monarch "The project was implemented rapidly, with minimal overheads to Monarch staff, and with no issues. Since the launch, the system has proven extremely reliable; generating both increased revenue and increased customer service." Laurie Diffey Group Head of IT Development

ETIHAD AIRWAYS "In our DCC provider, we were looking for a deep knowledge of GDSs and Reservation Systems; innovation in the wider payments and acquiring space; a significant airline customer base; a dedicated DCC travel platform, development, and support team; a compliant risk managed DCC solution." Ricky Thirion Vice President Treasury

info@continuumcommerce.com | +353 66 7100 700 | www.continuumcommerce.com

TAKE OFF WITH A NEW REVENUE STREAM TODAY...

FEXCO DCC (Dynamic Currency Conversion) generates revenue from international VISA & MasterCard transactions

WWW.FEXCOMS.COM

...and join our 45,000 customers in 19 countries

FEXCO

- The world's leading DCC provider
- Inventor and originator of DCC in 1996
- Local representation in all markets
- 1650 staff worldwide
- Profitable since its inception in 1981

FEXCO Merchant Services
Part of the FEXCO Group

Currency Conversion Solutions

FEXCO

www.fexco.com

Location	HQ Ireland. 17 offices worldwide
About	Established in Ireland in 1981, FEXCO is today an internationally admired & respected organisation employing 1650 people across its operations in Europe, the Americas, Asia, the Pacific and the Middle East. Over its thirty year history, FEXCO has been a true pioneer and innovator in the broad arenas of Dynamic Currency Conversion, Global Payments, Foreign Exchange, Transaction Processing and Business Process Outsourcing.. For more information about FEXCO, visit www.fexco.com
Regions	Europe, Asia, Middle East and Americas
Sample list of Airline customers	45,000 merchant globally including Qantas, JetStar and Aer Lingus
Contact	Airline Sales airlinesales@fexco.com

Consulting & Research

Edgar, Dunn & Company	www.edgardunn.com
Baudon Nortier Consulting	www.baudon-nortier-consulting.com
Glenbrook	www.glenbrook.com
Prologis	www.prologis.aero
Skaiblu	www.skaiblu.com
Tiralis Global	www.tiralisglobal.com
TELCHAR	www.telchar.nl
Travel Technology Research	www.t2rl.com
Vidamore	www.vidamore.com
XXL Solutions	www.xxlsolutions.us

Fraud Management Solutions

| 41st Parameter | www.glenbrook.com |

| Accertify | www.accertify.com |

Alaric International

www.alaric.com

Location	Headquartered in London, UK with offices in Kuala Lumpur, Malaysia; Melbourne, Australia; and Dallas, Texas
About	Alaric is a supplier to the global payments industry of advanced technology products & services. Alaric offers solutions for SOA-based and conventional multi-channel payments integration, card authorization, switching and routing and payment fraud risk management. Used together, Alaric's Authentic and Fractals products constitute the highest performance payment switching and fraud prevention solution available today.
Regions	Europe, Middle East, Africa, Asia Pacific and the Americas
Sample list of Airline customers	SITA, UATP, collectively servicing 180 airlines worldwide
Contact	Peter Parke (Director) 5-13 Great Suffolk Street London SE1 0NS pparke@alaric.com Tel: +44 (0) 207 593 2200

| ethoca | www.ethoca.com |

| DataCash | see also page 315 | www.datacash.com |

alaric

Less fraud, less cost, more business

Fraud detection at the heart of payments

Fractals self learning fraud detection technology, only from Alaric

www.alaric.com

Cybersource Corporation

www.cybersource.com

Location	San Francisco, CA
About	CyberSource simplifies payment management for airline merchants. CyberSource provides a complete portfolio of payment services that simplify your daily payment operations: domestic and international payment processing, fraud management and payment security services. The company, a wholly owned subsidiary of Visa Inc., is headquartered in San Francisco with regional headquarters in Singapore; Tokyo, Miami/Sao Paulo, and Reading, U.K.. CyberSource operates in Europe under agreement with Visa Europe. For more information, please visit www.cybersource.com.
Regions	North America, Europe, Asia, Latin America, Middle East & Africa. CyberSource operates in Europe under agreement with Visa Europe.
Sample list of Airline customers	Air France, Ryanair, Air Canada, Korean Air, Aeromexico, Emirates, Air China, British Airways, LAN and many more.
Contact	Rennie Pelkie, Sr. Director of Sales P.O. Box 8999 San Francisco, CA 94128-8999 +1 650 432 7350 sales@cybersource.com

CyberSource®
the power of payment

THE
GLOBAL LEADER
IN
AIRLINE FRAUD MANAGEMENT

20 of the 100 largest airlines worldwide depend on CyberSource to manage fraud and help grow their business globally.

+ Reduce fraud with the world's largest fraud detection radar

+ Rely on our experienced team of experts to optimize your fraud management metrics and processes

SECURITY

FRAUD

GLOBAL PAYMENTS

See what's new at www.cybersource.com/travel

© 2012 CyberSource Corporation, a Visa company. All rights reserved.

ReD

www.redworldwide.com

Location	Headquarters in Surrey, UK
About	ReD is a world leader in fraud prevention and payment services. Independent of any card scheme, ReD is present at every stage of the payments value chain, supporting merchants and PSPs, issuers and acquirers, processors and switch networks in the fight against fraud. ReD employs some the world's leading risk and fraud analysts and gathers data from more than 190 countries.
Regions	Worldwide
Sample list of Airline customers	Air China, Singapore Airlines, Air Pacific, Amadeus, Saudi Airlines, Air Caraibes, Royal Jordanian, Air Meridiana, KLM
Contact	Manish Patel, Regional President ReD House, Cemetery Pales, Brookwood, Surrey, GU24 0BL, UK +44 (0) 1483 728 700 info@redworldwide.com

Gift Cards / Prepaid Cards

AccessPrepaid Worldwide	www.accessprepaidworldwide.com
Citi	www.citigroup.com
Contis Group	www.contisgroup.com
PayLife Bank	www.paylife.at

Take control of the board.
For a strategic advantage in the fight against payments fraud, call Manish Patel on +44 (0) 1483 728700 or email info@redworldwide.com.
www.redworldwide.com
RED
MAKING PAYMENTS SIMPLE AND SECURE.

Payment Technology & Integrators

AirPlus

www.airplus.com

Alaric International

www.alaric.com

Location	Headquartered in London, UK with offices in Kuala Lumpur, Malaysia; Melbourne, Australia; and Dallas, Texas
About	Alaric is a supplier to the global payments industry of advanced technology products & services. Alaric offers solutions for SOA-based and conventional multi-channel payments integration, card authorization, switching and routing and payment fraud risk management. Used together, Alaric's Authentic and Fractals products constitute the highest performance payment switching and fraud prevention solution available today.
Regions	Europe, Middle East, Africa, Asia Pacific and the Americas
Sample list of Airline customers	SITA, UATP, collectively servicing 180 airlines worldwide
Contact	Peter Parke (Director) 5-13 Great Suffolk Street London SE1 0NS pparke@alaric.com Tel: +44 (0) 207 593 2200

Airlines Reporting Corporation (ARC)

www.arccorp.com

Payment TECHNOLOGY & Integrators

Amadeus IT Group

http://www.amadeus.com/airlineit/ solutions/ sol_2stand_4payment.html

Location	Amadeus has his central sites in Madrid (corporate headquarters), Nice (development) and Erding (Operations-data processing centre) and regional offices in Miami, Chicago Buenos Aires, Sao Paolo, Frankfurt Bangkok, Singapore and Dubai. At market level, Amadeus maintains customer operations through 70 local Amadeus Commercial Organizations (ACO) covering 193 countries.
About	Amadeus is the leading technology partner and transaction processor for the global tourism and travel industry. Amadeus Travel Payments is a dedicated team that will help all travel merchants streamline their payment acceptance and front/mid/ back office processes, across all channels. Amadeus Travel Payments offers an end to end, PCI compliant payment portfolio, fully integrated into the selling and ticketing flows and processes. Through travel and payments expertise travel merchants will reduce operational complexity whilst increasing revenues by establishing the right payment strategy.
Regions	Worldwide
Sample list of customers	Airlines, Airline IT customers and Distribution customers, rails, travel agencies, around 300 payment customers.
Contact	Celia Pereiro Head of Travel Payments BU Amadeus IT Group SA T: +34 911 771 034 celia.pereiro@amadeus.com Group email: travel.payments@amadeus.com

eNett	www.enett.com

Hahn Air	www.hahnair.com

Amadeus Payment Platform

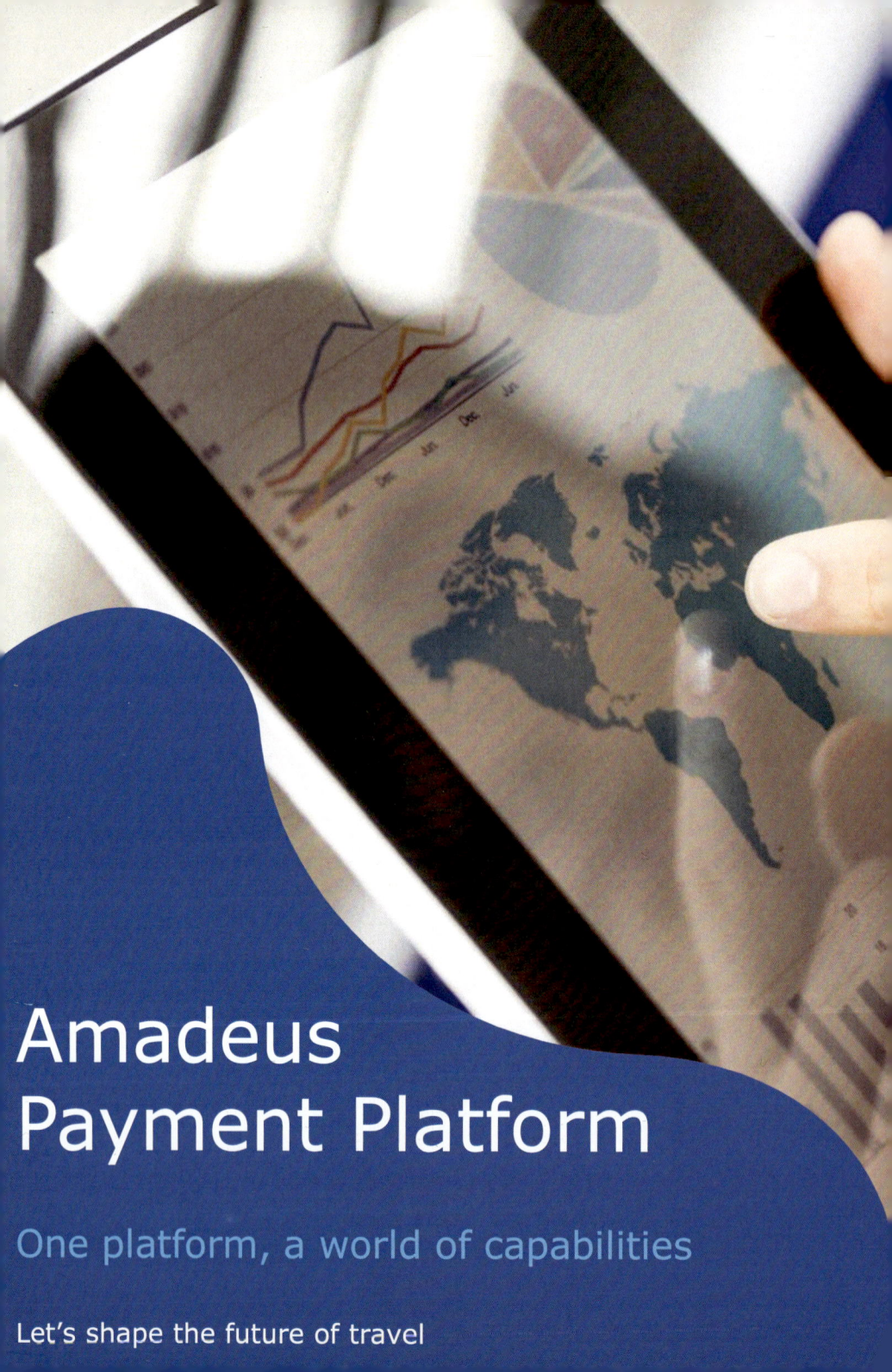

One platform, a world of capabilities

Let's shape the future of travel

Our solutions

- **Security Checks**
- **Acceptance**
- **Clearing and settlement**
- **Sales and bank reconciliation**

aMaDEUS

Payment Technology & Integrators

IATA	www.iata.org

Navitaire	www.navitaire.com

Sabre Holdings	www.sabre.com

SITA

www.sita.aero

Create success. Together

Location	HQ: London, Atlanta, Geneva
About	SITA is the world's leading specialist in air transport communications and IT solutions. SITA delivers and manages business solutions for airline, airport, GDS, government and other customers over the world's most extensive network, which forms the communications backbone of the global air transport industry. SITA has a 25 year history in travel payments including credit card authorization services that manage more than 24 million transactions per year from GDSs and airline reservations systems to all major credit card schemes.
Regions	Worldwide
Sample list of Airline customers	SITA provides services for over 550 air transport industry members and 3,200 customers in over 200 countries and territories.
Contact	SITA 1 London Gate 252-254 Blyth Road Hayes, Middlesex UB3 1BW United Kingdom

Travelport	www.travelport.com

Media and Publications

Flightglobal — www.flightglobal.com

Glenbrook — www.glenbrook.com

Low Cost & Regional Airline Business Magazine and Airline Payments

www.lowcostandregional.com

Location	London, UK
About	Low Cost & Regional Airline Business is a features-based quarterly magazine that delivers in-depth, strategic industry analysis. Covering a range of topics, from aircraft and ancillary revenues, to business practices and the latest technology, as well as regional focuses, we provide analysis that helps executives expand their airlines in this competitive sector. Staying at the forefront of the challenges facing the industry, we have launched the Airline Payments supplement, offering dedicated coverage of this business-critical subject
Regions	Worldwide
Sample list of Airline customers	
Contact	Air Transport Publications, 16 Hampden Gurney St, London W1H 5AL +44 207 724 3456 Media Sales Director: Kate Sloan kate@airtransportpubs.com

Payment News — www.paymentsnews.com

The Paypers — www.thepaypers.com

airline PAYMENTS

LOW COST & REGIONAL airline business

For high-flyers in the low-cost and regional industry

Low Cost & Regional Airline Business is the first quarterly magazine offering strategic analysis of these markets. Our editorial helps senior airline executives expand their companies in a competitive environment.

Airline Payments

Payment solutions are at the core of an airline's operations. In order to give regular coverage on this key issue, we have launched a dedicated supplement – *Airline Payments*.
To join our mailing list, email circulation@airtransportpubs.com

www.lowcostandregional.com

On-board Retail Solutions

ASiQ Ltd	www.asiq.com
Dutyfly Solutios	www.dutyflysolutions.vpweb.fr
Gate Retail Onboard	www.gateretailonboard.com
GuestLogix	www.guestlogix.com
Novo Ivc.	www.novoivc.com
Retail inMotion	www.retailinmotion.com
MI Airline	www.miairline.com

Airline Information

www.airlineinformation.org

Location	UK/US
About	The best place to network and understand the key issues for airline and travel payments is at an Airline Information event. These take place regularly throughout the world. Full details at www.AirlineInformation.org/events
Regions	Worldwide
Sample list of Airline customers	Delegates from all major airlines, hotels and travel companies attend our events. In addition, major suppliers, press and publications all attend and subscribe to our events.
Contact	Michael Smith – conference speaking, consultancy msmith@aiglobal.org Chris Staab – conference sponsorship and organisation cstaab@aiglobal.org

Airline Distribution	www.uatp.com
Airline Payments 101	www.bardowgroup.com
Airline Travel Payments Summit	www.airlineinformation.org

Payment Conferences and Courses

Innovation in Airline Distribution	www.flightglobalevents.com
Glenbrook Payment Boot Camps	www.glenbrook.com
IATA	www.iata.org

Global Payment Schemes

American Express		www.americanexpress.com
China Union Pay		www.en.unionpay.com
DinersClub		www.dinersclubus.com
Discover		www.discover.com
Japan Credit Bureau		www.jcbcard.com
MasterCard	see also DataCash, page 315	www.mastercard.com
PayPal		www.paypal.com
Visa	see also CyberSource, page 300	www.visa.com

UATP

www.uatp.com

Location	Washington DC, Geneva, Singapore
About	UATP is a global travel payment solution issued by the world's airlines and accepted by thousands of merchants for air, rail, hotel and travel agency payments. It is a low-cost payment option that airlines offer to corporate customers so that both can reduce the high cost of credit card use and travel spend. Other card brands have high charges for merchant service fees, currency conversion, surcharges and government and policy induced fees – UATP does not. UATP embraces its goal of lowering distribution costs for the airline and travel industry in all aspects. The solution provides low-cost processing while offering programs, options and benefits to corporations loyal to UATP and its member airlines. UATP's network of airline, rail and hotel connectivity provides travel and procurement managers with the data they need to effectively manage and control their travel programs. UATP tracks itinerary level data including carrier, destination and full itinerary details: Level III Data. This makes UATP the leader in the managed travel industry, offering better cost control and easy reconciliation to travel and procurement managers.
Regions	Worldwide
Sample list of Airline customers	Issuers include: Delta Air Lines, United, JAL, Air New Zealand, American Airlines, Etihad, Hahn Air, China Eastern, Qatar, Lufthansa Airplus
Contact	Wendy L. Ward Vice President, Marketing & Communications UATP 1301 Pennsylvania Ave., NW Washington, DC 20004 +1 202 626 4000

Solving travel payment needs

UATP

With the resurgence of corporate travel and the growing need for accurate and detailed information, UATP's corporate program and data tools are fulfilling the need for sophisticated travel management systems. For airline, rail and hotel data, UATP is the one provider that stands out, supplying Level III Data for all air and rail travel; and folio-level data for hotel stays

UATP is a global travel payment solution issued by the world's airlines and accepted by thousands of merchants for air, rail, hotel and travel agency payments. It is a low-cost payment option that airlines offer to corporate customers so that both can reduce the high cost of credit card use and travel spend. Other card brands have high charges for merchant service fees, currency conversion, surcharges and government and policy induced fees – UATP does not. UATP embraces its goal of lowering distribution costs for the airline and travel industry in all aspects. The solution provides low-cost processing while offering programs, options and benefits to corporations loyal to UATP and its member airlines.

DATASTREAM
UATP's proprietary billing system which enables airline Issuers to provide its own state-of-the-art invoicing

DATAMINE
Secure online tool that allows Issuers and its Corporate Subscribers to view all transaction level details

DATAVIEW
UATP's dashboard providing summary level data for instant program review

UATP is accepted by airlines, agencies, rail, cruise lines and hotels around the world

UATP's network of airline, rail and hotel connectivity provides travel and procurement managers with the data they need to effectively manage and control their travel programs. UATP tracks itinerary level data including carrier, destination and full itinerary details: Level III Data. This makes UATP the leader in the managed travel industry, offering better cost control and easy reconciliation to travel and procurement managers. For travel program management, this detailed data is imperative, serving as the window to the program and identifying travel patterns that management can utilise for better negotiations with suppliers, and to ensure compliance with company travel policy. The data enables the corporation and the Issuer to be informed in their negotiations and to find a win-win situation for both.

UATP.COM **marketing@uatp.com**

Payment Service Provider

Acculynk	www.acculynk.com

Adyen BV

www.adyen.com

Location	Amsterdam (HQ), Boston, Sao Paulo, Singapore
About	Adyen is the leading provider of global Internet payment and e-commerce solutions for mid, large and enterprise e-commerce merchants. Adyen's revolutionary Internet Payment Solution enables merchant to significantly increase online conversion by optimizing the online payment process. This "one-stop" solution can be implemented within days and highly optimises all commercial and operational processes.
Regions	Global
Sample list of Airline customers	KLM, Transavia, LAN, Sky Airline, Ukraine International Airlines
Contact	Adyen BV PO Box 10095 1001 EB Amsterdam The Netherlands Sander Maertens (VP International Sales – Travel) +31 20 2401 240

Alipay	global.alipay.com

Caledon Card Services	www.caledoncard.com

Cardinal Commerce	www.cardinalcommerce.com

Datacash	www.datacash.com
Digital River	www.digitalriver.com
eMerchantPay	www.emerchantpay.com
First Atlantic Commmerce	www.firstatlanticcommerce.com
GlobalCollect	www.globalcollect.com
MintWireless	www.mintwireless.com

Ogone Payment Pervices

www.ogone.com

Location	Brussels, Belgium (HQ), Other offices in: United Kingdom, The Netherlands, France, Switzerland, Germany, Austria and India
About	Ogone is one of the leading European PSP's with more than 33.000 clients across 45 countries. Ogone delivers manual to fully integrated solutions for managing electronic payments in several domains including e-commerce, ticketing, call centers, airlines and travel in both B2C or B2B environments. The service offering of Ogone is probably one of the most comprehensive available today.
Regions	Global
Sample list of Airline customers	Brussels Airlines, EgyptAir, Royal Air Maroc, Olympic Air, Martinair, Kenya Airways, TAM Airlines, Jetairfly.com, Grupo SATA, Malev
Contact	Ogone Pyment Services Woluwedal 102 B-1200 Brussels, Belgium +32 2 286 96 11 sales@ogone.com Patrick van der Knoop (Key Account Manager) pvk@ogone.com

Make Airline Payments Safe and Efficient

SEAMLESS & SECURE PAYMENT SOLUTIONS

From reservation and reconciliation to securing payments all the way, Ogone Airline Solutions help you streamline and optimise all your payment operations. With flexible integration into your system and advanced management services, processing payments has never been so safe and efficient.

Ogone Airline Solutions are built on our state-of-the art SSL payment platform, which optimises your existing online and call centre reservation systems.

With years of experience in the airline sector, our dedicated teams develop custom solutions that drive payments for numerous airlines all over the world, including Brussels Airlines, Kenya Airways, Martinair and Olympic Air.

Find out how Ogone can drive your business.
Contact us at **sales@ogone.com** or give us a call: +32 (0)2 286 96 11. www.ogone.com

With Ogone you can accept the above payment methods and many more.

Payment processed by **ogone**

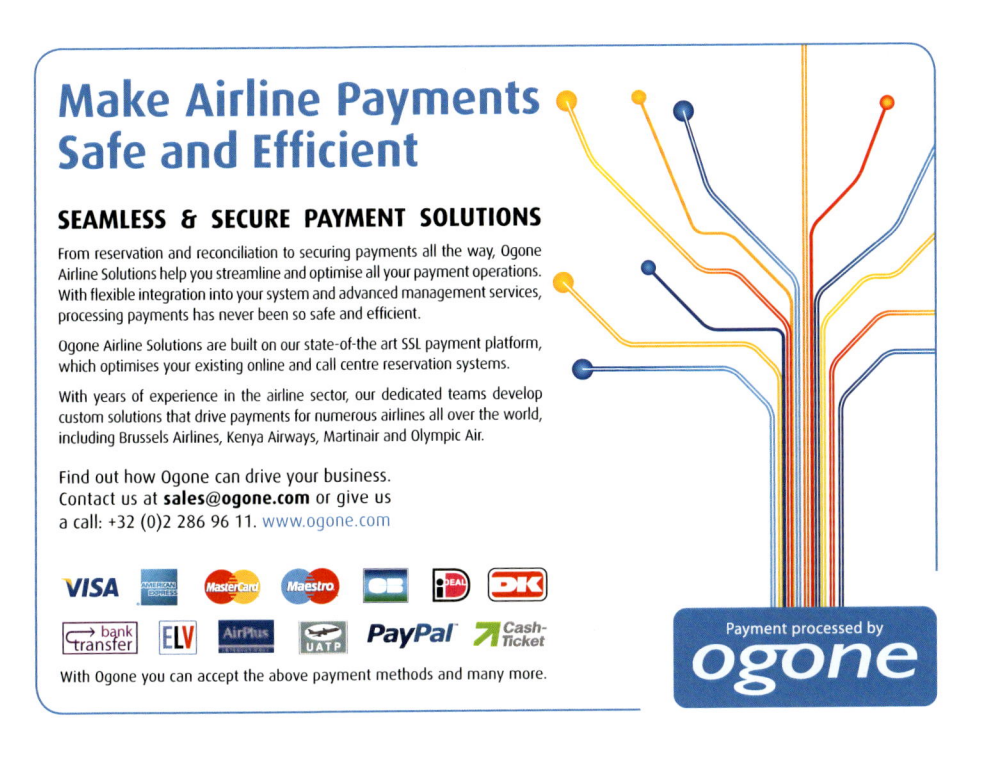

Payment Service Provider

Optimal Payments	www.optimalpayments.com
Realex Payments	www.realexpayments.com
SafetyPay	www.safetyPay.com
UseMyService	www.usemyservices.com

Your online payment

We understand the e-commerce needs of airlines like yours...
That's why, at Paygate, we provide innovative, simple and secure payment solutions that are tailored specifically to the airline industry's online requirements.

Airline Payments Expertise

When you choose your onboard catering or fueling service, you look for a partner that understands the needs and challenges of the airline industry. Naturally. So when you select an online payments solutions partner, we'd recommend you do the same.

- Reliable infrastructure with an excellent uptime record for 24/7/365 bookings.
- Multiple payment methods (subject to availability).
- User friendly airline booking engine integrations with a full testing environment.
- Fraud prevention and risk analysis services with a focus on the airline industry.
- Comprehensive tools to easily reconcile and manage your booking payments.
- Free technical support from our highly trained airline payments support team.

challenges solved.

An established partner like PayGate: a leading payment services provider specialising in the airline industry and with over 10 years of relevant experience and a reputation for service excellence.

PAYGATE

www.paygateinternational.com

Payment Service Provider

PayGate International

www.paygateinternational.com

Location	Cape Town, South Africa
About	PayGate International was founded way back in 1996 when the earth was cooling. Airlines are our VIP's. ur job is to convert your enquiries to tieckets sold - reliably, securely, cost-effectively. Our global links and online payment solutions give you the competitive edge our customers love us. The feeling is mutual.
Regions	Africa, UK, Europe, Asia, Australia, Middle East
Sample list of Airline customers	Air Namibia, TAAG, LAM, Iberia, American Airlines, Rwanda Air, Air Kenya, Air Botswana
Contact	Peter Harvey (Director Airlines) info@paygateinternational.com www,paygateinternational.com +27 21 712 7842

Notes

Payment Service Provider

Wirecard AG

www.wirecard.com

Location	Headquarters: Munich, Germany
About	Wirecard AG is one of the leading international providers of electronic payment and risk management solutions. The Wirecard Group supports various companies from diverse industry segments in their efforts to automate their payment processes and minimize cases of default. Wirecard Bank AG is Principal Member of Visa, MasterCard, licensed acquirer for Discover/Diners, China UnionPay, JCB and operates as a credit card acquirer.
Regions	Europe, Middle East, Asia Pacific, North America
Sample list of Airline customers	airberlin, Jet Airways, Malaysia Airlines, S7 Airlines, Turkish Airlines
Contact	Wirecard AG Einsteinring 35 D-85609 Aschheim / Munich Jörg Möller (Executive Vice President Travel & Transport) airline@wirecard.com (+49 89 4424 1680)

POS & Hardware Provider

| Motorola Enterprise Mobility Solutions | www.motorolasolutions.com |

| pks services | www.pksservices.co.uk |

wirecard

virtual terminal
fraud detection BSP solutions
banking service
IATA strategic partner
card acceptance
terminals virtual terminal
payment
Principal Member of VISA,
MasterCard and JCB
risk management
IATA strategic partner fraud detection
BSP solutions
payment terminals
risk management
virtual terminal
banking service

Payment, risk management, banking services:

Solutions from a single source

Wirecard AG provides complete payment and risk management systems and numerous offers that are specific to the airline sector: for example BSP-special solutions for airlines, the integration of payment solutions in booking systems and innovative risk management systems. Speak to our experts – we can simplify your business and make you more efficient.

THE WIRECARD BENEFITS:

- Integration with Amadeus, Sabre, Raddix, SITA, EB2, 2E system, Ypsilon.net

- Covers all sales channels: E-Commerce, BSP, POS, Mobile, Call Center

- Wirecard AG is an IATA Strategic Partner

You need more information about our airline-portfolio? Simply send an e-mail to:

airline@wirecard.com

Processors

Accelya	www.accelya.com

Transaction Network Services	www.tnsi.com

Recruitment Companies

Headcount

www.head-count.com

Location	London, UK
About	Headcount is a well established and leading provider of recruitment services to the: Card Payments, ePayments & mPayments industry sectors Worldwide. Headquartered in the City/London headcount's client base includes leading: Card Issuers (Commercial Card/Corporate, Card/Credit/Debit/Prepaid/Contactless), Acquirers, Payment Processors, PSP's, Associations/Schemes and Vendors of software/hardware/consultancy services positioned around a transaction from beginning to end.
Regions	UK, Europe, Asia, US
Sample list of Airline customers	WorldPay, PayPal, Datacash Cybersource, Moneybookers, Sagepay, Global Payments, Western Union, MasterCard Worldwide, Visa Europe/Inc.
Contact	Neill Butcher Managing Director Headcount Longcroft House 2/8 Victoria Avenue London EC2M 4NS Switchboard: +44(0)20 3206 1260 DDI: +44(0)20 3206 1262 Fax: +44(0)20 32061101 Mobile: +44 (0)7812 333160 neill.butcher@head-count.com

Recruitment Companies

Card and Payment Jobs	www.cardandpaymentjobs.com
IDPP	www.idpp.com

Notes

Notes

Index

3D Secure, 44
    call centre and, 162
    mobile payments, 174
    shift of liability, 93
Acquirer, 51
    commercial proposal, 237
    compliance, 232
    PSPs and, 53
    risks and responsabilities, 89
    selection process, 228
    technical Integration, 238
Acquiring bank. *See* Acquirer
Air Travel Card. *See* Universal Air Travel Plan
Airline Clearing House (ACH), 110, 112
Airline data, 62
Airline Reporting Corporation (ARC), 114
Airport Handling Agents (AHA), 110
Airport Ticket Office (ATO), 158

Alternative payment methods, 128
    PSPs and, 244
Amadeus, 120
American Express (Amex), 32, 43, 45, 50, 63, 98, 144, 200
    Descriptive Billing Information (DBI), 63
    Expresspay, 46
Ancillary services
    taking payments for, 202
Arbitration process, 70
ATO. *See* Airport Ticket Office
Authorisation, 56
    airlines and, 142
    code, 59
    floor limits, 58
    history of, 41
    pre-authorisation, 56
    referral, 59
    request, 56, 145
    response, 59

Authorisation Service Provider, 115, 145
Automated Teller Machine (ATM)
history of, 34
Bank transfers, 130
real-time, 129
BankAmericard, 32
Black lists/ white lists, 255
Blended rate, 77
Buyer, 36
Call Centre, 162
Cancellation, 64
Capture process, 65
Card association. *See* Payment scheme
Card operations, 214
Card scheme
fees, 76
Card Security Code (CSC), 42
card-not-present and, 43
travel agency and, 154
Cardholder, 48
billing, 67
fees, 74
risks and responsabilities, 91
Card-not-present, 154
Cash, 125
Cash payments, 130
Charge cards, 30
Charge-back, 68
Card Security Codes and, 43
collection process, 215
second, 70
Check-in desk, 161
Cheque cards, 33
Cheques, 125

Chip and PIN, 43
Chip Authentication Program (CAP), 46
CID. *See* Card Security Code (SCS)
City Ticket Office (CTO), 158
Clearing, 65
Clearing house, 54
Co-branded cards, 128
Collection, 215
Common Use Self Service (CUSS), 179, 184
Compensation payments, 197
prepaid cards and, 199
Contactless payments, 46
EMV and, 46
Conversion, 226
Credit cards, 32
adoption of, 34
call centres and, 162
IATA approved, 125
validation before check-in, 217
Credit transaction, 64
CRQ message, 145
CTO. *See* City Ticket Office
CTR message, 148
Currency exchange services, 262
DCC. *See* Dynamic Currency Conversion
fees, 264
rates look-up, 262
CVC2. *See* Card Security Code (SCS)
CVV1. *See* Card Security Code (CSC)

CVV2. *See* Card Security Code (SCS)
CVV3, 47
Data entry mode, 75
DCS. *See* Departure Control System
Debit cards, 128
 and PIN, 34
 history of, 33
Delivery of goods, 61
Departure Control Systems (DCS), 161
Descriptive Billing Information (DBI), 144
Device fingerprint, 257
Diners Club, 31, 32, 42, 184
Direct debit, 130
Direct distribution
 travel agency, 155
Domestic payment instruments
 IATA approved, 125
Dual-merchant payments, 72
Durbin amendment, 103
Dynamic Currency Conversion (DCC), 82
 benefits, 83
 compliance, 86
 provider selection, 263
Dynamic Data Authentication (DDA), 47
Dynamic Password Authentication (DPA), 46
E-commerce, 166
 3D Secure and, 172
 PCI-DSS and, 169
Electronic Miscellaneous Document (EMD), 123
Electronic wallets, 131
EMV
 history, 98
 shift of liability, 93
e-Nett, 122
Eurocard, 34
Europay, 34, 44, 98
European Payment Council (EPC), 104
 magnetic stripe and, 44
Expresspay, 46
False positives, 252
Floor limits, 58
Form of Payment Identifier (FOP ID), 123, 144
Fraud
 cheque cards and, 33
 consumer dissatisfaction, 95
 cost of, 96
 credit & return, 96
 friendly fraud, 68, 95
 skimming, 94
 types of, 94
Fraud management, 278
 evaluation process, 224
 order screening, 210
Fraud management solutions, 252
 fees, 261
 integration options, 258
 managed service, 253
 management console, 259
 provider selection, 252
 tools, 254
Frequent flyer
 pay with miles, 135
General Sales Agent (GSA), 110

Gift cards, 136
Global Distribution System (GDS), 120
  bookings through, 152
Guarantor, 36
Hand-Off Tape (HOT) file, 107, 149
Hologram, 37
Imprinter, 41
Interactive Voice Recognition (IVR), 164
Interchange, 74
  interchange+, 78
  parameters, 74
  preferential rates, 76
International Air Travel Association (IATA), 106
  Billing and Settlement Plan (BSP), 106, 149
  card number as a form of identification (FOID), 102
  CardAXS, 111
  CardClear, 110
  Clearing House (ICH), 110
  Data Processing Centre (DPC), 107
  form of payment codes, 123
  Passenger Service Conference Resolution Manual, 105
  PCI-DSS Work Group (PDWS), 102
  Perseuss, 112
  RFID and, 46
iPad, 173, 186
Issuer, 50
  risks and responsabilities, 90

IVR. *See* Interactive Voice Recognition
J/Secure, 45
Key Performance Indicators (KPIs), 225
Kiosks, 176
  bank certification, 183
  Common Use Self Service (CUSS) standards, 179, 184
  Magnetic stripe card reader and, 178
  PCI-DSS compliance, 179
  POS terminals and, 180
  selling at, 176
Level II data, 63
Level III data, 63
Lounge access, 197
Luhn digit, 40
Maestro, 34
Magnetic stripe
  removal of, 44
  track 1, 2 and 3, 42
Mail Order - Telephone Order (MOTO), 89
MasterCard
  DataCash and, 54
  history of, 32
  holograms and, 37
  magnetic stripes and, 41
  PayPass, 46
  SecureCode, 45
Merchant, 51
  risks and responsabilities, 88
  settlement, 67
Merchant acquirer. *See* Acquirer
Merchant Category Code (MCC), 150

Merchant discount rate. *See* Mechant service fee
Merchant of Record, 51
  airline as, 153
  travel agency as, 152
Merchant service fee, 76
  blended rate, 77
  tiered pricing, 78
Miscellaneous Cash Order (MCO), 123
Mobile applications, 172
  for agents, 185
Mobile devices, 186
Mobile money transfers, 134
Mobile payments, 134
  contactless, 134
  limitations, 173
  mobile as POS, 134
  operator billing, 135
  remote payments, 134
Monitoring, 281
Multiple transaction sequencing, 71
Navitaire, 121
Near Field Communication (NFC), 47
Network Service Providers (NSP), 79
On us, 66
On-board retail, 187
  chip & PIN devices, 191
  GSM technology, 192
  Point of Sale (POS) devices, 190
  real-time authorisation, 192
On-board telephone, 196
Order screening, 210

Passenger Service Systems (PSS) providers, 115
  supplier integration, 269
Pay before, 50
Pay later, 50
Pay now, 50
Payment Card Industry (PCI), 99
  IATA and, 102
  Payment Application Data Security Standard (PA-DSS), 100
  PIN Transaction Security (PTS), 100
  Security Standard Council (PCI SSC), 99
  version 2.0, 99
Payment cards, 30
  history of, 29
  origins of, 30
Payment confirmation, 60
Payment methods
  costs, 272
  integration of, 274
  regulatory requirements, 273
  risk, 272
  selecting, 270
Payment project, 221
  implementation, 275
  starting a, 221
Payment scheme, 52
  risks and responsabilities, 90
  rules, 98
Payment Service Directive (PSD), 104
Payment Service Provider (PSP), 53, 167, 240
  acquiring business, 54

    categories of, 242
    direct integration, 168
    fees, 244
    full service provider, 242, 245
    infrastructure, 247
    integration options, 168, 250
    payment institution and, 242
    re-direct integration, 170
    reporting, 246
    Service Level Agreement (SLA), 248
Payment technology, 36
Payment transactions
    asynchronous, 276
    correction processes, 214
    cost reduction, 226
    domestication, 231
    initiation of, 36
    reconciliation, 213
PayPal, 114, 132, 167, 170, 172
PayPass, 46
PayWave, 46
PCI. *See* Payment Card Industry
Perseuss, 112
Personal Identification Number (PIN)
    history of, 34
    on-line verification, 182
    validation by the chip, 44
Pick up card, 60
Plastic cards, 37
Point of Sale (POS) terminals, 34
    acquiring banks and, 232
    level 2 certification, 181
    terminal management, 183
    virtual, 164

POS terminals. *See* Point of Sale terminals
Prepaid cards, 133
Processor, 53
PSP. *See* Payment Service Provider (PSP)
Qualified Security Assessor (QSA), 99
Radio-frequency Identification (RFID), 46
Reconciliation, 213, 279
Re-direct, 171
Refund, 64
    manual, 64
Re-presentment. *See* Second presentment
Request for copy, 68
Request for information, 68
RET files, 149
Reversal, 64
Risk, 88
    acquiring an airline, 233
    evaluation process, 234
    un-flown tickets, 233
Sabre, 122
SafeKey, 45
Second presentment, 69
Secure design elements, 37
Self-Service Kiosks. *See* Kiosks
Seller, 36
SEPA. *See* Single European Payment Area (SEPA)
Settlement, 65, 149
Shift of liability, 92
    U.S. in the, 94
Signature, 36, 37
    strip, 37

Single European Payment Area (SEPA), 104
SITA, 115
   credit card authorisation service, 115
Split payments, 70
Staff travel office, 196
Strategy development, 225
Surcharging, 80
Testing, 280
Third party booking, 217
Ticket desk, 158
   POS terminal, 158
Ticket sales process, 144
Token solutions, 268
   provider selection, 268
Transaction
   cost model, 73
   cost of, 72
   dispute process, 68
   ID, 151
   late presentment, 70
   polling, 65
   second (re-) presentment, 69
   submission, 65, 149
   unmatched, 150
Transaction processing company, 53
Travel agency
   charge-back risk, 152
   credit risk management, 156
   payments at, 151
Travelport, 122
UATP. *See* Universal Air Travel Plan
Universal Air Travel Plan (UATP), 31, 112
   airline data, 113
   alternative payment methods and, 113
   PayPal and, 114
Verified by Visa, 45
Visa
   CyberSource and, 54
   history of, 33
   holograms and, 37
   magnetic stripe and, 41
   PayWave, 46
Vouchers, 136
Western Union, 30

Table of Figures and Tables

1 Tables

Table 1: Examples of Level II and Level III Airline Data 63
Table 2: Chart of Airlines Charging Credit Card Surcharges in the UK Market (Courtesy of Airline Information) 81
Table 3: The 12 PCI-DSS Requirements (Source: PCI Security Standards Council, 2011) 101
Table 4: IATA Approved Form of Payment Codes 124
Table 5: IATA Approved International Payment Cards 125
Table 6: IATA Approved Payment Instruments, Domestic Usage Only.. 126
Table 7: IATA Defined Authorisation Messaging Format (Source: IATA, SITA) 145
Table 8: IATA Defined Approval/Denial Codes (Source: IATA, SITA) 148
Table 9: List of Fraud Screening Tools 255

2 Figures

Fig 1: The "Air Travel Card", Predecessor of the UATP Card (Courtesy of UATP) 30
Fig 2: First Diners Club Card (Courtesy of Diners Club) 31
Fig 3: MasterCharge Logo 32
Fig 4: Preferred Online Payment Methods in Germany, Europe and Brazil (Courtesy of DataCash) 35
Fig 5: Secure Design Elements (Courtesy of AustriaCard) 38
Fig 6: Manual Imprinter 41
Fig 7: Example of MasterCard SecureCode Screen 45
Fig 8: Antenna in RFID enabled Cards (Courtesy of AustriaCard) 47
Fig 9: Participants in the Payment Transaction Life Cycle – Overview 49
Fig 10: Authorisation Request and Response Transaction Flow 57
Fig 11: Clearing and Settlement Flow 66
Fig 12: Example of Split Payment Processing 71
Fig 13: Who Earns What? Transaction Cost Model 73
Fig 14: Illustration of Blend Fee Pricing (Courtesy of Adyen) 77
Fig 15: Illustration of Interchange+ Pricing (Courtesy of Adyen) 78
Fig 16: Surcharge Amount depending on the Payment Method 80
Fig 17: Sample Text for a MasterCard on-line DCC Transaction (Courtesy of FEXCO) 84
Fig 18: Sample Receipt (Courtesy of FEXCO) 86
Fig 19: Airline Fraud (Source: Airline Online Fraud Report 2011- Courtesy of CyberSource) 96
Fig 20: BSP Card Sales Process (Courtesy of IATA) 108
Fig 21: SITA Horizon Payment Services (Courtesy of SITA) 116
Fig 22: Amadeus Travel Payments Portfolio (Courtesy of Amadeus) 120
Fig 23: Real-time Bank Transfer Payment Screen 129
Fig 24: Example of an Electronic Wallet Payment Screen: CashU 132
Fig 25: Example of a Prepaid Card: Paysafecard (Courtesy of Paysafecard) 133
Fig 26: The World of Mobile Payments (Courtesy of Edgar, Dunn & Company – modified) 134
Fig 27: Kenya Airways and Mobile Payments (Courtesy of Kenya Airways) 135
Fig 28: KLM Airline Gift Card (Courtesy of KLM) 136

Fig 29: Traditional Airline Payment Transaction Flow 143
Fig 30: Airline Ticket Desk 159
Fig 31: Check-in Desk 161
Fig 32: Example of a Directly Integrated Payment Page 169
Fig 33: Example of a Re-direct Payment Page (Courtesy of PayGate) ... 171
Fig 34: Example of a Mobile Payment Screen (Courtesy of SITA/Malaysia Airlines) 175
Fig 35: Ryanair Self Service and Sales Kiosk at Stansted Airport 177
Fig 36: Kiosk with Integrated POS Terminal (Courtesy of SITA) 181
Fig 37: Motorola Handheld Device with Chip & PIN Snap-On Mobile Payment Module for Check-in and taking Payments (Courtesy of Motorola/SITA) 185
Fig 38: Apple iPads used as Payment Devices with Integrated PIN Pad (Courtesy of pks services) 186
Fig 39: Using iPads for On-board Retailing (Courtesy of MI Airline) 190
Fig 40: Two Generations of British Airways Compensation Cards: ChipCash and Cash Passport (Private; Courtesy of AccessPrepaid Worldwide) 199
Fig 41: AUA Compensation Card with Card Carrier (Courtesy of Paylife Bank) 200
Fig 42: Typical Order Screening Process for E-commerce Transactions (Courtesy of DataCash) 211
Fig 43: Example of a Case Management Screen (Courtesy of DataCash) 212
Fig 44: Typical Charge-back Recovery Rate (Source: CyberSource) 216
Fig 45: Example of an Authorisation Letter from the Cardholder (Courtesy of Oman Air) 218
Fig 46: Sample Flow Chart for a Payment Project 222
Fig 47: Example of a Merchant Acquiring Information Request Form ... 236
Fig 48: Example of a Risk Management Console (Courtesy of Adyen) ... 260
Fig 49: DCC Transaction Flow (Courtesy of Continuum Commerce) 266
Fig 50: Why a better Payment Selection needs to be on every Airline's Radar (Perfect Passenger Payments - Courtesy of WorldPay) 271
Fig 51: Selecting Payment Methods (Courtesy of DataCash) 273
Fig 52: Transaction Monitoring Page (Courtesy of SITA/Malaysia Airlines) 282

References

Airline Information/GuestLogix. *Selling in the Sky: The Onboard Retail Potential.* Toronto: GuestLogix Inc., 2011.

Amadeus. *Amadeus Travel Payments, 2014.* http://www.amadeus.com/airlineIT/solutions/sol_2stand_4payment_1payment.html (accessed 2011 December).

Board of Governors of the Federal Reserve System. *Press Release.* 2011. http://www.federalreserve.gov/newsevents/press/bcreg/20110629a.htm (accessed 2011 October).

CBSNews. "Number of Cell Phones Worldwide Hits 4.6B." 2010 18-February. http://www.cbsnews.com/stories/2010/02/15/business/main6209772.shtml (accessed 2012 January).

Cohen, Amon. "Payment." *Business Travel News.* 2011 14-October. http://www.businesstravelnews.com/Business-Globalization/Airlines-May-Consider-Card-Surcharge-Revisions-After-EU-Ministers-Approve-New-Directive/?a=trans (accessed 2001 November).

CyberSource. *Payment Security Practices and Trends Report.* Mountain View, CA: CyberSource, 2011.

CyberSource. *Airline Online Fraud Report.* Mountain View, CA: CyberSource, 2011.

CyberSource. *Fact Sheet: Payer Authentication*. Mountain View, CA: CyberSource, 2005.
CyberSource. *Insider's Guide to ePayment Management*. Mountain View, CA: CyberSource, 2011.
CyberSource. *UK Online Fraud Report*. Reading: CyberSource, 2011.
DATALOSS db. *Largest Incidents*. 2011. http://datalossdb.org/ (accessed 2012 January).
Diners Club. *Company History*. 2012. https://www.dinersclubus.com/home/about/dinersclub/company-history?nav=left (accessed 2012 January).
Edgar, Dunn & Company. *Advanced Payments Report*. London: Edgar, Dunn & Company, 2011.
EMVCo. *A guide to EMV*. EMVCo, 2011.
Eurocheques. *Geschichte der Eurocheques und EC-Karte*. 2011. http://www.eurocheques.de/history.html (accessed 2012 January).
European Central Bank. *SEPA - Single Euro Payments Area*. 2011. http://www.ecb.int/paym/sepa/html/index.en.html (accessed 2011 December).
European Commission. *Directive on Payment Services (PSD)*. 2011. http://ec.europa.eu/internal_market/payments/framework/index_en.htm (accessed 2011 November).
European Payments Council. " Preventing Card Fraud in a Mature EMV Environment ." *EPC documents*. 2011 31-01. http://www.europeanpaymentscouncil.eu/knowledge_bank_detail.cfm?documents_id=480 (accessed 2011 November).
—. "EPC Deliverables in the Area of Cards." *SEPA Vision for Cards*. 2011. http://www.europeanpaymentscouncil.eu/content.cfm?page=sepa_vision_for_cards (accessed 2011 November).
Evans, David, and Richard Schmalensee. *Paying with Plastic*. Cambridge: Massachusetts Institute of Technology, 2005.
First Data*First Data Facts*2012http://www.firstdata.com/en_us/about-first-data/media/first-data-facts.html
GSMA; Booz & Company. *Socio-economic benefits of SIM-based NFC*. London: Booz & Company; GSMA, 2011.
Harteveldt, Henry H. *Why Smartphones Will Become One Of Travel's Two Most Important Touchpoints*. Forrester Research, 2011.

Hock, Dee. *Birth of the Chaordic Age.* San Francisco, CA: Berrett-Koehler Publishers, INC., 1999.
HSN Consultants INC. *The Nilsen Report.* Carpinteria, CA: HSN Consultants INC, Various Issues 2010, 2011.
IATA31st Joint ATA/IATA Passenger Services Conference (JPSC)*BOOK OF FINALLY ADOPTED RESOLUTIONS & RPs*SingaporeIATA2012
IATA. *BSP Data Interchange Specifications Handbook.* Geneva: IATA, 2010.
—. "Passenger Services Conference Resolution Manual." Canada: IATA, 2009.
King, Mark. "Debit and credit card surcharges under OFT microscope." *The Guardian.* 2011 28-June. http://www.guardian.co.uk/money/2011/jun/28/debit-credit-card-surcharges-oft?INTCMP=SRCH (accessed 2011 November).
Lindsey, Ian. *Credit cards, the authoritative guide to credit and payment cards.* Bedfordshire: Rushmere Wynne Ltd., 1994.
Mandell, Lewis. *The Credit Card Industry: A History.* Twayne Publishers, 1990.
MasterCard. *Company Milestones.* 2011. http://www.mastercard.com/us/company/en/ourcompany/company_milestones.html (accessed 2011 July).
Navitaire. *New Skies Payments Engine.* 2011. http://www.navitaire.com/res_and_dist/newskies.asp (accessed 2011 December).
NFC Forum. *The Near Field Communication (NFC) Forum.* http://www.nfc-forum.org (accessed 2011 November).
PCI Security Standards Council. *PCI SSC Data Security Standards Overview.* 2011. https://www.pcisecuritystandards.org/security_standards/index.php (accessed 2011 October).
Putzger, Ian. "Cutting out the crooks." *Low Cost & Regional - Payment Supplement*, 2011: 38-40.
Putzinger, Ian. "Cashing in on technology." *Low Cost & Regional - Payment Supplement*, 2011: 46-48.
Sabre. *Credit Suite.* 2011. http://www.sabreairlinesolutions.com/home/products_services/product/credit_suite (accessed 2011 November).

Sienkiewicz, Stan. *Credit Cards and Payment Efficiency.* Philadelphia: Federal Reserve Bank of Philadelphia, 2001.
SITA. *Airline IT Trend Survey.* Geneva: SITA, 2011.
Smart Card Alliance. *Card Payments Roadmap in the United States: How Will EMV Impact the Future Payments Infrastructure?* Smart Card Alliance Payments Council, 2011.
Smith, Michael. "Getting mobile." *Low Cost & Regional - Airline Payments Supplement,* 2011 December: 8.
The Paypers and PaySys Consultancy. *SEPA/PAYPERS.* Frankfurt: The Paypers and PaySys Consultancy, Various Issues 2010, 2011.
The Paypers. *PSP Buyer's Guide.* The Paypers BV, 2010, 2011.
Travelport. *Payment Solutions.* 2011. http://www.travelport.com/solutions/Payment%20Solutions.aspx (accessed 2011 November).
UATP. *UATP - About Us.* 2011. http://www.uatp.com/about-us/index.html (accessed 2012 January).
VISA. "Airline Fraud Analysis." *IATA Card Fraud Working Group.* VISA, 2008.
Worldpay. *Perfect Passenger Payments.* London: Worldpay, 2012.